The One Year®
MAKE IT Stick DEVOTIONS

Dr. Emmett Cooper
Creator of the *HoneyWord® Bible*

Interior Illustrations by Joel Hickerson

TYNDALE KiDS

Tyndale House Publishers, Inc.
Carol Stream, Illinois

W9-AYK-019

Visit Tyndale's exciting Web site for kids at www.cool2read.com

Also see the Web site for adults at www.tyndale.com

TYNDALE is a registered trademark of Tyndale House Publishers, Inc.

The One Year is a registered trademark of Tyndale House Publishers, Inc.

Tyndale Kids logo is a trademark of Tyndale House Publishers, Inc.

The One Year Make-It-Stick Devotions

Copyright © 2007 by Dr. Emmett Cooper. All rights reserved.

All devotions, including Bible-book introductions and HoneyWord lessons (daily devo slogans) with discussions and make-it-stick activities, are based on the HoneyWord features, copyright © 2004 by Dr. Emmett Cooper, created and written by Dr. Emmett Cooper for the *HoneyWord Bible*, copyright © 2004 by Tyndale House Publishers, Inc., Carol Stream, Illinois 60188.

The following material was written by Betty Free Swanberg and edited by Dr. Emmett Cooper: prayers for each devotional; optional weekend activity ideas; and make-it-stick activities for the book-introduction devotionals, including the just-for-fun activities.

Cover illustration by Joel Hickerson. Copyright © by Dr. Emmett Cooper. All rights reserved.

Interior illustrations by Joel Hickerson. Interior illustrations copyright © 2004, 2007 by Dr. Emmett Cooper. All rights reserved.

Designed by Jacqueline L. Noe

Edited by Betty Free Swanberg

All Scripture quotations are taken from the Holy Bible, New Living Translation, copyright © 1996, 2004. Used by permission of Tyndale House Publishers, Inc., Carol Stream, Illinois 60188. All rights reserved.

HoneyWord is a registered trademark of HoneyWord Foundation, Inc., and Dr. Emmett Cooper. All rights reserved.

The HoneyWord logo is a registered trademark of HoneyWord Foundation, Inc., and Dr. Emmett Cooper. All rights reserved.

Making God's Word Stick is a registered trademark of HoneyWord Foundation, Inc., and Dr. Emmett Cooper. All rights reserved.

HoneyWord cartoons, visual concepts, characters, character names, number symbols, the 246 Click-ers, the 246 daily devo slogans, and all other related elements are the intellectual property of Dr. Emmett Cooper. Copyright © 2004 and 2007. All rights reserved.

The One Year Make-It-Stick Devotions is published in association with the literary agency of Alive Communications, Inc., 7680 Goddard Street, Suite 200, Colorado Springs, CO 80920.

Library of Congress Cataloging-in-Publication Data

Cooper, Emmett, date.
    The one year make-it-stick devotions / Emmett Cooper ; interior illustrations by Joel Hickerson.
        p. cm.
    Includes index.
    ISBN-13: 978-1-4143-1551-5 (sc)
    ISBN-10: 1-4143-1551-1 (sc)
    1. Children—Prayers and devotions—Juvenile literature. 2. Devotional calendars—Juvenile literature. I. Hickerson, Joel. II. Title.
    BV4571.3.C66 2007
    242'.62—dc22   2007009462

Printed in the United States of America

13   12   11   10   09   08   07
 7   6   5   4   3   2   1

DEDICATION

To those rare souls—
family, friends, and fellow warriors—
who saw the dream and joined the fight.
I couldn't have made it without you.

EMMETT THE ANT

CONTENTS

CONTENTS

BOOKS OF THE BIBLE
with Their Sound-Alike Animal Names

OLD TESTAMENT
DEVOTIONS FROM:

Genesis	Genny the Jellyfish	Weeks 1–2
Exodus	Elks-odus	Weeks 2–3
Leviticus	Levi the Lamb	Weeks 4–5
Numbers	Num-Bee	Weeks 5–6
Deuteronomy	Doodlebug-eronomy	Weeks 6–7
Joshua	Jaws-chew-ya	Weeks 7–8
Judges	Judge the Jaguar	Weeks 8–9
Ruth	Ruthie the Raccoon	Week 9
1 Samuel	Sam Mule the 1st	Weeks 9–10
2 Samuel	Sam Mule the 2nd	Week 11
1 Kings	Captain Kingaroo the 1st	Weeks 11–12
2 Kings	Captain Kingaroo the 2nd	Week 12
1 Chronicles	Davey Cricket the 1st	Weeks 12–13
2 Chronicles	Davey Cricket the 2nd	Weeks 13–14
Ezra	Ezra-triever	Week 14
Nehemiah	Nehemiah the Butterfly-ah	Weeks 14–15
Esther	Esther the Starfish	Week 15
Job	Joe B. Buffalo	Week 16
Psalms	Singer the Psalm-Bird	Weeks 16–20
Proverbs	Professor Wowl	Weeks 20–22
Ecclesiastes	Eagle-easy-astes	Weeks 22–23
Song of Songs	Swans-a-Swimming	Week 23
Isaiah	Isaiah the Irish Setter	Weeks 23–25
Jeremiah	Jerry the Jackrabbit	Weeks 25–26
Lamentations	Mama Llama	Week 26
Ezekiel	E. Zeek Eel	Week 27
Daniel	Dan O. Saur	Week 27
Hosea	Hosea the Horse	Week 28
Joel	Joel the Mole	Week 28

Amos	Amos the Moose	Weeks 28–29
Obadiah	O-bad-eye-ah the Ostrich	Week 29
Jonah	Jonah the Moan-ah Fish	Week 29
Micah	Micah the Cat	Week 30
Nahum	Na-hum-ing-bird	Week 30
Habakkuk	Habakkuk the Hawk	Week 30
Zephaniah	Zeph the Zebra	Week 31
Haggai	Haggai the Hedgehog	Week 31
Zechariah	Zack the Yak	Weeks 31–32
Malachi	Mala-gator	Week 32

**NEW TESTAMENT
DEVOTIONS FROM:**

Matthew	Matt the Mouse	Weeks 32–34
Mark	Mark the Monkey	Weeks 34–35
Luke	Luke the Lion	Weeks 35–36
John	John the Giraffe	Weeks 37–38
Acts	Emmett the Ant	Week 39
Romans	Roman the Rhino	Weeks 40–41
1 Corinthians	Cori Chameleon the 1st	Weeks 41–42
2 Corinthians	Cori Chameleon the 2nd	Week 42
Galatians	Sea-gull-atians	Weeks 42–43
Ephesians	Ele-phesians	Weeks 43–44
Philippians	Philip the Firefly	Week 44
Colossians	Colossians the Collie	Weeks 44–45
1 Thessalonians	Sloth-a-lo-nians the 1st	Week 45
2 Thessalonians	Sloth-a-lo-nians the 2nd	Weeks 45–46
1 Timothy	Timmy Tiger the 1st	Week 46
2 Timothy	Timmy Tiger the 2nd	Weeks 46–47
Titus	Titus the Tortoise	Week 47
Philemon	Philemon the Flamingo	Week 47
Hebrews	Hebrews the Hippo	Weeks 47–48
James	James the German Shepherd	Weeks 48–49
1 Peter	Peter Panda the 1st	Weeks 49–50
2 Peter	Peter Panda the 2nd	Week 50
1 John	Johnny Giraffe the 1st	Weeks 50–51
2 John	Johnny Giraffe the 2nd	Week 51
3 John	Johnny Giraffe the 3rd	Week 51
Jude	Jude the Donkey Dude	Weeks 51–52
Revelation	Rev. the Rooster	Week 52

Dear Young Friend,

If you could somehow dive into the middle of my heart, you'd see how I've dreamed and dreamed of this moment, when you'd be holding *The One Year Make-It-Stick Devotions* in your hands and reading it with your eyes.

You'd also see how I've prayed and prayed with all my heart that God will strengthen you to dig big in his Word. For if you stick like glue to what God says to do:

You'll tie and apply his Word to your heart.
You'll feel God's smile and go the extra mile.
You'll be in the crowd that follows God's cloud
And start growing like a sprout inside and out.
You'll carry God's map inside your thinking cap
And find you're a major piece of God's master puzzle.
Your heart will open the door to the poor,
And you'll dwell on what's behind the shell.

You won't dillydally in the valley of decision,
And you'll have the sense to stay off the fence.
You'll love God's honey more than money
And find God has the power to provide all your flour.
Your faith will stay in grape shape,
And you'll go out on a limb for him.
You'll glitter God's glory,
And like the lone leper you'll pepper God with praise.

So let's bee-lieve in God's perfect weave,
And one day meet on Easy Street.

I'll see you then, if not before.

Love,

Emmett

P.S. Please come visit us at www.HoneyWord.org or call us at 1-800-HoneyWord (1-800-466-3996).

Dear Grown-Up Friend,

Have you ever thought about why the "lessons" tied to McDonald's golden arches, Nike's swoosh, and Disney's Mickey Mouse ears really stick to our hearts and minds? The answer is simple: This *tie-a-message-to-a-symbol* educational method is solidly based on the spiritual technology of Deuteronomy 6:7-9:

> *Repeat* [God's commands] again and again to your children. *Talk* about them when you are at home and when you are on the road, when you are going to bed and when you are getting up. *Tie* them to your hands and wear them on your forehead as reminders. *Write* them on the doorposts of your house and on your gates *(italics added).*

Throughout Scripture, God uses concrete, make-it-stick reminders of his powerful promises, like the rainbow in Genesis 9, the twelve stones in Joshua 4, and the bread and cup in 1 Corinthians 11. Everything God teaches in his Word can be tied to a symbol—a picture in our minds. And whatever can be pictured in our minds can be placed in our hands and permanently *stuck* to our hearts.

Each daily devo saying in this *One Year Make-It-Stick Devotions* is tied to a "Click-er," something that kids see or think about all the time. These visual symbols make God's Word "click and stick" in your child's mind and heart. And by seeing or thinking about them every day, your family is constantly reminded to stick like glue to what God says to do.

With all my heart I hope these make-it-stick devotions help you, your kids, and your grandkids discover the sweetness of God's Word. Then, like David in Psalm 19:9-10, you'll feel and bee-lieve:

> "The laws of the LORD . . . are sweeter than honey."

If I can help you in any way, please contact me at www.HoneyWord.org or 1-800-HoneyWord (1-800-466-3996).

Making God's Word Stick,

Emmett Cooper

At Home with the HoneyWord Way of Learning

When you see a jar of honey, you probably think about how sweet and sticky it is! In the book of Psalms, Chapter 19 (verses 9-10) God tells us that his Word is sweeter than honey. So the HoneyWord way of learning is getting God's Word to stick like honey in your mind and heart. Here's how the HoneyWord way works.

The week and day help you keep track of which devo to do each day.

In *The One Year Make-It-Stick Devotions*, you'll find 66 book introductions—one for each book of the Bible.

Each book introduction features an animal with a sound-alike Bible-book name.

The animal shows up in each cartoon of the book it represents. When you see the cartoon in your mind, the animal helps you remember which book the daily devo is from.

A HoneyWord animal might be like the person who wrote that book of the Bible. Or it might be like the people whom the book is about.

HoneyWord chapter-number symbols appear near the animal in every cartoon. They help you recall which chapter the daily devo is from. (See the list of symbols on page 15.)

For a quick picture of what a Bible book is about, just read the second paragraph of the book-introduction page.

A make-it-stick activity helps you remember the Bible book and what it's about. You can look up some Bible verses from that book in your Bible "just for fun," then close your devotional time with a prayer.

Week 6, Wednesday

BOOK OF DEUTERONOMY
Doodlebug-eronomy

Doodlebug-eronomy sounds like *Deuteronomy*. Like people who doodle things on paper again and again, Moses spelled out God's Word one more time before the people entered the Promised Land. When you see Doodlebug-eronomy in a picture, you'll know the daily devo is from Deuteronomy. Connected to Doodlebug-eronomy are number symbols. (See page 15.) They make the chapter location of the devo click and stick.

The people of God were right back where they had started. Forty years earlier, they had camped in this same place by the Jordan River. But instead of trusting God and entering the Promised Land, they had shrunk back in fear. To keep them strong this time, Moses put together a scrapbook of faith, which we call Deuteronomy. Like a human doodlebug writing the same thing over and over, Moses told story after story to remind the people again and again of God's love and faithfulness. Then he challenged the people to step out in faith as they watched God step in and provide.

MAKE IT STICK
Make a tab to mark the book of Deuteronomy in your Bible. (See Week 1, Monday, for directions.)

Have you ever tried doodling? The next time you watch TV or listen to your favorite CD, get out a pencil and notepad and write a name or word over and over. Or draw a simple picture of a favorite flower or animal again and again. Doodling helps the word or picture you're thinking about really stick in your mind, doesn't it? Aren't you glad Moses was like a doodlebug, writing again and again about God's love?

Whenever you see a picture of a doodlebug or think about one, remember Doodlebug-eronomy and the book of Deuteronomy. (There really are tiny doodlebugs. You can read about them on page 60.)

JUST FOR FUN
You can look up Moses' last words to God's people. You'll find them in Deuteronomy, Chapter 33 (verses 26-29). Tell someone what you learned about God from these words.

PRAYER
Thank you, God, for having people like Moses write your words. I'm glad your words are written down for me to read in the Bible. Amen.

Daily verses are printed below the book and chapter location.

The 246 daily devos help you dive deep for treasure to keep. Every devo starts with a fun saying that will help you learn and remember the meaning of one small slice of the Bible.

One word in each devo (like glue) is called a Click-er. Whenever you see or think about it, the truth of the daily devo will click in your brain.

The short paragraph that follows helps you understand how to tie and apply this devo to your life.

Doing the fun activity and praying the prayer help you stick like glue to what God says to do.

When you look at this picture of a big glue stick, the devo saying "I stick like glue to what God says to do" is triggered in your mind.

Whenever Doodlebug-eronomy shows up in a cartoon, you know the devo is from Deuteronomy. The six-pick-up-stix lets you know that this daily devo is from chapter 6.

At the top of each daily devo page you'll find the book and chapter location of each verse the daily devo (HoneyWord lesson) is about.

Week 6, Saturday/Sunday 59

DEUTERONOMY, CHAPTER 6 (VERSES 6–8)
You must commit yourselves wholeheartedly to these commands that I am giving you today. Repeat them again and again to your children. Talk about them when you are at home and when you are on the road, when you are going to bed and when you are getting up. Tie them to your hands and wear them on your forehead as reminders.

DAILY DEVO
I stick like glue **to what God says to do.**
God wants his words to click and stick in our hearts. He shows parents how to make this happen. He tells them to talk about his words at all kinds of fun times. Did you ever tie a string around your finger so you wouldn't forget something important? Well, God told his people long ago to tie his commands to their hands, to wear them on their foreheads, and even to write them on their doors and gates (verse 9)! As you look at the Click-ers you're learning about in this book, you, too, will see reminders of God's Word everywhere you go. And you'll stick like glue to what God says to do.

MAKE IT STICK
Think about some fun times when you and your family read and talked about God's Word together. Then gather some of the Click-ers that are helping you remember God's Word. Choose a smaller one, such as a dime or a cereal flake, and dab the back of it with a glue stick. Then glue the item to a piece of paper. That's a picture of how God's Word is meant to stick in your heart.

PRAYER
Thank you, God, for all the things around me that remind me of your Word. I want to stick like glue to what you say to do. Amen.

CLICK-ER: **GLUE STICK**
Whenever you see or use a *glue stick*, let this daily devo cling to your mind as it clicks and sticks. Doodlebug-eronomy with six-pick-up-stix reminds you that the devo is from Deuteronomy, Chapter 6.

For extra click-and-stick power, read the words below the Click-er, so the cartoon can help you race to the right place every time.

For each weekend, you'll see some review activity ideas. There's also a related daily devo you might want to do on Sunday.

Whenever you're ready, you can meet and greet your first Old Testament animal friend, Genny the Jellyfish, on page 19.

HONEYWORD CHAPTER-NUMBER SYMBOLS

Here are the names for each chapter-number symbol. It's easy to see why the symbols make sense. Notice how the key has the number 3 on it, the floorboard has 4 boards, the hive-hat has 5 layers, and so on.

	One-on-a-bun	=	Chapter 1
	Two-blue-shoes	=	Chapter 2
	Three-is-the-key	=	Chapter 3
	Four-on-the-floorboard	=	Chapter 4
	Five-on-a-hive-hat	=	Chapter 5
	Six-pick-up-stix	=	Chapter 6
	Highway-seven-to-heaven	=	Chapter 7
	Eight-under-skates	=	Chapter 8
	Nine-foot-pine	=	Chapter 9
	(A halo-is-a-hero-as-a-zero)	=	0
	One-on-a-bun plus a halo-is-a-hero-as-a-zero	=	Chapter 10
	One-on-a-bun plus another one-on-a-bun	=	Chapter 11
	One-on-a-bun plus two-blue-shoes	=	Chapter 12

You get the idea! Check out a cartoon to see if you can read the chapter-number symbols.

Jesus is my friend to THE END!

God's gift of his Son, Jesus, is the greatest gift he's ever given. Believe that Jesus died for you! Then reach out to receive him—just like a gift at Christmas. That's it. Simply believe and receive. His gift is your one and only lift to heaven.

Jesus gave super-clear directions on getting to God. He said, "No one can come to the Father except through me." That means he is THE only complete, one-way street to heaven.

How many ways are there to the top of a mountain? Probably several. But for this bike hike, there's only one. And the serpent doesn't want you to follow it. But remember, it's always a mistake to listen to any kind of snake.

Week 1, Monday

BOOK OF GENESIS

Genny the Jellyfish

Jellyfish sounds like *Genesis*. A jellyfish is clear, just like everything God created in the beginning. When you see Genny the Jellyfish in a picture, you'll know the daily devo is from Genesis. Connected to Genny are number symbols. (See page 15.) They make the chapter location of the devo click and stick.

Genesis is a book about beginnings. At first everything was perfect and out in the open. There was no sin to cover up. Everything was pure and clear, like a see-through jellyfish floating in crystal blue water. But it didn't stay that way. Adam and his madam, Eve, disobeyed God, and their sin muddied the water for all of us. Things have been cloudy ever since. One day God's Son, Jesus, will return. Then God will create a new earth, and we'll get back to clear blue see-through everything.

 MAKE IT STICK

To make a tab for the book of Genesis in your Bible, tear off a sheet from a self-stick notepad. Cut a strip about one-half inch deep. At the sticky end, print *Genny the Jellyfish*. At the non-sticky end, draw a tiny jellyfish. (Or find a picture that you can make smaller on a copier and paste it to the tab.) Stick your tab on the upper right corner of the page in your Bible where Genesis begins.

Whenever you see a *jellyfish* or think about one, remember Genny the Jellyfish and the book of Genesis.

JUST FOR FUN

To learn about the two children born in the Garden of Eden, find Genesis, Chapter 4, in your Bible. You can read verses 3-16 to learn about the first family. Who disobeyed God? What happened then?

PRAYER

Dear God, I'm glad there was no sin in the beginning. And I'm glad there will be no sin when Jesus returns. But I'm sorry that sin even came into the world at all. Help me not to cover up my sins. Please forgive me for _____. In Jesus' name I pray. Amen.

GENESIS, CHAPTER 1 (VERSE 1)

In the beginning God created the heavens and the earth.

DAILY DEVO

In the beginning, God's call got the ball rolling.

Did you know that a very long time ago nothing was around except God? Then, when God decided the time was just right, he created everything. God made the sun, the moon, and the stars. He made the little ball we live on called Planet Earth. He made every living thing on Earth. He also created the sky above and the oceans below. God made the call to create every fish, bird, and animal. And when it was time to make people, God made that call too. None of this was an accident. In the big beginning, only God was big enough to make the call that got the ball rolling. And he's the only one big and powerful enough to keep it going, day after day.

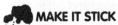 **MAKE IT STICK**

Roll a ball across your kitchen floor or somewhere outdoors. Then ask yourself, *Who made the call to get that ball rolling?* Obviously, you made the decision to roll it. In the same way, God made the decision to create the universe and set it in motion. Your made-from-something ball stopped, but God's made-from-nothing "Earth-ball" just keeps rolling and rolling. Isn't God great?

PRAYER

Dear God, thank you for getting the ball rolling when you created the world. And thanks for keeping it rolling day after day and season after season. In Jesus' name, amen.

CLICK-ER: BALL

Whenever you see, play with, or think about a *ball*, let this picture roll through your mind as the daily devo clicks and sticks. Genny the Jellyfish with her one-on-a-bun will remind you that the devo is from Genesis, Chapter 1.

GENESIS, CHAPTER 1 (VERSE 27)

So God created human beings in his own image. In the image of God he created them; male and female he created them.

DAILY DEVO

Mirror, mirror, on the wall, God's image is in us all.

A mirror on its own is just a piece of glass with a special coating. What makes a mirror really special is the way it shows the figure or image in front of it. You probably used a mirror this morning to get ready for the day. Maybe you brushed your hair and made sure your clothes were on just right. Your mirror's job was to show or reflect your image. When God made people, he gave us the job of reflecting his image like a mirror. That's extra special, isn't it? Everyone—including you—has God's image inside. You reflect what God is like just as your mirror reflects how you look!

MAKE IT STICK

Mirror, mirror, on the wall,
God's image is in us all.

Are you able to read the words above? Probably not! To see clearly what the words say, hold them up to a mirror. Then you'll be able to read and understand them. When we are kind and forgiving, we allow God's love to be "reflected" off our life like a mirror reflects the way we look. Then everyone can understand God better.

PRAYER

Dear God, please help me to be more like you. I want people to see what you are like when they look at what I do and say each day. In Jesus' name, amen.

CLICK-ER: **MIRROR**

Whenever you see, use, or think about a *mirror*, let your mind reflect on this picture as the daily devo clicks and sticks. Genny the Jellyfish holding a one-on-a-bun will remind you that the devo is from Genesis, Chapter 1.

GENESIS, CHAPTER 3 (VERSE 1)

The serpent was the shrewdest of all the wild animals the Lord God had made. One day he asked the woman, "Did God really say you must not eat the fruit from any of the trees in the garden?"

DAILY DEVO
I make a mistake when I listen to the snake.

Satan is tricky and speaks through whatever gets our attention. The Bible says that in the beginning, snakes didn't have to crawl on the ground. They were very smart and very clever. So Satan used a snake to sneak up on Eve and ask: "Did God really say that?" Whenever any voice tells us not to believe God's words in the Bible, remember that the devil is behind it—coiled and hissing at us like a snake. Don't listen. Don't even get close! Call out to God for help to understand Satan's tricks. And be ready to go the other way.

 **MAKE IT STICK**

Coil an old shoelace on a table. Pretend that the plastic tip is the head of a snake. While holding the tip between two fingers, remember a way Satan has tried to trick you. (Has he ever said it was okay to steal? Or to be unkind?) As soon as you remember Satan's lie, say: "I make a mistake when I listen to the *snake*." Then sweep the pretend snake off the table and step on it. That's a picture of God's promise in Romans 16:20 to "crush Satan under your feet."

PRAYER

Dear God, thank you for helping me listen to your words in the Bible so I won't believe anything Satan tries to tell me. In Jesus' name I pray. Amen.

CLICK-ER: SNAKE

Whenever you see, touch, or think about a *snake*, let this picture slither through your mind as the daily devo clicks and sticks. Genny the Jellyfish with a three-is-the-key is a reminder that the devo is from Genesis, Chapter 3.

GENESIS, CHAPTER 7 (VERSE 18)

As the waters rose higher and higher above the ground, the boat floated safely on the surface.

DAILY DEVO

God is the lifeboat that keeps me afloat.

Genesis 6:5 says that in Noah's time people's thoughts were "consistently and totally evil." Noah was the only person who always tried to please God and do exactly what God asked. God trusted Noah, so God told him to build a big boat that would float way above the Flood that was going to cover everything. Noah obeyed. God's directions became the lifeboat that kept Noah and his family alive. God is still in the lifeboat business today. He's always looking for someone who will climb aboard and get involved in his big plan for the world. And he'll be there to help in time of trouble. He wants to float your boat. Will you let him?

 MAKE IT STICK

Form a piece of aluminum foil into the shape of a boat. Then watch it float in a pool, a bucket of water, or a bathtub. It floats because it has sides that keep the water out. Now flatten the sides and see what happens. It sinks! When we don't obey God, it's like taking away the sides of our boat. But when we obey God, he becomes the boat that keeps us afloat.

PRAYER

Dear God, sometimes my problems seem so big that I feel like I'm going to sink. But when I obey you, Lord, you keep my life afloat. Thank you! Amen.

CLICK-ER: BOAT

Whenever you see, ride in, or think about a *boat*, let this picture float through your mind as the daily devo clicks and sticks. Genny the Jellyfish holding a highway-seven-to-heaven sign reminds you that the devo is from Genesis, Chapter 7.

GENESIS, CHAPTER 9 (VERSES 13, 16)

I have placed my rainbow in the clouds. It is the sign of my covenant with you and with all the earth. . . . When I see the rainbow in the clouds, I will remember the eternal covenant between God and every living creature on earth.

DAILY DEVO

God's rainbow is the seal of his special deal.

The Flood may have been the first rain anybody ever saw. And what a rain it was! Can you imagine 40 days and 40 nights of nonstop rain? When Noah and his family finally got their feet back on the ground, they probably hoped there would never be another storm like that! Well, God promised he would never again send a flood to destroy all living things. And God sent a rainbow as a sign that his promise is real. He gave Noah and his family—and us—a permanent deal and sealed it with a rainbow.

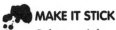 **MAKE IT STICK**

Color a rainbow, cut it out, and punch a hole near one end. Tie a string to the hole. Punch another hole at the top of a paper circle (the seal) on which you've written "His Special Deal." Tie the other end of the string to that paper. Then punch a hole through the top center of the rainbow and put another string through it. You can hang your rainbow from a kitchen cabinet. As you reach for a glass to get a drink of water, let the rainbow remind you of God's promise.

PRAYER

Thank you, Lord, for beautiful rainbows. Every time I see one in the sky, I'll remember that you always keep your promises. Amen.

CLICK-ER: **RAINBOW**

Whenever you see or think about a *rainbow* (paper or real), let this picture flood your heart as the daily devo clicks and sticks. Genny the Jellyfish on a nine-foot-pine reminds you that the devo is from Genesis, Chapter 9.

WEEKEND ACTIVITY IDEAS

(1) Highlight the verses for Week 1 in your Bible. (2) Find Genny the Jellyfish in each picture for this week and identify the chapter-number symbols. (3) Start a collection of Click-ers—real items or pictures of them. (4) Say the daily devos for Week 1. (5) Check out Saturday/Sunday of Week 3 for a related devo on being in the crowd that follows God's cloud.

WATER, WATER, WATER

The jellyfish is 99 percent water and so clear that
the organs inside it can easily be seen.

GENESIS, CHAPTER 22 (VERSE 17)

I will certainly bless you. I will multiply your descendants beyond number, like the stars in the sky and the sand on the seashore.

DAILY DEVO

God's blessings for me are like the sand by the sea.

Blessings are special gifts from God, including special things he does for people. Abraham wanted God to bless him with children. God told Abraham that his kids, grandkids, great-grandkids, and everyone else born into his family would number more than the grains of sand by the sea! God has blessings for you, too: healthy days, people to love you, food to eat, pets to love, God's Word to guide you, life with God forever—and so much more! God gives everyone who believes in him as many blessings as there are grains of sand by the sea!

MAKE IT STICK

Write down your blessings from God. Be specific: List each friend separately, name each person in your family, and so on. On the back of your paper, draw a beach scene without sand. Then, for each blessing you listed, put a dot of sand on your beach with a crayon or marker. Each time you think of a new blessing, add it to your list and add a grain of sand to your beach. Pretty soon you won't be able to count the grains of sand! God's blessings are also too many to count.

PRAYER

Wow, God, I never knew I had so many blessings from you! You must love me a lot. Thank you for all of these special gifts. In Jesus' name, amen.

CLICK-ER: SAND

Whenever you see or think about *sandy* beaches, let this picture sift through your mind as the daily devo clicks and sticks. Genny the Jellyfish holding two pairs of two-blue-shoes reminds you that the devo is from Genesis, Chapter 22.

GENESIS, CHAPTER 37 (VERSE 5)

One night Joseph had a dream, and when he told his brothers about it, they hated him more than ever.

DAILY DEVO

Jealousy opens the gate to hate.

Brothers and sisters often fight because no one wants to share the spotlight. That's the way it was with Joseph and his 10 older brothers. Joseph was his daddy's favorite, and that made his brothers very jealous. The jealousy grew into hatred, and they finally sold Joseph as a slave to some men going far away to Egypt. Sometimes parents and other family members do things that are unfair. But the message to us is pretty clear: Allowing ourselves to become jealous can open the gate to hate.

 MAKE IT STICK

On a piece of paper, draw a stone fence with a double-door gate. Cut around the top, bottom, and the center edge between the doors. With the doors folded open, tape your fence drawing on top of a blank piece of paper. Then, behind the left gate, draw someone who is jealous and upset. Behind the right gate, draw the same person with a happy face. Now shut the gates. When you open each one, think about your attitude. When you're jealous, do you see smiles or frowns? When you're not jealous, what do you see?

PRAYER

Dear God, I'm thankful for everything you do for me. Forgive me when I get jealous of things you do for others. I know you love everyone. Help me to do that too. Amen.

CLICK-ER: GATE

Whenever you see, open, or think about a *gate*, let this picture open your mind as the daily devo clicks and sticks. Genny the Jellyfish with her three-is-the-key and highway-seven-to-heaven sign reminds you that the devo is from Genesis, Chapter 37.

GENESIS, CHAPTER 50 (VERSE 20)

You intended to harm me, but God intended it all for good. He brought me to this position so I could save the lives of many people.

DAILY DEVO

Only God can look under the hood and turn bad to good.

When we're born, we're kind of like a brand-new car—bright, shiny, and ready to roll. Over time, however, bad things happen to a car, and a mechanic needs to fix it. When bad things happen to a person, God is the only "mechanic" who can get under the "hood" and fix what's wrong. Often it's just an attitude that needs to be changed. Joseph and his brothers all suffered a lot. They didn't like that or understand it, but the Good Mechanic helped the older brothers adjust their attitudes. They went from being jealous of Joseph to being thankful for him. And God turned bad to good by using Joseph to keep many people, including his own family, from starving.

 MAKE IT STICK

When it's convenient, ask if your dad or mom will open the hood of the family car and show you the engine. Even if you can name some of the parts, you probably wouldn't know how to fix them if they broke. God loves it when you bring that I-don't-know-what-to-do feeling to him. He wants you to depend on him for the right attitude so he can take the bad things that happen and use them for good.

PRAYER

Dear God, I don't understand why bad things happen sometimes. But I know I can trust you to find a way to turn the bad to good. Thank you! In Jesus' name, amen.

CLICK-ER: CAR HOOD

Whenever you see, touch, or think about a *car hood*, let this picture open your heart as the daily devo clicks and sticks. Genny the Jellyfish with her five-on-a-hive hat and halo-is-a-hero-as-a-zero reminds you that the devo is from Genesis, Chapter 50.

Week 2, Thursday

BOOK OF EXODUS
Elks-odus

Elks-odus sounds like *Exodus*. Like an elk sheds its antlers, God's people shed their slavery as they left Egypt, following the exit signs. When you see Elks-odus in a picture, you'll know the daily devo is from Exodus. The number symbols (see page 15) connected to Elks-odus make the chapter location of the devo click and stick.

Exodus is a book about timing. For over 400 years God's people cried out for freedom from slavery in Egypt. Like an elk that sheds its antlers every year, the Israelites wanted to shed slavery and start a new life in a new place. Finally, along came Moses, and God was ready to launch his master plan. It was as if God held up a big neon exit sign and said, "Let's go. It's time to leave." When God says, "Go," we need to move out and not pout, knowing he's leading us to the right place at the right time.

 MAKE IT STICK

Make a tab for the book of Exodus just as you did for Genesis. (See Week 1, Monday.)

You can read all about elks on the Internet or in an encyclopedia. You can also make antlers from play dough. Placing them on your head and then removing—or shedding—them will remind you of the time when God's people left Egypt and shed the slavery that had kept them there for 400 years.

Whenever you see a picture of an elk or think about one, remember Elks-odus and the book of Exodus.

JUST FOR FUN

You may want to find Exodus, Chapters 7–11, in your Bible. Make a list of the 10 plagues that God sent to the Egyptian people so that Pharaoh would let the Israelite slaves go.

PRAYER

Thank you, God, for sending Moses to lead your people from slavery to freedom. I pray that my family and I will follow you wherever you lead us. In Jesus' name, amen.

EXODUS, CHAPTER 2 (VERSE 3)

When she could no longer hide him, she got a basket made of papyrus reeds and waterproofed it with tar and pitch. She put the baby in the basket and laid it among the reeds along the bank of the Nile River.

DAILY DEVO

Wherever my basket lands, I'm in God's hands.

Times were bad when Moses was born. God's people, the Hebrews, were slaves who belonged to the Egyptian people. A bad Egyptian ruler called Pharaoh had also made a very bad rule: Every Hebrew baby boy had to be killed. Trusting God more than they feared Pharaoh, Moses' parents put their little boy in God's hands by placing him in a basket-boat. They were trusting God, not knowing what would happen. As we, too, learn to walk by faith, God will also ask us to trust him when we don't understand his plan. If times are bad for you or your family, talk to God about it. No matter where your basket lands, just like Moses you are in God's hands.

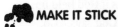 **MAKE IT STICK**

Find an old basket and pretend it has some of your most valuable possessions in it. Repeat this daily devo as you throw the basket in the air and let it land on the ground. Remember, there's a big difference between how you handle your basket and how God handles you in his "basket." To throw your basket, you have to let go. But God never lets go of you. Never, ever. You'll always be safe in his hands.

PRAYER

Dear God, please help me to trust you when I don't know what's going to happen next. Thanks for keeping me safe wherever I end up. Amen.

CLICK-ER: BASKET

Whenever you see, carry, or think about a *basket*, let this picture weave itself into your heart as the daily devo clicks and sticks. Elks-odus with his two-blue-shoes is a reminder that the devo is from Exodus, Chapter 2.

EXODUS, CHAPTER 3 (VERSE 4)

When the LORD saw Moses coming to take a closer look, God called to him from the middle of the bush, "Moses! Moses!" "Here I am!" Moses replied.

DAILY DEVO

God can use a burning bush whenever I need a push.

What does it take for God to get your attention? Do you check out God's Word to see what he wants you to do? Do you listen to your parents and teachers? Or does it take something bigger for you to follow him? God will do whatever it takes to get our attention. One day when Moses was minding his own business, God showed up in a burning bush that didn't burn up. God told Moses to go back to Egypt and lead his people out of slavery into the Promised Land. God used that burning bush to push Moses into action. How is God trying to get your attention? Whatever he does, stop and listen. Then do what he says. You'll be glad you did.

 MAKE IT STICK

Draw a picture of the burning bush as you imagine Moses saw it. Draw a second picture of Moses walking to Egypt—doing what God pushed him into doing. Now draw a third picture of something God might use to push you into action. What do you think the picture of you obeying God will look like?

PRAYER

I'm glad that you care about me, God, and you do whatever it takes to get me to obey you. Give me the push I need today. In Jesus' name, amen.

CLICK-ER: BUSH

Whenever you see, touch, or think about a *bush*, let this picture stir a fire in your heart as the daily devo clicks and sticks. Elks-odus with a three-is-the-key reminds you that the devo is from Exodus, Chapter 3.

WEEKEND ACTIVITY IDEAS

(1) Highlight the verses for Week 2 in your Bible. (2) Find the HoneyWord animal in each picture for this week and identify the chapter-number symbols. (3) Add to your collection of Click-ers. (4) Say the daily devos for Week 2. (5) Check out Wednesday of Week 26 for a related devo on the kind of fires God admires.

RACK 'EM, PACK 'EM, & STACK 'EM

Every year an elk grows a rack of antlers 5 feet wide. Just 10 years of racks stacked tip to tip would be 50 feet high—as tall as a 5-story building.

Week 3, Monday

EXODUS, CHAPTER 5 (VERSE 13)

The Egyptian slave drivers continued to push hard. "Meet your daily quota of bricks, just as you did when we provided you with straw!" they demanded.

DAILY DEVO

When I hit a brick wall, I call out to God.

As slaves, the people of God were "up against a brick wall." Pharaoh gave them the impossible task of making the same number of bricks each day, even though they now also had to find their own straw. At times, we, too, run into what seems like a brick wall. We lose a pet. Our parents fight and talk about getting a divorce. A friend gets a serious illness. Whenever life makes us feel like we're up against a brick wall, it may seem that we're all alone. But we're not—God is with us. He promises to hear our prayers and put peace back in our heart. Have you hit a brick wall? Call out to God. He'll help you know what to do.

MAKE IT STICK

The next time you're near a brick wall, lean against it as hard as you can. No matter how hard you try, you know you can't make it move. That's a picture of how strong and faithful God is. We all have times when the only way out is to look up . . . to God in prayer. Lean hard one more time while repeating this daily devo.

PRAYER

Dear God, whenever I feel alone, I'll remember that you are with me. Thank you for the peace you give. In Jesus' name I pray. Amen.

CLICK-ER: **BRICK WALL**

Whenever you see, touch, or think about a *brick wall*, let your heart lean hard on this daily devo as it clicks and sticks. Elksodus with his five-on-a-hive-hat reminds you that the devo is from Exodus, Chapter 5.

EXODUS, CHAPTER 6 (VERSE 9)

*Moses told the people of Israel what the L*ORD* had said, but they refused to listen anymore. They had become too discouraged by the brutality of their slavery.*

DAILY DEVO

Every diary on slavery is filled with heartache and bravery.

God's people worked hard as slaves in Egypt. Again and again they cried out to God: "When can we get out of here?" But he was silent for over 400 years. While they all waited, individuals fought hard to maintain their strength and dignity. They did many kind and heroic things to help their family, friends, and fellow slaves. If they had kept a detailed diary, it would have been full of stories of personal courage and bravery. As you grow older, you'll learn more about the harsh history of slavery. Let the stories of brave slaves challenge you to live boldly for the Lord. It's the only way to live, regardless of your circumstances.

 MAKE IT STICK

Make a small diary by folding a piece of paper in half. Write "Diary on Slavery" on the cover. On the inside, draw a picture of a slave being kind to another slave or doing something brave. Then explain your picture to your family. Ask your parents to tell you any stories they might know about brave slaves.

PRAYER

Dear God, I feel sad when I think about how hard life was for people who were slaves. Whether my life is easy or hard, help me always to be your brave follower. In Jesus' name, amen.

CLICK-ER: DIARY

Whenever you see, write in, or think about a *diary*, let your heart store up this daily devo as it clicks and sticks. Elks-odus with his six-pick-up-stix reminds you that the devo is from Exodus, Chapter 6.

EXODUS, CHAPTER 16 (VERSE 14)

When the dew evaporated, a flaky substance as fine as frost blanketed the ground.

DAILY DEVO

God is good, God is great, for making 40 years of frosted flakes.

Can you imagine waking up to a backyard full of FREE frosted flakes every morning? That's exactly what happened to God's people in the book of Exodus. Each day, six days a week, for 40 years, all they had to do was roll out of their tents, pile high their cereal bowls, and eat as much manna as they wanted. This all-you-can-eat buffet breakfast is a picture of how God promises to take care of us as we trust him day by day. Whenever you start your day with cereal flakes of any kind, grin from ear to ear as you remember that God promises to provide everything you need.

 MAKE IT STICK

Politely ask your dad or mom if you can do a cereal-flake hunt outside. Take a bowl of cereal and spread the flakes out on the ground. Then pick up as many flakes as you can and place them in a dish for the birds or a pet to eat. This will remind you of God's goodness when he fed his children in the desert for 40 years.

PRAYER

Even when I thank you for my food, God, I sometimes forget that you are the one who always provides what I need. With your help, I promise to do a better job of remembering. Amen.

CLICK-ER: CEREAL FLAKES

Whenever you see, eat, or think about *cereal flakes*, let your mind munch on this daily devo as it clicks and sticks. Elks-odus with his one-on-a-bun and six-pick-up-stix will remind you that the devo is from Exodus, Chapter 16.

EXODUS, CHAPTER 20 (VERSES 1-17)

(Verses 1-3): God gave the people all these instructions: "I am the LORD your God, who rescued you from the land of Egypt, the place of your slavery. "You must not have any other god but me. . . ."

DAILY DEVO

I need to heed godly speed.

Speed limits mean you can't always go as fast as you'd like to go. But speed limits also keep everyone safer while traveling on or near a street. That's why it's important for everyone to obey them. God gave "speed limits" to his people when he gave us the Ten Commandments. (The first is printed above. You'll find the rest in your Bible.) Sometimes we'd rather not obey God's limits. But his commandments help us to get along better with the people around us. They also show us how to honor God. Just like speed limits for cars, God's limits are meant for everyone. And if everyone followed them, we'd all be much happier.

 MAKE IT STICK

On a piece of paper, make a speed-limit sign that says "God's Big Ten Speed Limits." On the other side of the paper, list the numbers one through ten. Then look for the Ten Commandments (do's and don'ts) in Exodus, Chapter 20 (verses 3-17). At the end of the day, see if you and your family can name ways you have obeyed each of the commandments.

PRAYER

Dear God, I'm happier when I obey you. But it's not always easy. Thank you for your Son, Jesus, who shows me how to love you and others each day. In Jesus' name I pray. Amen.

CLICK-ER:
SPEED-LIMIT SIGN

Whenever you see, pass by, or think about a *speed-limit sign*, let this picture drive through your mind as the daily devo clicks and sticks. Elks-odus with two-blue-shoes and a halo-is-a-hero-as-a-zero is a reminder that the devo is from Exodus, Chapter 20.

Week 3, Friday

EXODUS, CHAPTER 28 (VERSE 29)

Aaron will carry the names of the tribes of Israel on the sacred chestpiece over his heart when he goes into the Holy Place. This will be a continual reminder that he represents the people when he comes before the LORD.

DAILY DEVO

God keeps my name in a special picture frame.

When Aaron, the high priest, went into the presence of God, he always wore the names of the 12 tribes of Israel over his heart. This was the way God wanted Aaron to keep the people of God lifted up before the Lord in prayer. This is such a wonderful picture of how Jesus, our High Priest, keeps our names close to God. You are so important to God that he has your name in a picture frame over his heart all the time. And it's even spelled right! God knows all of his followers by name and keeps us close to his heart.

MAKE IT STICK

Make a name frame by writing your name on a small piece of paper or cardboard and drawing a picture frame around the edges. Punch a hole in each of the upper two corners. Then cut a piece of string (or yarn) so it's long enough to reach around your neck and hold your name above your heart. Put one end of the string through each hole and tie it. As you wear your name-in-a-frame, stand in front of a mirror and say this daily devo.

PRAYER

You are the great Creator, God. Yet I'm so important to you that you let your Son, Jesus, bring my name before you at all times. Thank you for making me feel so special. Amen.

CLICK-ER:
PICTURE FRAME

Whenever you see, hold, or think about a *picture frame*, let this daily devo frame your heart as it clicks and sticks. Elks-odus with his two-blue-shoes and eight-under-skates, reminds you that the devo is from Exodus, Chapter 28.

EXODUS, CHAPTER 40 (VERSE 36)

Now whenever the cloud lifted from the Tabernacle, the people of Israel would set out on their journey, following it.

DAILY DEVO

I'm in the crowd that follows God's cloud.

Maybe you've seen a white cloud that was so thick and fluffy you felt that if you could just get up there, you could lie down on it. God used a cloud like that to lead his family, the people of Israel, as they traveled in the desert. They didn't lie down on the cloud. But they did follow it for 40 years. When the cloud moved, they moved. When it didn't, they stayed put. That's a picture of how God wants everyone in his Kingdom, including you, to follow him day by day. Are you part of a church crowd that follows the cloud of God? If so, stay put. Keep following. Stay involved. If not, tell God. He'll show you how to find the right crowd.

 MAKE IT STICK

Draw a cloud and cover it with cotton balls. Then politely ask your dad or mom if you can hang it from the rearview mirror in your family car for one week. Every time you get into the car, look at your cloud and repeat the daily devo. Thank God for your church or ask him to help you find a church crowd he'd like you to become part of.

PRAYER

I'm thankful for the crowd that follows you, God. It's the only crowd I want to be in. Please help me to stay with your crowd as I grow up. In Jesus' name I pray. Amen.

CLICK-ER: CLOUD

Whenever you see or think about a *cloud*, let this picture float through your heart as the daily devo clicks and sticks. Elks-odus with his four-on-the-floorboard and halo-is-a-hero-as-a-zero tells you that the devo is from Exodus, Chapter 40.

WEEKEND ACTIVITY IDEAS

(1) Highlight the verses for Week 3 in your Bible. (2) Find Elks-odus in each picture for this week and identify the chapter-number symbols. (3) Add to your collection of Click-ers—real items or pictures. (4) Say the daily devos for Week 3. (5) Check out Saturday/Sunday of Week 1 for a related devo on the rainbow seal of God's special deal.

HEAVY HEADS

A boy elk is called a bull. Only the bulls have antlers.

A rack of antlers can weigh up to 40 pounds.

Week 4, Monday

BOOK OF LEVITICUS

Levi the Lamb

Levi the Lamb sounds like *Leviticus*. A sweet, harmless lamb reminds us of the perfect lambs that God, who is perfect, asked his people to give him. When you see Levi the Lamb in a picture, you'll know the daily devo is from Leviticus. The number symbols (see page 15) connected to Levi make the chapter location of the devo click and stick.

Having safely left Egypt, God's people, the Israelites, took a yearlong pit stop at the foot of Mount Sinai. While they were refueling, God gave them rules for the road. This huge handbook of holy living called Leviticus contains rules for everything. Because God is holy, or perfect, his people had to be holy. It was that simple. And that hard. God asked for perfect animals to be offerings or sacrifices for sin. This painted a picture of the best sacrifice of all—Jesus, God's Son. As the perfect Lamb of God, Jesus would one day come to take away our sins once and for all.

 MAKE IT STICK

Make a tab for the book of Leviticus in your Bible. (See Week 1, Monday, for directions.)

Try to find out as much as you can about lambs. You can find books in a library or enter words such as *sheep* and *behavior* in a search engine on your computer. Draw pictures of lambs doing things that might be typical of what a real lamb would do. Think about how Jesus was like a lamb. How are you like a lamb? How are you different from one?

Whenever you see a lamb or a picture of one, think about Levi the Lamb and the book of Leviticus.

JUST FOR FUN

To find a list of offerings, use the Table of Contents in your Bible to look up Leviticus. In chapters 1–4, how many kinds of offerings can you find? What kinds of gifts do you offer God?

PRAYER

Trying to be perfect is hard, God. But you are perfect, and so is your Son, Jesus. Thank you for sending Jesus, who offered his perfect life to take away my sins. In Jesus' name I pray. Amen.

LEVITICUS, CHAPTER 1 (VERSE 4)

*Lay your hand on the animal's head, and the L*ORD *will accept its death in your place to purify you, making you right with him.*

DAILY DEVO

Jesus paid my price for paradise.

Do you like animals? Do you have a favorite pet? Then you understand why nobody likes to see or hear about animals dying. That's especially true of us pet lovers. So why was God so big on animal sacrifices? Even though it's kind of hard to understand, God wanted his people to offer animals as gifts to him so they would feel and remember the high price of sin. That price was death. Every time a sweet, harmless animal died, God was painting a picture of how Jesus would one day die on the cross for all our sins—past, present, and future. His death was the full and final price for paradise (another name for heaven). And that's why no more animals have to die as sacrifices for sin. Now that's good news!

MAKE IT STICK

The next time you're in a store with your dad, mom, or a friend, find something that costs a lot. Remember that Jesus paid a high price to take away your sins. Point to the price tag and say to yourself, *Jesus paid my price for paradise.*

PRAYER

Dear God, I want to live with you in paradise someday. But I could never be good enough to get there. I'm so glad that Jesus made it possible for me to go to heaven when he died on the cross. Amen.

CLICK-ER: PRICE TAG

Whenever you see, buy, or think about something with a *price tag*, let this picture register in your mind as the daily devo clicks and sticks. Levi the Lamb with a one-on-a-bun reminds you that the devo is from Leviticus, Chapter 1.

LEVITICUS, CHAPTER 11 (VERSES 21-22)

You may . . . eat winged insects that walk along the ground and have jointed legs so they can jump. The insects you are permitted to eat include all kinds of locusts, bald locusts, crickets, and grasshoppers.

DAILY DEVO

It's gross, but clean, to eat grasshoppers that are green.

Have you ever swallowed a flying bug by mistake? That's not very tasty, and not much fun either! It's hard to believe, but there are places in the world where people crunch grasshoppers like we munch popcorn. It sounds gross, but God's Word has always allowed it. In the Old Testament, God was kind and thoughtful to tell his people what they could and couldn't eat. Nobody understands all the reasons why some animals were okay to eat and some weren't. But we do know this for sure: God has always cared about his children, wanting their bodies and hearts to be pure and clean. Is your heart clean from the dirt of sin? Eating clean, green grasshoppers won't hurt your body, but keeping your heart clean from sin is way more important.

 MAKE IT STICK

Roll sugar-cookie dough into logs about the size of grasshoppers, sprinkle on green sugar, and bake. As you pop one in your mouth, say the daily devo and enjoy eating *"grasshoppers* that are green."

PRAYER

Dear God, I'm glad you know what's pure and clean and good for me. Most of all, I pray that you will help me keep my heart clean from sin. In Jesus' name, amen.

CLICK-ER:

GRASSHOPPERS

Whenever you see, try to grab, or think about *grasshoppers,* let this daily devo hop through your mind as it clicks and sticks. Levi the Lamb with a one-on-a-bun on either side of his belt reminds you that the devo is from Leviticus, Chapter 11.

LEVITICUS, CHAPTER 16 (VERSE 10)

*The scapegoat chosen by lot . . . will be kept alive, standing before the L*ORD*.*
When it is sent away to . . . the wilderness, the people will be purified and made
*right with the L*ORD*.*

DAILY DEVO

Jesus, my scapegoat, took my "sin coat."

Sometimes we blame others for things we do wrong. Instead of admitting our sin, we make another person the "scapegoat." In the Old Testament, the high priest would use his hands to picture himself moving the sins of the people to the head of a goat. The scapegoat was then sent out into a wild area to die. This may sound unkind and unfair, but it is a powerful picture of how God would one day move our sin to his Son, Jesus, and make him the scapegoat for our sin. The problem of sin would be like a heavy coat on him.

 MAKE IT STICK

Draw the front and back of a coat on the front and back of an upside-down paper bag. On a piece of paper, list some sins to tape to the coat. Then draw a picture of a goat. Place it inside the bag after cutting out a hole in the bottom of the bag for its head. Carry it to a faraway corner in your garage, basement, or backyard. Later, throw the bag away. This will help you remember how God put the coat of your sin on the scapegoat of his Son.

PRAYER

Dear God, thank you for Old Testament lessons that help me understand the New Testament lessons about Jesus. Thank you, Jesus, for carrying my sins away when you died on the cross. Amen.

CLICK-ER: COAT

Whenever you see, wear, or think about your *coat*, let this picture warm your heart as the daily devo clicks and sticks. Levi the Lamb with his one-on-a-bun and six-pick-up-stix is a reminder that the devo is from Leviticus, Chapter 16.

LEVITICUS, CHAPTER 19 (VERSE 32)

Stand up in the presence of the elderly, and show respect for the aged. Fear your God. I am the LORD.

DAILY DEVO

I always say hi and look my elders in the eye.

Do you have a favorite grandparent, great-aunt, great-uncle, or elderly neighbor? Sometimes we forget how special older people really are, and how important it is to honor them. But God doesn't forget. He wants us to use good manners to show our elders we respect them. Besides saying "please," "thank you," and "you're welcome," God wants us to honor older people by standing up in their presence. When an older person walks into a room, stop what you're doing, stand up, smile, look the person in the eye, and say "Hi!" This may sound like a little thing to you, but it's a big thing to elderly people. They'll be impressed, and you'll be blessed.

MAKE IT STICK

The next time you run into your grandparents, some elderly neighbors, or some older folks at church, smile, say hi, and look them in the eye. Watch what happens. Your show of respect may impress them so much that they'll want to know how you learned to act that way. Then you can tell them about this verse.

PRAYER

Thank you, God, for the elderly people in my life. I know you care about them and want me to do the same. Help me remember to do that. In Jesus' name, amen.

CLICK-ER: EYE

Whenever you use, see in a mirror, or think about your *eye*, let this daily devo on respect stand up in your mind as it clicks and sticks. Levi the Lamb with his one-on-a-bun and nine-foot-pine reminds you that the devo is from Leviticus, Chapter 19.

LEVITICUS, CHAPTER 20 (VERSE 6)

I will turn against those who . . . [put] their trust in mediums or in those who consult the spirits of the dead. I will cut them off from the community.

DAILY DEVO

I won't march to the drum of a medium.

The devil uses all kinds of tricks to try to get us off track with God. One of the tricks has to do with people called *mediums*. These people say they can talk with the spirits of the dead. Mediums want us to think they speak for God. They don't. They speak for the devil. Please obey God, and don't ever talk to a medium or listen to one. You don't need to. God is always with you, and you can talk to him in prayer at any time. You can read his Word, the Bible, to find out more about what you should do every day of your life. Listen to God's voice. Follow his ways. Stay far from the drum of a medium.

 MAKE IT STICK

The use of drums in music is common these days. Tune in to your favorite radio station or put on a favorite CD or DVD and listen for the drums. When you hear them, tap along with a drumstick or a pencil and repeat this daily devo. Remember, as a Christian your new heart does not beat to the tune of the world around you. It beats to a different drummer: the Spirit of God.

PRAYER

Dear God, I'm so glad I can talk to you. And I can read your directions to me in the Bible. Thank you for warning me about mediums. I'll stay far away from them. Amen.

CLICK-ER: DRUM

Whenever you see or hear a *drum*, let this daily devo beat in your heart as it clicks and sticks. Levi the Lamb with his two-blue-shoes and halo-is-a-hero-as-a-zero reminds you that the devo is from Leviticus, Chapter 20.

WEEKEND ACTIVITY IDEAS

(1) Highlight the verses for Week 4 in your Bible. (2) Find Levi the Lamb in each picture for this week and identify the chapter-number symbols. (3) Add to your collection of Click-ers. (4) Say the daily devos for Week 4. (5) Check out Saturday/Sunday of Week 10 for a related devo on the itch of a witch. You can also read what God said about mediums and witches in Deuteronomy, Chapter 18 (verses 9-11).

HEAVY-DUTY HAIRCUT

Sheep are shorn only once a year by hair cutters called sheep shearers. The wad of hair, called wool, that is collected from each sheep every year weighs almost eight pounds. From sheep hides and wool we make baseballs, tennis balls, carpet, and clothes.

Week 5, Monday

LEVITICUS, CHAPTER 24 (VERSE 11)

During the fight, this son of an Israelite woman blasphemed the Name of the LORD with a curse. So the man was brought to Moses for judgment.

DAILY DEVO

It's never cool to cuss, not even on the school bus.

Some kids think it sounds cool to cuss. Others get into the habit because they hear it on TV, in movies, on the playground, and maybe even at home. How can we keep our words under control and please God? The main thing to think about is that God's third commandment reminds us not to misuse his name. (See Exodus, Chapter 20, Verse 7.) God knows that not being respectful of his name hardens our hearts and shrinks our souls. We soon forget that we should speak respectfully to other people too, because they are made in God's image. Cussing isn't cool. It hurts you and others, including God. Don't cuss, but do pray for those who do.

 MAKE IT STICK

If you struggle with cussing, ask God for strength to stop. Come up with other words, such as "rats" or "drat," to replace the ones you no longer want to say. If you don't struggle with cussing, pray for someone who does have that habit. Your prayers could make all the difference.

PRAYER

Dear God, your name is holy. Help me to never forget that. When I say your name, may it always be in prayer or praise to show my love and respect for you. In Jesus' name I pray. Amen.

CLICK-ER: SCHOOL BUS

Whenever you see, ride, or think about a *school bus*, let this picture cruise through your mind as the daily devo clicks and sticks. Levi the Lamb with his two-blue-shoes and four-on-the-floorboard reminds you that the devo is from Leviticus, Chapter 24.

Week 5, Tuesday

BOOK OF NUMBERS
Num-Bee

Num-Bee sounds like *Numbers*. A bee that won't buzz off reminds us of the nonstop nagging of God's people in the book of Numbers. When you see Num-Bee in a picture, you'll know the daily devo is from Numbers. Connected to Num-Bee are number symbols. (See page 15.) They make the chapter location of the devo click and stick.

Numbers is a book about spiritual crybabies. It's also about God, who loved his people anyway. You would think everybody would have been ready to believe God after he led them out of Egypt. Instead, God's people buzzed around Moses, singing the blues day and night. When God told them to enter the Promised Land, they shrank back in unbelief and turned what could have been an 11-day hike into a 40-year nightmare. They never stopped buzzing until that whole complaining, unbelieving generation died. The children who grew up during those 40 years went into the Promised Land, trusting God to go with them.

MAKE IT STICK

Make a tab to mark the book of Numbers in your Bible. (See Week 1, Monday, for directions.)

Then ask your mom or dad where you can go to run around like a buzzing bee. Think about how you would feel if a bee chased you all day. If you wish, look up *bees* on the Internet. How many different kinds of bees can you find?

Whenever you see a bee or a picture of one, or hear a bee buzzing by, think about Num-Bee and the book of Numbers.

JUST FOR FUN
You can read about the complaining Israelites in Numbers, Chapter 11, and act out the story with your family. Talk together about what it's like to be around complaining people all the time.

PRAYER
Dear God, thank you for loving me even when I complain. But I don't want to be a complainer. I want to believe your promises and trust you to lead me every day. In Jesus' name, amen.

NUMBERS, CHAPTER 6 (VERSE 25)

May the LORD smile on you and be gracious to you.

DAILY DEVO

When I feel God's smile, I go the extra mile.

"Look at me!" is a phrase we've all thought and said a million times. All of us want the special people in our lives to see something we've done, smile, and say: "Way to go!" "Good job." "I love you." "You're a cool kid!" "Are you totally awesome, or just awesome?" If you often hear words like that, you probably feel like doing your best in everything you do. The truth is, though, the important people in our lives do not always talk to us this way. But God does. Every day he looks forward to smiling down on you and saying great things about you. Just follow him. And when you do something that doesn't please him, tell him you're sorry. You'll feel God's smile, and it'll help you go the extra mile, day after day.

 MAKE IT STICK

Get a smiley-face sticker or draw and cut out a happy face. Put the sticker or drawing inside one of your shoes. As you walk around your house, neighborhood, school, or church and feel the smiley face with your toes, repeat this daily devo.

PRAYER

I love you, God. You are totally awesome! And it makes me really happy to know that's how you feel about me. Thank you! In Jesus' name, amen.

CLICK-ER: SMILEY FACE

Whenever you see someone's *smile* or look at a *smiley-face sticker*, let this picture lighten your heart as the daily devo clicks and sticks. Num-Bee with his six-pick-up-stix reminds you that the devo is from Numbers, Chapter 6.

NUMBERS, CHAPTER 11 (VERSE 4)

Then the foreign rabble who were traveling with the Israelites began to crave the good things of Egypt. And the people of Israel also began to complain. "Oh, for some meat!" they exclaimed.

DAILY DEVO

When I complain, my attitude goes down the drain.

The people of Israel had a lot to be thankful for. God had brought them out of Egypt, where they had been slaves. He was feeding them all they could eat and keeping their clothes from wearing out. But the only thing the people could think about was what God *wasn't* doing. They needed an attitude adjustment! Do you? If you feel your attitude of gratitude going down the drain, why not stop, pray, and praise? Begin by thanking God for everything you can think of—even basic stuff like the air you breathe. If you do this, you'll be amazed to discover that God will plug the drain in your heart and fill it up again with thanksgiving to him.

 **MAKE IT STICK**

Plug the drain in a sink and fill the sink with water. Then pull the plug for a couple of seconds and repeat this daily devo. Next, plug the drain again and turn on the water for a few seconds while thanking God for one thing he has done for you. Have fun doing this over and over again. It will help you understand how complaining drains your heart, while thanking God fills it.

PRAYER

Dear God, I praise you for who you are and thank you for what you do. I pray that my attitude will always be filled with gratitude. In Jesus' name, amen.

CLICK-ER: DRAIN

Whenever you see, watch, or think about water going down a *drain*, let this daily devo fill your heart as it clicks and sticks. Num-Bee water skiing on two one-on-a-bun skis reminds you that the devo is from Numbers, Chapter 11.

NUMBERS, CHAPTER 13 (VERSE 23)

They cut down a branch with a single cluster of grapes so large that it took two of them to carry it on a pole between them! They also brought back samples of the pomegranates and figs.

DAILY DEVO

My faith is in grape shape.

Moses' 12-member "God squad" of special spies saw some amazing things during the 40 days they looked at the Promised Land. Everything they saw was "giant-this" or "giant-that." As proof, they brought back a cluster of grapes so large that two men had to carry it on a pole between them! These giant-sized grapes are a picture of the giant-sized faith that Joshua and Caleb had. Their faith in God stayed strong and fresh like a juicy grape, while the hearts of their spy buddies shriveled up like dried grapes, otherwise known as raisins. If you're not trusting God for something right now, your faith might be close to getting "raisin-ized." Don't let it happen. Ask God for help to keep your faith in "grape shape"!

 MAKE IT STICK

Ask your mom if you can have grapes for lunch sometime soon. After you thank God for this special treat, start popping the grapes into your mouth one by one! Just for fun, say this daily devo for every grape you eat. Then ask God for big faith to help you trust him.

PRAYER

Thank you, God, for the giant-sized faith of people like Joshua and Caleb. I pray that my trust in you will grow each day and never shrivel up. In Jesus' name, amen.

CLICK-ER: GRAPES

Whenever you see, eat, or think about *grapes*, let this daily devo get your spiritual juices flowing as it clicks and sticks. Num-Bee with his one-on-a-bun and three-is-the-key reminds you that the devo is from Numbers, Chapter 13.

NUMBERS, CHAPTER 16 (VERSES 19, 31)

Korah had stirred up the entire community against Moses and Aaron. . . .
The ground suddenly split open beneath them.

DAILY DEVO
Whenever I'm a rebel, I'm like a pebble in a shoe.

If you try to hike with pesky pebbles in your shoes, it's not too likely you'll get where you're going. The pain will make you want to quit and go home. Korah was like a pebble in a shoe. His bad attitude brought pain to the entire nation of Israel. Somehow he got everyone to rebel against Moses and Aaron. It was ugly. As God's leader, Moses wasn't about to roll over and play dead. So he announced a showdown at sunrise the next day. When the moment arrived, the lines were drawn. Suddenly the ground around Korah and his followers split apart, and they all disappeared. This story may sound scary, but it shows how important it is not to fight against God or his leaders. Don't side with rebels. They'll only bring you down.

MAKE IT STICK
Find a pebble, place it in your shoe, and keep it there for as long as you can stand it. As you feel the pain of that little stone in your shoe, think about the story of Korah, who tried to fight against God and Moses. When you finally remove the pebble, say this daily devo one more time.

PRAYER
Dear God, I don't want to be like a pebble in a shoe. Help me to obey you and never be a rebel at home, at school, or at church. In Jesus' name I pray. Amen.

CLICK-ER: **PEBBLE**
Whenever you see, feel, or think about a *pebble* in your shoe, let this daily devo send a pointed message to your heart as it clicks and sticks. Num-Bee with his one-on-a-bun and six-pick-up-stix reminds you that the devo is from Numbers, Chapter 16.

WEEKEND ACTIVITY IDEAS

(1) Highlight the verses for Week 5 in your Bible. (2) Find the HoneyWord animal in each of the pictures for this week and identify the chapter-number symbols. (3) Add to your collection of Click-ers. (4) Say the daily devos for Week 5. (5) Check out Friday of Week 8 for a related devo on how God warns with thorns.

BUSY BUZZER

Buzzing bees stay busy building six-sided boxes called honeycombs. The chapter-number symbol for six in this book of devos (six-pick-up-stix) is shaped like a honeycomb.

NUMBERS, CHAPTER 18 (VERSE 26)

Give these instructions to the Levites: When you receive from the people of Israel the tithes I have assigned as your allotment, give a tenth of the tithes you receive—a tithe of the tithe—to the LORD as a sacred offering.

DAILY DEVO

For every dollar, God gets a dime every time.

Old Testament Levites, like pastors today, were paid from the tithes of God's people. So didn't the Levites have to tithe? Yep. All God's people, then and now, are to give God one dime for every 10 dimes—every dollar—they get. Really, everything belongs to God. He's placed what we have in our care and only asks for a tenth of it back. That's so easy, you'd think all Christians would do it all the time. But they don't. Know why? Because we all struggle with selfishness when it comes to our money. Don't fall into that trap. God promises to give big-time blessings to anyone who faithfully tithes. Start tithing today. Give God one dime every time you get one dollar.

MAKE IT STICK

Show your family that you understand how to give God a tithe. Put a dollar bill on the table. Next to it make a stack of ten dimes to take the place of the dollar. Then pick up one dime and say this daily devo. If you have money in a piggy bank, count the dollars. Knowing this daily devo will help you figure out how much money to give to God!

PRAYER

Dear God, you know that I can be selfish. But you also know that I love you and want to please you. Teach me the joy of giving you one dime from every dollar I ever get. Amen.

CLICK-ER: DIME

Whenever you see, spend, or think about a *dime*, let this daily devo make change in your mind as it clicks and sticks. Num-Bee with his one-on-a-bun and eight-under-skates reminds you that the devo is from Numbers, Chapter 18.

NUMBERS, CHAPTER 22 (VERSE 32)

"Why did you beat your donkey those three times?" the angel of the LORD demanded. "Look, I have come to block your way because you are stubbornly resisting me."

DAILY DEVO

When God blocks my way, he wants me to obey.

Do you ever feel like doing something you know you shouldn't? That feeling is called *temptation*. It happens to everyone. Just ask Balaam. Though he knew better, he caved in when King Balak hired him to curse God's people. Why did he give in? Money. The love of money often steers people off God's path. But God loves us so much that when we are tempted to disobey him, he sometimes sends an angel to block our way. Then we can either turn around or keep going. Are you doing anything that might cause God to block your way? If so, turn around and obey. It'll be one of the best decisions you'll ever make.

 MAKE IT STICK

Get a block and a toy car. Place the block near the edge of a table. Roll the car toward the block, letting the block stop it. What would have happened if the block had not stopped the car? It's a good thing God stops us from rolling in the wrong direction! Roll your car toward the block again and try to say this daily devo before it reaches the block.

PRAYER

Dear God, I don't like to have my way blocked. But when it's you doing the blocking, I know it's a good thing. Make me willing to turn around and follow you. In Jesus' name I pray. Amen.

CLICK-ER: WOOD BLOCK

Whenever you see, play with, or think about a *wood block*, let this daily devo square away in your mind as it clicks and sticks. Num-Bee with his two pairs of two-blue-shoes reminds you that the devo is from Numbers, Chapter 22.

Week 6, Wednesday

BOOK OF DEUTERONOMY
Doodlebug-eronomy

Doodlebug-eronomy sounds like *Deuteronomy*. Like people who doodle things on paper again and again, Moses spelled out God's Word one more time before the people entered the Promised Land. When you see Doodlebug-eronomy in a picture, you'll know the daily devo is from Deuteronomy. Connected to Doodlebug-eronomy are number symbols. (See page 15.) They make the chapter location of the devo click and stick.

The people of God were right back where they had started. Forty years earlier, they had camped in this same place by the Jordan River. But instead of trusting God and entering the Promised Land, they had shrunk back in fear. To keep them strong this time, Moses put together a scrapbook of faith, which we call Deuteronomy. Like a human doodlebug writing the same thing over and over, Moses told story after story to remind the people again and again of God's love and faithfulness. Then he challenged the people to step out in faith as they watched God step in and provide.

 MAKE IT STICK

Make a tab to mark the book of Deuteronomy in your Bible. (See Week 1, Monday, for directions.)

Have you ever tried doodling? The next time you watch TV or listen to your favorite CD, get out a pencil and notepad and write a name or word over and over. Or draw a simple picture of a favorite flower or animal again and again. Doodling helps the word or picture you're thinking about really stick in your mind, doesn't it? Aren't you glad Moses was like a doodlebug, writing again and again about God's love?

Whenever you see a picture of a doodlebug or think about one, remember Doodlebug-eronomy and the book of Deuteronomy. (There really are tiny doodlebugs. You can read about them on page 60.)

JUST FOR FUN

You can look up Moses' last words to God's people. You'll find them in Deuteronomy, Chapter 33 (verses 26-29). Tell someone what you learned about God from these words.

PRAYER

Thank you, God, for having people like Moses write your words. I'm glad your words are written down for me to read in the Bible. Amen.

DEUTERONOMY, CHAPTER 4 (VERSE 2)

Do not add to or subtract from these commands I am giving you. Just obey the commands of the LORD your God that I am giving you.

DAILY DEVO

Like a recorder, I speak the Word in order.

Have you ever made a recording of yourself singing or speaking? Did you think that recording sounded like you? Perhaps you've seen yourself on a home video. Did you think the video looked like you? The best recorders make recordings that sound and look like the real you. God wants us to be good recorders of his Word. There's no room to add extra things. There's no reason to subtract anything either. God wants us to simply record it clearly in our hearts so we can live and speak it clearly also. Be a walking recorder. Speak God's Word in order. That way, you'll remind yourself and the people around you how God really wants us all to live!

 ### MAKE IT STICK

If you or your family has a boom box, a camcorder, a digital camera that records sound, or a computer and a microphone, politely ask someone to record your voice. Find a favorite Bible passage and record yourself reading it. Have fun playing it back—then find a way to *do* what this passage is teaching!

PRAYER

Lord, thank you for teaching me that nothing is to be added to or subtracted from your commands. Help me learn where to find your commands, and teach me to say them and obey them. In Jesus' name, amen.

CLICK-ER: RECORDER

Whenever you see, make a recording on, or think about a *recorder*, let your mind speak this daily devo in order as it clicks and sticks. Doodlebug-eronomy with its four-on-the-floorboard reminds you that the devo is from Deuteronomy, Chapter 4.

DEUTERONOMY, CHAPTER 5 (VERSE 19)

You must not steal.

DAILY DEVO

I won't steal even an orange peel.

Maybe you've heard a news story about someone who robbed a bank and took other people's money. Perhaps a person in your town stole a car. You might think stealing big things is worse than stealing little things. But stealing is stealing. Some people start taking a penny here and a nickel there. They keep taking what isn't theirs until they take more and more things. You don't have to start that habit. God is very clear about stealing. One of his commandments says, "You must not steal." This means even little things. When you're tempted to steal something that belongs to someone else, even if it's as small as an orange peel, don't take it. Leave it alone. Then you'll be pleasing God.

 **MAKE IT STICK**

Most grocery stores have a produce department full of fresh oranges and other fruit. The next time you're shopping with a parent, look for the oranges and say softly, "I won't steal even an *orange peel*." If your dad or mom asks what you're doing, explain that you are obeying God's commandment not to steal.

PRAYER

Dear God, you know how to help people get along together. Thank you for your command not to steal. Help me to obey it no matter how much I want something that doesn't belong to me. Amen.

CLICK-ER: ORANGE PEEL

Whenever you see, pull off, or think about an *orange peel*, let this daily devo slice into your mind as it clicks and sticks. Doodlebug-eronomy with its five-on-a-hive-hat reminds you that the devo is from Deuteronomy, Chapter 5.

DEUTERONOMY, CHAPTER 6 (VERSES 6–8)

You must commit yourselves wholeheartedly to these commands that I am giving you today. Repeat them again and again to your children. Talk about them when you are at home and when you are on the road, when you are going to bed and when you are getting up. Tie them to your hands and wear them on your forehead as reminders.

DAILY DEVO

I stick like glue to what God says to do.

God wants his words to click and stick in our hearts. He shows parents how to make this happen. He tells them to talk about his words at all kinds of fun times. Did you ever tie a string around your finger so you wouldn't forget something important? Well, God told his people long ago to tie his commands to their hands, to wear them on their foreheads, and even to write them on their doors and gates (verse 9)! As you look at the Click-ers you're learning about in this book, you, too, will see reminders of God's Word everywhere you go. And you'll stick like glue to what God says to do.

 MAKE IT STICK

Think about some fun times when you and your family read and talked about God's Word together. Then gather some of the Click-ers that are helping you remember God's Word. Choose a smaller one, such as a dime or a cereal flake, and dab the back of it with a glue stick. Then glue the item to a piece of paper. That's a picture of how God's Word is meant to stick in your heart.

PRAYER

Thank you, God, for all the things around me that remind me of your Word. I want to stick like glue to what you say to do. Amen.

CLICK-ER: GLUE STICK

Whenever you see or use a *glue stick*, let this daily devo cling to your mind as it clicks and sticks. Doodlebug-eronomy with six-pick-up-stix reminds you that the devo is from Deuteronomy, Chapter 6.

WEEKEND ACTIVITY IDEAS

(1) Highlight the verses for Week 6 in your Bible. (2) Find Num-Bee or Doodlebug-eronomy in each picture for this week and identify the chapter-number symbols. (3) Add to your collection of Click-ers. (4) Say the daily devos for Week 6. (5) Check out Thursday of Week 7 for a related devo on the Master of plaster.

OODLES OF DOODLES

Doodlebugs don't eat strudel, can't sing "Yankee Doodle," and don't doodle oodles of noodles. (Only people can do those things.) But doodlebugs do exist in the real world of bugs. Like their cousin the roly-poly, they're tiny and can curl up into a small ball. They're also known as pill bugs or sow bugs.

DEUTERONOMY, CHAPTER 8 (VERSE 3)

He humbled you by letting you go hungry and then feeding you with manna. . . .
He did it to teach you that people do not live by bread alone; rather, we live by
*every word that comes from the mouth of the L*ORD.

DAILY DEVO

I love to chew whatever's on God's menu.

Everybody knows that if you want to eat in a restaurant, you have to order from
the menu. And unless you just order soup, the food that's served won't do you any
good unless you chew it. It's the same with God's Word. God has served up a huge
plate of spiritual food called the Bible. When you read and think about or "chew
on" God's Word, you learn about his love and his ways. God's spiritual food is free,
but it's not so easy to chew. There is much to think about. So start small. Think of
each page as one meal from God. Over time, as you chew on God's Word verse by
verse and story by story, he'll fill your soul and satisfy your heart.

 MAKE IT STICK

Fold a piece of paper in half to make a special menu. On the cover, print "Holy
Menu." On the inside, make a list of Click-ers that trigger your favorite daily devos.
Then show it to someone in your family, and let that person "order" as many daily
devos as he or she wants. For each Click-er that's ordered, say the daily devo along
with its book and chapter location.

PRAYER

Dear God, I want to think
about your Word all the time
so I'm always filled up with
your spiritual food. Thanks
for teachers who help me
understand the Bible. In Jesus'
name, amen.

CLICK-ER: MENU

Whenever you see, order from,
or think about a *menu*, let your
mind serve up this daily devo as
it clicks and sticks. Doodlebug-
eronomy with its eight-under-
skates reminds you that the devo
is from Deuteronomy, Chapter 8.

DEUTERONOMY, CHAPTER 15 (VERSE 11)
There will always be some in the land who are poor. That is why I am
commanding you to share freely with the poor and with other Israelites
in need.

DAILY DEVO
My heart opens the door to the poor.
The world is filled with millions of poor people. Someone who is poor doesn't have
enough money for food, clothes, or maybe even a place to live. We must ask God
for soft, caring hearts. If we close the door on poor people and don't love them, our
hearts will get hard, and soon we won't love God either. We can pray. We can give.
We can be kind. We can always do something, but we must never do nothing. God
loves poor people. When we help them, God helps us in everything we do.

 MAKE IT STICK
Draw and cut out a heart. Then draw and cut out the top, bottom, and one side of
a door in the center of the heart. Hold your paper heart up to your real heart. Then
open the little paper door and pray, "Lord, please show my heart how to open the
door to the poor." Once a day for the next several days, pray this prayer as you place
your paper heart over your real heart. Then wait for God to open a door. He'll show
you what to do.

PRAYER
Dear God, thank you for loving
poor people, rich people, and me!
Please give me a caring heart so
that I will love others like you do
and share what I have, whether it
is much or little. Amen.

CLICK-ER: DOOR
Whenever you see, open, or think
about a *door*, open your heart
to this daily devo as it clicks
and sticks. Doodlebug-eronomy
with its one-on-a-bun and five-
on-a-hive-hat reminds you that
the devo is from Deuteronomy,
Chapter 15.

DEUTERONOMY, CHAPTER 17 (VERSES 18-19)

When he sits on the throne as king, he must copy for himself this body of instruction on a scroll. . . . He must always keep that copy with him and read it daily as long as he lives. That way he will learn to fear the LORD his God by obeying all the terms of these instructions and decrees.

DAILY DEVO

I love to plunge like a sponge into the Word.

Back in the time of the Old Testament, the first order of business for new kings was to write out their own copy of God's Word. They had to do it themselves, in their own handwriting. Those kings were to have a heart like a sponge: They were to plunge into the Scripture and soak it up. What about you? Are you soaking up God's Word like a sponge? No one can do it for you. You have to jump in and learn for yourself what God says. When you do, you'll find it's like clean water. It's refreshing and life changing. Come on in. The water's great!

MAKE IT STICK

The next time you're ready for a bath, politely ask your dad or mom for a sponge. Once you're in the tub, squeeze out all the water and place the sponge on the side ledge. Then flick it into the water and say this daily devo. Watch how fast the sponge soaks up the water. That's a picture of how God wants you to soak up his Word. You can do it by reading your Bible and learning how to obey it every day.

PRAYER

Dear God, I'm glad you want everyone—even kings and queens and presidents—to know what your Word says. Help me to soak it up like a sponge so I'll always remember it. Amen.

CLICK-ER: SPONGE

Whenever you see, squeeze, or think about a *sponge*, let your mind soak up this daily devo as it clicks and sticks. Doodlebug-eronomy with its one-on-a-bun and highway-seven-to-heaven sign remind you that the devo is from Deuteronomy, Chapter 17.

DEUTERONOMY, CHAPTER 27 (VERSE 8)

You must clearly write all these instructions on the stones coated with plaster.

DAILY DEVO

God's Word on plaster reminds me who's Master.

The minute God's people crossed the Jordan River and entered their new land, they were to set up an altar of stones and plaster God's Word all over it. God's Word on plaster was a way of reminding them that God was the loving Master of their lives. God wants us to do the same thing today. We no longer use altars covered with plaster, but most homes today have walls covered with plaster or plasterboard. Maybe you or your parents have a plaque or a wall hanging with a Bible verse on it. Each day as you see it, God helps you believe it and obey it. His Word on your plaster reminds you that he's Master.

 MAKE IT STICK

Write out a favorite Bible verse along the top of a piece of paper. Underneath it, draw a picture that shows you obeying the verse. Now "plaster" it on your bedroom wall using sticky tack or another removable adhesive. Tonight when you go to bed, look at it and ask God to help you obey the verse tomorrow.

PRAYER

Dear God, thank you for your Word wherever I can read it—in the Bible, on a plaque, or on a handwritten paper. I want to read it often so I'll remember you are my Master. Amen.

CLICK-ER:

PLASTERBOARD

Whenever you see, touch, or think about *plaster* or a *plasterboard wall*, let this daily devo be "stucco-ed" to your mind as it clicks and sticks. Doodlebug-eronomy with its two-blue-shoes and highway-seven-to-heaven sign reminds you that the devo is from Deuteronomy, Chapter 27.

Week 7, Friday

BOOK OF JOSHUA

Jaws-chew-ya

Jaws-chew-ya sounds like *Joshua*. Fear chewed at the hearts of the people living in Canaan as Joshua and the Israelites attacked their land like a shark. When you see Jaws-chew-ya in a picture, you'll know the daily devo is from Joshua. Connected to Jaws-chew-ya are number symbols. (See page 15.) They make the chapter location of the devo click and stick.

As the book of Joshua opens, God's people were finishing the last lap of their 40-year desert marathon. They were tired and sunburned. Everybody was thinking: This time, will we trust God to help us take the land, or will we chicken out and run like before? The Israelites had learned to flex their faith muscles, and Joshua wasn't about to let anyone get flabby now. Under his leadership they stayed strong and courageous. Like an attacking shark, Joshua struck fear in the hearts of the people of Canaan. God gave Joshua victory after victory, helping him chew up the Canaanites' evil ways.

 MAKE IT STICK

Make a tab for the book of Joshua in your Bible. (See Week 1, Monday, for directions.)

Pretend you are a shark, attacking a wicked gang of robbers. What is it about you that makes the robbers afraid of you? Joshua became the leader of God's people after Moses died. Joshua was like a shark that only attacked the enemies of God.

Whenever you see a picture of a shark or think about one, remember Jaws-chew-ya and the book of Joshua.

JUST FOR FUN

The most famous story in the book of Joshua is in Chapter 6. You may want to read the first 20 verses with your family and see how many things you can learn about the battle of Jericho. Then act it out.

PRAYER

Thank you, God, for leaders like Joshua, who aren't afraid to fight wicked people. Give the leaders of my country and my city the courage to do what is right. And please give me that same courage. In Jesus' name I pray. Amen.

JOSHUA, CHAPTER 1 (VERSE 8)

Study this Book of Instruction continually. Meditate on it day and night so you will be sure to obey everything written in it. Only then will you prosper and succeed in all you do.

DAILY DEVO

I say YES! to God's cookbook for success.

When you first tried to ride a bike or swim, it was a little scary, wasn't it? Life is like that. Ask Joshua. When God told him to take over the Promised Land, he was a little scared. But instead of focusing on his fears, he focused on God. That's the secret. Josh knew his Bible and obeyed God's laws. He trusted God to make him strong and give him courage. Then he watched God do mighty things through him, again and again. God will do the same for you. Say YES! to his laws—the recipes in his cookbook. It's the only way to have real success.

MAKE IT STICK

Take a sheet of paper and fold it in half, then fold it in half again to make a booklet. On the cover, write "God's Cookbook." Inside, list these directions for God's favorite recipe: "Read Joshua 1:8. Understand it. Obey it. Succeed." Then show your booklet to your mom or dad and read Joshua 1:8 from your Bible. Talk about what it means to obey God and have success in his eyes.

PRAYER

Dear God, if I follow you, I'll have a lot of joy and peace, won't I? I may not get everything I'd like, but I'll get everything I need. I'll be truly successful. Thanks, God. In Jesus' name, amen.

CLICK-ER: COOKBOOK

Whenever you see, cook from, or think about a *cookbook*, let this daily devo simmer in your mind as it clicks and sticks. Jaws-chew-ya with his one-on-a-bun reminds you that the devo is from Joshua, Chapter 1.

WEEKEND ACTIVITY IDEAS

(1) Highlight the verses for Week 7 in your Bible. (2) Find the HoneyWord animal in each of the pictures for this week and identify the chapter-number symbols. (3) Add to your collection of Click-ers. (4) Say the daily devos for Week 7. (5) Check out Friday of Week 4 for a devo on saying hi—one of God's recipes for success.

NON-CHOOSY CHEWERS

Called the scavengers or hunters of the sea, sharks have been known to eat tires, boxes of nails, and tin cans. The great white shark can lose over 20,000 teeth during its lifetime.

JOSHUA, CHAPTER 3 (VERSES 15-16)

The Jordan was overflowing its banks. But as soon as the feet of the priests who were carrying the Ark touched the water at the river's edge, the water above that point began backing up a great distance away. . . . And the water below that point flowed on to the Dead Sea until the riverbed was dry. Then all the people crossed over near the town of Jericho.

DAILY DEVO

When I step out, God steps in.

How were 2 million people, with all their camping gear, going to get across a flooded river? God had a plan, and Joshua agreed to follow it. The priests, carrying the Word of God, were to be strong in faith and step into the water. Then God would roll it back. When they stepped out, God stepped in with an incredible miracle. Not only did the water roll back, but the river bottom dried up, and everyone walked over on dry ground! What impossible river is God asking you to cross? What hard thing does he want you to do? Step out in faith. And watch God step in with power!

MAKE IT STICK

Find a pan in the kitchen and take it to your bathroom. Pour an inch or two of water into the pan and place it on the floor. Take off your shoes and socks. Close your eyes as you step into the water and imagine being one of the priests in this Bible story. Before opening your eyes, say this daily devo.

PRAYER

Dear God, when I have a hard thing to do, I know you want me to step out and start doing it. Then you'll step in and help. Please give me the courage to take the first step. Thanks, God! In Jesus' name, amen.

CLICK-ER: STEP

Whenever you *step* into a tub, *step* over a puddle, or walk down a *step*, let your mind step up to this daily devo as it clicks and sticks. Jaws-chew-ya with his three-is-the-key reminds you that the devo is from Joshua, Chapter 3.

JOSHUA, CHAPTER 4 (VERSES 21-22)

Then Joshua said to the Israelites, "In the future your children will ask, 'What do these stones mean?' Then you can tell them, 'This is where the Israelites crossed the Jordan on dry ground.'"

DAILY DEVO

I like submarining for deep meaning in the Word.

Some of the first submarines were used in the Civil War. These amazing machines are used not only by our navy, but by scientists who explore deep water. Small robot-controlled submarines with cameras were used to explore the wrecked *Titanic*. Others found fish thought to no longer exist. Just like explorers in an ocean, we can "submarine" into God's Word and find answers to things we wonder about. Exploring God's Word is an adventure you can start now and enjoy throughout your life. The deeper you "submarine" for meaning in God's Word, the more you'll discover there is to find. Dive in!

 MAKE IT STICK

Find several small stones. Use a permanent marker to write or draw the Click-er for one daily devo on each stone (for example, a submarine). Pour some water into a pail and put the stones at the bottom. Pull out one stone as you pretend your hand is the arm on a submarine that retrieves stuff from the ocean bottom. See if you can remember the meaning of the picture or word on the stone. Try it with a friend.

PRAYER

I like to explore everything in the world you made, God. Thank you for the adventures I can look forward to enjoying as I explore your Word, too. In Jesus' name I pray. Amen.

CLICK-ER: SUBMARINE

Whenever you see, draw, or think about a *submarine*, let this daily devo sink deep into your mind as it clicks and sticks. Jaws-chew-ya with his four-on-the-floorboard reminds you that the devo is from Joshua, Chapter 4.

JOSHUA, CHAPTER 24 (VERSE 15)

If you refuse to serve the LORD, then choose today whom you will serve. Would you prefer the gods your ancestors served beyond the Euphrates? Or will it be the gods of the Amorites in whose land you now live? But as for me and my family, we will serve the LORD.

DAILY DEVO

Lord, give me the sense to stay off the fence.

Fences are everywhere, and we're always on one side or the other of a fence. Joshua knew the same is true about friendship with God. Joshua wanted the people of Israel to stay on the Lord's side. But the choice was theirs. Joshua couldn't decide for them. And no one can decide for you. Whose side are you on? It's the most important question you'll ever answer. You can't be on both sides of the fence at the same time. If you're already on God's side, keep believing, trusting, and obeying. If you're on the other side, come on over. If you're trying to live on both sides, ask God for the sense to get off the fence. That's a prayer he loves to answer.

 **MAKE IT STICK**

Build a fence from dominoes, blocks, or sticks. Write words on small pieces of paper or sticky notes to describe actions or attitudes that please God. Put these on one side of the fence. Write down actions or attitudes that *don't* please God, and put those on the other side. Then decide which side of the fence you want to live on.

PRAYER

Dear God, thank you for letting me choose whether or not to follow you. I need your help to make the right choice so I'm always on the side that pleases you. Amen.

CLICK-ER: FENCE

Whenever you see, climb, or think about a *fence*, let this daily devo make sense in your mind as it clicks and sticks. Jaws-chew-ya with his two-blue-shoes and four-on-the-floorboard reminds you that the devo is from Joshua, Chapter 24.

Week 8, Thursday

BOOK OF JUDGES

Judge the Jaguar

Jaguar begins with the same letter as *Judges*. Like a jaguar pacing in its cage at the zoo, the Israelites went back and forth—sometimes obeying God, but most of the time not caring whether they obeyed or not. When you see Judge the Jaguar in a picture, you'll know the daily devo is from Judges. Connected to Judge the Jaguar are number symbols. (See page 15.) They make the chapter location of the devo click and stick.

The book of Judges is a story about the wishy-washy hearts of God's people. After Joshua died, they couldn't make up their minds about following God. One day they loved him. The next day they didn't. Their hearts roamed back and forth like a restless jaguar. Each time they turned away from God, he let their enemies win. But when they cried out for help, he chose special leaders called judges to help them. God doesn't want an on-again, off-again, halfhearted relationship with you. He wants you to follow him every day, loving him with all your heart.

 MAKE IT STICK

Make a tab to mark the book of Judges in your Bible. (See Week 1, Monday, for directions.)

We have judges and juries today who help decide whether a person is innocent or guilty of a crime. Talk with your family about how this works.

Today's judges are not exactly the same as the judges of the Old Testament. God gave his people judges to show them how to do what was right. But the people wouldn't always listen to them. And after a while they would stop obeying God.

Whenever you see a picture of a jaguar or think about one, remember Judge the Jaguar and the book of Judges.

JUST FOR FUN

Look up what the Bible says about the judges in the book of Judges, Chapter 2 (verses 16-19).

PRAYER

Lord, I want to show my love for you every day. Forgive me for times when I've forgotten about you, following my own path instead of yours. Keep me closer to you. Thanks, God. In Jesus' name, amen.

JUDGES, CHAPTER 2 (VERSE 3)

I will no longer drive out the people living in your land. They will be thorns in your sides, and their gods will be a constant temptation to you.

DAILY DEVO

I listen when God warns and don't get stuck with thorns.

In the book of Judges, God probably gave his people more spankings per page than in any other book of the Bible. He loved them. He knew what was best for them. He told them over and over what he wanted them to do. And when they didn't do it, he disciplined them like any loving father would do. He let their enemies upset and hurt them like thorns stuck in their skin. It was painful, but it got their attention. This might sound hard to believe, but spankings can be a good thing when backed by a heart of love. God loves you and knows what's best for your life. Are you obeying him? If not, he may send you a loving thorn of warning. When he does, listen. He's only trying to protect you and keep you on track.

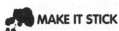 **MAKE IT STICK**

Look for a bush with thorns or for an encyclopedia photo of a thorn. Talk with your family about how much a sharp thorn can hurt. You may want to pantomime cutting a rose and getting stuck with a thorn. Then talk about why God sometimes needs to get our attention with a sharp warning.

PRAYER

Dear God, thank you for being my heavenly Father and for loving me enough to discipline me when I don't obey you. Being disciplined isn't fun. But I know that you do only what's best for me. Thanks, God. Amen.

CLICK-ER: THORNS

Whenever you see, get stuck by, or think about a *thorn*, let this daily devo prick your mind as it clicks and sticks. Judge the Jaguar with his two-blue-shoes reminds you that the devo is from Judges, Chapter 2.

JUDGES, CHAPTER 5 (VERSES 16-18)

Why did you sit at home among the sheepfolds? . . . Gilead remained east of the Jordan. And why did Dan stay home? Asher sat unmoved at the seashore, remaining in his harbors. But Zebulun risked his life, as did Naphtali, on the heights of the battlefield.

DAILY DEVO

I get out of my chair when a friend needs care.

Deborah was a great woman who trusted God and did whatever God asked of her. As one of Israel's judges, she knew it was time to lead the people of God into battle. She and a man named Barak called for everyone to help fight the Canaanites. But some of God's people were like couch potatoes. They just sat at home and didn't lift a finger. Yeah, they escaped the dangers of war, but they missed out on the joys of victory. Stuck-in-their-chair people miss out on everything. They sit and won't commit to anything. They don't experience the power of God. If you have a friend who needs care, don't just sit in your chair. Get up and help!

MAKE IT STICK

Sit in a chair and quietly ask God to help you think of a family member or a friend who needs help. When God brings someone to mind, get out of your chair and offer to help that person. God will see your good deed and be very pleased.

PRAYER

Dear God, when someone needs my help, please show me what to do. In Jesus' name, amen.

CLICK-ER: CHAIR

Whenever you see, sit in, or get out of a *chair*, let this daily devo be seated in your mind as it clicks and sticks. Judge the Jaguar in the picture with his five-on-a-hive-hat reminds you that the devo is from Judges, Chapter 5.

WEEKEND ACTIVITY IDEAS

(1) Highlight the verses for Week 8 in your Bible. (2) Find the HoneyWord animal in each of the pictures for this week and identify the chapter-number symbols. (3) Add to your collection of Click-ers. (4) Say the daily devos for Week 8. (5) Check out Friday of Week 51 for a related devo on hanging hats over welcome mats.

TALE OF A TAIL

A jaguar can use the tip of its tail to get a fish to come
to the surface, and then snag it with its claws.

JUDGES, CHAPTER 6 (VERSES 39-40)

Gideon said to God, "Please don't be angry with me, but . . . this time let the fleece remain dry while the ground around it is wet with dew." So that night God did as Gideon asked. The fleece was dry in the morning, but the ground was covered with dew.

DAILY DEVO

I don't need morning dew to know what to do.

The life of Gideon makes it clear that God can turn any scaredy-cat into a mighty warrior. As the story opens, Gideon was hiding from the Midianites. When the angel of the Lord tapped him on the shoulder and called him to lead God's people, the angel ignored the sound of Gideon's knocking knees. He saw Gideon's future and called him "mighty hero." When Gideon started piling on excuses about why he was the wrong guy, God showed him a morning-dew-on-fleece miracle to make his faith strong. But one miracle wasn't enough. So the next morning God very kindly gave him a morning-dew-on-the-ground miracle. Do you need proof that God will do what he says before you will obey him? Sometimes he gives it, and sometimes he doesn't. Either way, you have to decide: Are you going to obey God or not?

 MAKE IT STICK

Grab a handful of grass and place it on a sheet of paper. Then drip a few drops of water on the blades of grass to give it that wet-morning-dew look. When you have "dew-ed" it the way you want it, repeat this daily devo.

PRAYER

Dear God, thank you for the times when you make it clear just what you're going to do. But even when you don't, help me to make right choices and do what you say. In Jesus' name, amen.

CLICK-ER:
MORNING DEW

Whenever you see, walk through, or think about *morning dew* on grass, let this daily devo soak into your mind as it clicks and sticks. Judge the Jaguar with six-pick-up-stix reminds you that the devo is from Judges, Chapter 6.

Week 9, Tuesday

BOOK OF RUTH

Ruthie the Raccoon

Raccoon begins with the same letter as *Ruth*. A raccoon is good at finding food, even at night. Ruth found food in a field. And she trusted God to help her as she curled up at the feet of Boaz one night.

When you see Ruthie the Raccoon in a picture, you'll know the daily devo is from Ruth. Connected to Ruthie are number symbols. (See page 15.) They make the chapter location of the devo click and stick.

The book of Ruth is a powerful picture about hanging on to God when everything looks hopeless. Ruth's husband was dead, and she had nothing. But she did have faith in God, and she had one friend who believed in God—her mother-in-law, Naomi. That was enough. Sometimes life knocks the wind out of us. But God helps us get back on our feet. Like a raccoon finding food on a dark night, we can find help from God when things look dark. If hard times hit and you feel like giving up, let Ruth's story help you keep on keeping on.

MAKE IT STICK

Make a tab to mark the book of Ruth in your Bible. (See Week 1, Monday, for directions.)

Politely ask your dad or mom if you can go to the library and check out some books with stories about raccoons. Maybe you'll learn how they find corn in fields just as Ruth found a grain called *barley* in a field.

Whenever you see a picture of a raccoon or think about one, remember Ruthie the Raccoon and the book of Ruth.

JUST FOR FUN

You may want to find the book of Ruth, Chapter 1 in your Bible. You and your family can take turns reading it to discover who Ruth was. Chapter 2 tells you about Boaz. His name is also in Luke 3:32. He was an ancestor of Jesus!

PRAYER

Dear God, thank you for making corn and barley and all the other crops that grow in farmers' fields. And thanks for helping people know how to make bread and cereal from them. In Jesus' name, amen.

RUTH, CHAPTER 2 (VERSE 11)

"Yes, I know," Boaz replied. "But I also know about everything you have done for your mother-in-law since the death of your husband. I have heard how you left your father and mother and your own land to live here among complete strangers."

DAILY DEVO

I'm willing to go out on a limb for him.

If we compare trusting God to climbing a tree, we could say that God is always calling us to climb out farther on a limb. God makes sure that we will never outclimb or outgrow our need for trust. Ruth is a beautiful picture of someone who kept trusting God during the worst time of her life. When everything within her wanted to climb down and quit, she kept climbing and trusting. Are you climbing up to God in faith, or are you climbing down away from him in fear? Be willing to "go out on a limb" for God by trusting him. He'll calm your fears and meet your needs. That's a promise.

 MAKE IT STICK

Think about something you need to trust God to handle. Maybe it's a problem at home or at school. Find a low-hanging limb to hang from. When you get as far out on the limb as you feel comfortable going, let your hands go. As you drop safely to the ground, repeat this daily devo. Then thank God by faith for the way he's going to help you.

PRAYER

Sometimes I feel afraid, God. Please give me the strength to keep going. Teach me to count on you to be there for me in both the bad times and the good. Amen.

CLICK-ER: **TREE LIMB**

Whenever you see, hang from, or think about a *tree limb*, let this daily devo climb into your heart as it clicks and sticks. Ruthie the Raccoon with her two-blue-shoes reminds you that the devo is from Ruth, Chapter 2.

Week 9, Thursday

BOOK OF 1 SAMUEL

Sam Mule the 1st

Sam Mule sounds like *Samuel*. Like a stubborn mule, God's people dug in their feet, turned down his rule over them, and called for a king. When you see Sam Mule the 1st in a picture, you'll know the daily devo is from 1 Samuel. Connected to Sam Mule the 1st are number symbols. (See page 15.) They make the chapter location of the devo click and stick.

First Samuel is a book about the BIG difference between outside looks and inside attitudes. From the outside, Saul looked like Mr. Everything—tall, handsome, and brave. He talked and dressed like a king. David, on the other hand, didn't look at all like a king. He was small and barely old enough to shave. He was Mr. Nobody from Nowhere. But things aren't always as they seem. Saul, who looked like a king on the outside, was as stubborn as a mule on the inside. David, who looked like a no-big-deal kid on the outside, had a heart inside that loved God. Guess who became Israel's greatest king? David.

 MAKE IT STICK

Make a tab to mark the book of 1 Samuel in your Bible. (See Week 1, Monday, for directions.)

Look up "animal idioms" on a search engine. You'll learn what "stubborn as a mule" means, as well as what other expressions related to animals mean. Do you think God's people were wise to be stubborn like a mule? Was Saul wise when he was as stubborn as a mule?

Whenever you see a mule and picture it wearing the number *one*, remember Sam Mule the 1st and the book of 1 Samuel.

JUST FOR FUN

Check out 1 Samuel 8:4-9 to see why it was wrong for God's people to ask for a king.

PRAYER

Dear God, I'm glad you are a good king. When I let you rule my life, everything turns out for the best. Help me not to be stubborn about letting you be my Lord and King in everything. In Jesus' name, amen.

1 SAMUEL, CHAPTER 2 (VERSE 26)

The boy Samuel grew taller and grew in favor with the LORD and with the people.

DAILY DEVO

I'm growing like a sprout, inside and out.

Every year Hannah sewed Samuel a new coat. She had to. Like all children, he sprouted taller and taller, year after year. But while he was growing tall on the outside physically, he was also growing tall on the inside spiritually. He was learning to love God and to be like him. That's how God wants every child—including you—to grow. Physical growth usually just happens. But spiritual growth is different. Each of us has to choose whether or not we want to begin growing spiritually. Don't wait until you're a grown-up. Start growing to be more like God now. Do what Samuel did. Be among the few who are growing like a sprout, inside and out.

 MAKE IT STICK

Draw a picture of yourself planted in a garden from the waist up. All around you are sprouts just starting to grow. Label these sprouts with words that tell how you're growing to be like God: *loving*, *kind*, *helpful*, *patient*, *caring*, and so on. (There are more words like these in the book of Galatians, Chapter 5, verses 22-23.) Show your picture to your parents or grandparents and say the daily devo.

PRAYER

Dear God, it's fun to grow bigger and taller. But growing to be like you is even more important. Show me one area where I need to make some changes. Thanks, God. In Jesus' name, amen.

CLICK-ER: SPROUT

Whenever you see, touch, or eat any kind of *sprout*, let this daily devo shoot up in your mind as it clicks and sticks. Sam Mule the 1st with his two-blue-shoes reminds you that the devo is from 1 Samuel, Chapter 2.

1 SAMUEL, CHAPTER 3 (VERSES 19-20)

As Samuel grew up, the LORD was with him, and everything Samuel said proved to be reliable. And all Israel . . . knew that Samuel was confirmed as a prophet of the LORD.

DAILY DEVO

My words untie lots of knots.

Do you ever feel "all tied up in knots"? That's the feeling you can get when you are worried and don't know what to do. As a young boy, Samuel learned to love and obey God. As Samuel prayed day after day, he didn't just *talk* to God, he also *listened*. He heard wise words from God that hit the spot. Samuel shared God's wise words with others and "untied knots" in people's hearts. Be like Samuel. Trust God to help you say words that fit and hit the needs of other people. You'll find that God will use you, as he did Samuel, to untie lots of knots in people's worried hearts.

MAKE IT STICK

Tie a piece of rope or string into knots. Then untie the knots while saying this daily devo. How many times did you need to say this daily devo before all your knots were untied? Sometimes it takes time to untie knots in worried hearts, too. But God is pleased when we keep on sharing the wise things we learn about him and his love.

PRAYER

Dear God, please help me find ways to tell my family and friends how much you love them. In Jesus' name I pray. Amen.

CLICK-ER: KNOT

Whenever you see, untie, or think about a *knot*, let your mind tie this daily devo to your heart as it clicks and sticks. Sam Mule the 1st with his three-is-the-key reminds you that the devo is from 1 Samuel, Chapter 3.

WEEKEND ACTIVITY IDEAS

(1) Highlight the verses for Week 9 in your Bible. (2) Find the HoneyWord animal in each picture for this week and identify the chapter-number symbols. (3) Add to your collection of Click-ers. (4) Say the daily devos for Week 9. (5) Check out Wednesday of Week 21 for a related devo on words that give life or cut like a knife.

WHEN MARES MARRY

A mule is the baby of a mare (girl horse) and a jackass (boy donkey).

1 SAMUEL, CHAPTER 10 (VERSES 21-22)

[Samuel] brought each family of the tribe of Benjamin before the LORD, and . . . Saul son of Kish was chosen. . . . They asked the LORD, "Where is he?" And the Lord replied, "He is hiding among the baggage."

DAILY DEVO

I can't hide from God's grace, even in a suitcase.

The time had come for Saul to be crowned king of Israel. Everybody was excited. And everybody was there . . . except Saul! The people asked the Lord where he was. "Hiding in the baggage!" the Lord said. Saul knew God had picked him to be king, so why did he hide? Was it the shy-guy thing or what? Nobody knows for sure. But like Saul, we often hide when God wants us to do something for him. Perhaps we don't want to fail. Or maybe we're afraid of what others might think. Sometimes we're just not sure what to do. Don't run from the stuff God has asked you to do. It's no use. He'll find you. And when he does, he'll love you because of his kindness—his grace. And he'll help you, step by step.

MAKE IT STICK

Get a large cardboard box that you can hide in. Pretend that it's a suitcase. Then play hide-and-seek with your dad, mom, brothers, sisters, or friends. Let your "suitcase" be home base. Each person who gets home free must say the daily devo.

PRAYER

I'm sorry, God, about trying to hide instead of helping or sharing or doing something else you wanted me to do. Thanks for loving me anyway, but please help me do what you want today. In Jesus' name, amen.

CLICK-ER: SUITCASE

Whenever you see, carry, or think about a *suitcase*, let your mind unpack this daily devo as it clicks and sticks. Sam Mule the 1st with his one-on-a-bun and halo-is-a-hero-as-a-zero reminds you that the devo is from 1 Samuel, Chapter 10.

1 SAMUEL, CHAPTER 16 (VERSES 6-7)

Samuel took one look at Eliab and thought, "Surely this is the LORD's anointed!" But the LORD said to Samuel, "Don't judge by his appearance or height, for I have rejected him. The LORD doesn't see things the way you see them. People judge by outward appearance, but the LORD looks at the heart."

DAILY DEVO

I dwell on what's behind the shell.

TV shows, movies, and magazine covers try to show us how our outside shells should look. If we've got the right face, body, and clothes, we have "the Look" and we're cool. If we don't, we're out. It's nothing new. When Samuel dropped by Jesse's house, he went there to anoint the second king of Israel. He would pour oil on the person God had chosen. The minute Samuel saw Jesse's son Eliab, he thought, *Whoa, this is the guy!* But Samuel was wrong. While Eliab had "the Look," David had "the Heart." So God told Samuel to anoint David. Your outside shell is what people see first. But with God, what you're like inside is a much bigger deal. Don't worry about the shell. Worry about what's behind it—in yourself and others.

MAKE IT STICK

Draw your favorite seashell. Then tell your family what you learned from the story of Samuel and David. (If you're fortunate enough to live near a beach, or if you have a shell collection, find your favorite shell instead and do the same thing.)

PRAYER

Dear God, I like to look nice on the outside, but I know that the thoughts and attitudes inside of me are what matter to you. When I choose my friends, I pray that those things will be most important to me, too. Amen.

CLICK-ER: SEASHELL

Whenever you see, pick up, or think about a *seashell*, let your mind shell out this daily devo as it clicks and sticks. Sam Mule the 1st with his one-on-a-bun and six-pick-up-stix reminds you that the devo is from 1 Samuel, Chapter 16.

1 SAMUEL, CHAPTER 17 (VERSES 48-49)

As Goliath moved closer to attack, David quickly ran out to meet him. Reaching into his shepherd's bag and taking out a stone, he hurled it with his sling and hit the Philistine in the forehead. The stone sank in, and Goliath stumbled and fell face down on the ground.

DAILY DEVO

I can hit the spot with my spiritual slingshot.

Each of us, just like David, has to fight our own battles with evil every day. It takes courage. David knew God would help him fight Goliath. But Saul's king-size armor didn't work. (See verses 38-39.) David trusted God to help him fight in his own way, with his own sling. One of the hardest things to learn is how to find what God wants each of us to do. Too many of us look at our "giant" problems and shrink back, instead of looking to God for help and charging forward. Don't be a wimp. Trust God to help you hit your problem spots with your "slingshot."

MAKE IT STICK

To make a slingshot, find a small branch in the shape of a *Y*. Stretch a rubber band across the top of the *Y*. Now keep folding a little piece of paper until it's about the size of a nickel. Place the fold of the paper against the front of the rubber-band strands, pull the paper toward you, aim, and let go. Each time you hit your target, name a problem God can help you knock down.

PRAYER

When my problems seem like giants, help me, God, to trust you. I know you can teach me how to knock down my problems as easily as David knocked down Goliath. I'm glad nothing is too hard for you. Amen.

CLICK-ER: SLINGSHOT

Whenever you see, use, or think about a *slingshot*, let this daily devo hit the spot as it clicks and sticks. Sam Mule the 1st with his one-on-a-bun and highway-seven-to-heaven sign reminds you that the devo is from 1 Samuel, Chapter 17.

1 SAMUEL, CHAPTER 18 (VERSES 3-4)

Jonathan made a solemn pact with David, because he loved him as he loved himself. Jonathan sealed the pact by taking off his robe and giving it to David, together with his tunic, sword, bow, and belt.

DAILY DEVO
The true friends I gain are like a twin-engine plane.

Twin-engine airplanes have two engines for two reasons: (1) to fly faster, higher, and farther; and (2) to keep the plane in the air until it can land safely if one engine stops working. Great friends are like a twin-engine plane. They are heading in the same direction; the same things are important to them; and they help each other reach their goals. And if something bad happens to one, the other keeps the plane flying until they can safely get help. David and Jonathan had a very special twin-engine friendship, which grew as they went through many ups and downs. If God gives you a special friend, be sure to show God—and your friend—how thankful you are. And take good care of your twin-engine friendship!

 MAKE IT STICK

Look up the Wright brothers in an encyclopedia and read how they built the first successful airplane in 1903. The Wright brothers weren't just brothers. They were true Christian friends. Their friendship grew just like the twin-engine airplane industry they created.

PRAYER

Thank you, Lord, for special friends. Show us how to help each other through all of our ups and downs. In Jesus' name I pray. Amen.

CLICK-ER:
TWIN-ENGINE PLANE

Whenever you see, ride in, or think about a *twin-engine plane*, let this daily devo fly through your mind as it clicks and sticks. Sam Mule the 1st with his one-on-a-bun and eight-under-skates reminds you that the devo is from 1 Samuel, Chapter 18.

1 SAMUEL, CHAPTER 24 (VERSE 14)

Who is the king of Israel trying to catch anyway? Should he spend his time chasing one who is as worthless as a dead dog or a single flea?

DAILY DEVO

I'm not a flea; I'm Spirit-led me.

David was tired of running from King Saul, who didn't understand God's plans. David knew that the king had started seeing him as nothing more than a tiny flea, when in fact he was the next king of Israel. Sometimes the people around us or the hard times we face can make us think to ourselves, *I'm nobody. I'll never amount to anything.* But nothing could be further from the truth. Like David, you're God's child. You can't see God, but his Spirit is leading you. So when the devil hits you with the line, "You're nothing but a flea," don't believe it. Instead, trust God and say, "I'm not a flea; I'm Spirit-led me." Then the devil will back off, and you'll be ready to follow God's plans for you.

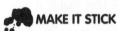 MAKE IT STICK

Did you ever have a dog or a cat with fleas? Did you ever look at a flea under a magnifying glass? Enter the words "picture of flea" in a search engine to find a Web site with a picture. Then stand in front of a mirror and repeat this daily devo as you imagine a flea sitting on the tip of your finger.

PRAYER

Dear God, thanks for creating me and letting me be your child. Thank you for sending your Holy Spirit to lead me. And thanks for this daily devo, which reminds me that David was not worthless, and neither am I. Amen.

CLICK-ER: FLEA

Whenever you see, get bit by, or think about a *flea*, let this daily devo jump into your mind as it clicks and sticks. Sam Mule the 1st with his two-blue-shoes and four-on-the-floorboard reminds you that the devo is from 1 Samuel, Chapter 24.

1 SAMUEL, CHAPTER 28 (VERSES 3, 5, 7)

Saul had banned from the land of Israel all mediums. . . . When Saul saw the vast Philistine army, he became frantic with fear. . . . Saul then said to his advisers, "Find a woman who is a medium, so I can go and ask her what to do."

DAILY DEVO
I don't itch to see a witch.

The green leaves of poison ivy don't look as if they would hurt you. But just touch one, and before you know it, you'll develop a skin rash so itchy you'll feel like climbing walls. All practices connected to the world of Satan are like poison ivy. They may look harmless, but they're off-limits. Don't touch them in any way. The devil would like nothing more than for you to believe that a witch is just an ugly old woman with a wart on her nose. Don't fall for that. A real witch, sometimes called a *medium*, is an evil person who worships Satan. A witch would like to turn you away from trusting God and his Word. No one can follow both a witch and God—they don't mix. So don't be like Saul. Don't ever give in to any itch to see a witch.

 MAKE IT STICK

Politely ask your dad or mom or a Sunday school teacher to help you find Deuteronomy 18:9-14 in your Bible. Read what God says there about witches and mediums. Then draw a picture of a witch to crumple up and throw away as you say this daily devo.

PRAYER
Dear God, I worship only you. I trust only you and your Word. Make my faith grow strong so that no one can ever convince me to turn away from you. In Jesus' name I pray. Amen.

CLICK-ER: WITCH
Whenever you see, read about, or think about a *witch*, let this daily devo scratch your brain as it clicks and sticks. Sam Mule the 1st with his two-blue-shoes and eight-under-skates reminds you that the devo is from 1 Samuel, Chapter 28.

WEEKEND ACTIVITY IDEAS

(1) Highlight the verses for Week 10 in your Bible. (2) Find the HoneyWord animal in each of the pictures for this week and identify the chapter-number symbols. (3) Add to your collection of Click-ers. (4) Say the daily devos for Week 10. (5) Check out Saturday/Sunday of Week 4 for a related devo on the drum of a medium.

MULE RULE

Mules are sterile. That means they are not able to have babies.

Week 11, Monday

BOOK OF 2 SAMUEL
Sam Mule the 2nd

Sam Mule sounds like *Samuel*. Like a stubborn mule that doesn't want to change, David would not change his mind about following God. So being stubborn can sometimes be a good thing! When you see Sam Mule the 2nd in a picture, you'll know the daily devo is from 2 Samuel. Connected to Sam Mule the 2nd are number symbols. (See page 15.) They make the chapter location of the devo click and stick.

The book of 2 Samuel looks at what King David was like inside. We learn why he was such a good friend of God's. It wasn't because he was perfect. Far from it. Like us, he did wrong things again and again. The key to David's friendship with God was this: Whenever David sinned, he admitted it. He had a lifelong, mulelike determination to tell God he was sorry about his sins. That may not sound like much, but telling God we're sorry about the bad things we've done is the first step to take if we want to stay friends with him. That was true for David, and it's true for us.

 MAKE IT STICK

Make a tab to mark the book of 2 Samuel in your Bible. (See Week 1, Monday, for directions.)

Think of a situation in which it would be good to be stubborn like a mule, and then act it out. Maybe a kid down the street tries to get you to disobey one of the Ten Commandments, perhaps by not listening to your parents, by lying, or by stealing, and you stubbornly refuse.

Whenever you see a mule and picture it wearing the number *two*, remember Sam Mule the 2nd and the book of 2 Samuel.

JUST FOR FUN

In Chapter 12 of 2 Samuel, verses 9 and 13, you can learn about something sinful that David did and admitted. Then, in Psalm 51, you'll find his prayer of confession. Choose one or several verses from the psalm that you can pray when you need to confess a sin.

PRAYER

Dear God, when it comes to obeying you, I want to be stubborn like a mule. But I know that just like everyone else, I sometimes do things that are wrong. So when I sin, help me confess it to you right away. In Jesus' name I pray. Amen.

2 SAMUEL, CHAPTER 4 (VERSE 4)

Saul's son Jonathan had a son named Mephibosheth, who was crippled as a child.

DAILY DEVO

Even with a crutch, I can do much.

Mephibosheth was only five years old when his dad (Jonathan) and granddad (Saul) were killed in a battle. Then his nurse dropped him. She didn't mean to do it, but after that he couldn't walk or run ever again. Over time Mephibosheth learned to love and trust God. Do you have to use crutches or braces to get around? Are you in a wheelchair? If so, don't let it steal your zeal for God. Talk to him about the things that bother you. After a while you'll discover that he is taking away any anger you may feel. You'll find that he is with you when you feel sad. You'll also learn from him that there are many things you still can do.

 MAKE IT STICK

If you need crutches, braces, or a wheelchair, name things God helps you do. If you don't need any of those medical helps, list what you could do with someone who does need them. Then make plans to do one of those things. (In 2 Samuel, Chapter 9, you and your family can read what King David did for his friend's son, Mephibosheth.) Repeat this daily devo as you thank God for his plan for your life.

PRAYER

Dear God, I wish no one would ever need a crutch, braces, or a wheelchair. But I know life won't be perfect until we get to heaven. So thank you for all the things my friends and I *can* do. In Jesus' name, amen.

CLICK-ER: CRUTCH

Whenever you see, use, or think about a *crutch*, let this daily devo support your mind as it clicks and sticks. Sam Mule the 2nd with his four-on-the-floorboard reminds you that the devo is from 2 Samuel, Chapter 4.

2 SAMUEL, CHAPTER 6 (VERSE 14)

David danced before the LORD with all his might.

DAILY DEVO

I'm a clean jumping jelly bean.

If David were living today, his church family, like his wife, might not understand him (verse 16). He was sort of wild when it came to worship. He loved to leap and dance and sing for the Lord. And he liked the sound of harps, tambourines, and cymbals—all kinds of celebration noisemakers. If drums had been big in his day, he probably would have had a full set. David's great love for God is a picture of God's great love for you. God is wild about you! When you worship him, he celebrates you. Go ahead. Be like David. Be a clean jumping jelly bean for God.

 MAKE IT STICK

The next time you're at a grocery store or drugstore, politely ask if you may buy a small bag of jelly beans. Whether or not your parents let you, they'll want to know why. When they ask, start jumping up and down and saying this daily devo. Tell the Bible story behind it too!

PRAYER

Dear God, I love you so much. And I love to worship you by jumping up and down, shouting, and clapping as I sing praises to you. Thank you for understanding me and for loving me back. Amen.

CLICK-ER: JELLY BEAN

Whenever you see, eat, or think about *jelly beans*, let this daily devo jump into your mind as it clicks and sticks. Sam Mule the 2nd with his six-pick-up-stix reminds you that the devo is from 2 Samuel, Chapter 6.

2 SAMUEL, CHAPTER 22 (VERSE 29)

O LORD, you are my lamp. The LORD lights up my darkness.

DAILY DEVO
God is my night-light.

Thinking about what's under our beds during the daytime is no big deal—stray socks, a leftover sandwich, maybe a hamster that escaped from its cage. But nighttime can be a different story. After the lights are out, we like to keep our arms and legs on the bed, at a safe distance from the edge. After all, who knows what kind of creepy crawlies might be hiding under the bed. You know the feeling. We all do. So does God. That's why he promises to be our light at night. If you find yourself feeling afraid at night, call out to God. He'll help you feel better, and he'll be like a light that will keep you safe all through the night, just as he was for David.

MAKE IT STICK

Draw a picture of a night-light. Then decorate it to remind you of God and his love for you. You might want to cover it with stars like the ones God made. If you have a real night-light, ask if you can decorate it. Then thank God for being with you and helping you feel safe all night, just like a night-light. (You might want to read another verse about God and his Word being like a light. See Psalm 119:105.)

PRAYER

Thank you, Lord, for staying awake all night so I don't need to. Thanks for keeping me safe in the same way that a light shows me the way in the dark. Amen.

CLICK-ER: NIGHT-LIGHT

Whenever you see, turn on, or think about a *night-light*, let this daily devo lighten your heart as it clicks and sticks. Sam Mule the 2nd with his two pairs of two-blue-shoes reminds you that the devo is from 2 Samuel, Chapter 22.

2 SAMUEL, CHAPTER 24 (VERSE 24)

The king replied . . . "I will not present burnt offerings to the Lord my God that have cost me nothing." So David paid [the man] fifty pieces of silver for the threshing floor and the oxen.

DAILY DEVO

I don't pinch pennies with God.

King David wanted to build a place to worship God, so a man offered to give David some of his land. The man said David could also have his oxen for an offering. But David wouldn't take the land or the oxen. He paid the man for these things. When you give money to God, do you give your own money? If you do, that's good. But if you just get money from your parents and hand it off to God, that's not giving. That didn't cost you a thing. Ask your parents if you can earn some money to share. David never pinched his money so tightly that he couldn't give it away. You shouldn't pinch pennies with God either. Follow David's example.

 MAKE IT STICK

Act out this drama in front of a mirror. Get two pennies: one from your dad or mom, and one from your own money. Pinch your penny while you hold up your parents' penny to the Lord, saying, "Here's my parents' money, God." Now loosen the grip on your own penny and say, "Here's my money, God." Can you see God's smile? Then point to yourself in the mirror and say this daily devo.

PRAYER

Thank you, God, for helping my family and me earn the money we need. I'm glad when I can share some of my money with you. In Jesus' name, amen.

CLICK-ER: PENNY

Whenever you see, hold, or think about a *penny*, let this daily devo register in your mind as it clicks and sticks. Sam Mule the 2nd with his two-blue-shoes and four-on-the-floorboard reminds you that the devo is from 2nd Samuel, Chapter 24.

Week 11, Saturday/Sunday

BOOK OF 1 KINGS

Captain Kingaroo the 1st

Kangaroo begins with the same letter as *Kings*. Captain Kingaroo the 1st is a picture of the hopping King Solomon had to do to meet the high expectations of his father, King David. Solomon also worked hard at hopping higher and higher to meet God's standards. When you see Captain Kingaroo the 1st in a picture, you'll know the daily devo is from 1 Kings. Connected to Captain Kingaroo the 1st are number symbols. (See page 15.) They make the chapter location of the devo click and stick.

If kangaroos wore shoes, they'd have to be big, because their paws grow three feet long! King David left kangaroo-size shoes for his son Solomon to fill. So Solomon asked God for wisdom, and God helped him become the wisest man in the world. But then he took his eyes off God. As a result, his kingdom was later split right down the middle. It was as if he hopped into a wall and busted everything. His sins made trouble for Israel for many years.

MAKE IT STICK

Make a tab to mark the book of 1 Kings in your Bible. (See Week 1, Monday, for directions.)

Ask a friend or family member to measure how high and how long you can hop. When Solomon asked God for wisdom, it was like hopping right up to God. You can do that too!

Whenever you see a kangaroo and picture it wearing the number *one*, remember Captain Kingaroo the 1st and the book of 1 Kings.

JUST FOR FUN

You can read Solomon's prayer for wisdom in Chapter 3 of 1 Kings (verses 7-14). How did God answer King Solomon?

PRAYER

Dear God, I need your wisdom, just as Solomon did, to understand what is right and wrong. Thank you for teaching me your ways as I read your Word and talk to you every day. Amen.

WEEKEND ACTIVITY IDEAS

(1) Highlight the verses for Week 11 in your Bible. (2) Find the HoneyWord animal in each picture for this week and identify the chapter-number symbols. (3) Add to your collection of Click-ers. (4) Say the daily devos for Week 11. (5) Check out Thursday of Week 20 for a daily devo on some words Solomon wrote about wisdom.

WHOPPER HOPPER

Kangaroos can hop at a whopping speed of forty miles per hour. While running, a kangaroo's hop can be nine feet high and thirteen feet long.

1 KINGS, CHAPTER 17 (VERSES 13–15)

Elijah said to [the woman], ". . . make a little bread for me first. Then use what's left to prepare a meal for yourself and your son. For this is what the LORD, the God of Israel, says: There will always be flour and olive oil left in your containers until the time when the LORD sends rain and the crops grow again!"

DAILY DEVO

God has the power to provide all my flour.

The food chain is one big, nonstop miracle of God's creative power. God mixes sunlight with water and makes wheat grow out of the dirt. We harvest the wheat, grind it into flour, and make bread to eat. Bread gives our bodies the power to work. Farmers use some of that power to plant more wheat, and the cycle goes on. When wheat and other crops won't grow, God still takes care of those who trust him. A widow gave Elijah her last piece of bread. She believed God would provide more food for her son and herself. And God did! He gave her flour the power to multiply and feed Elijah and her family. So trust God to give you all the food you need. He can do it!

 **MAKE IT STICK**

Politely ask your dad or mom for a cup of flour. With clean fingers, feel how finely it's been ground and name things we make out of flour. Then repeat this daily devo. (If you wish, make play dough by adding one-fourth cup each of salt and water to the flour. You can form the dough into tiny loaves.)

PRAYER

Dear God, thank you for the food you give me every day. Thanks for times when there is plenty and for times when there is just enough. Amen.

CLICK-ER:
SACK OF FLOUR

Whenever you see, feel, taste, or think about food made from *flour*, let this daily devo sift through your mind as it clicks and sticks. Captain Kingaroo the 1st with his one-on-a-bun and highway-seven-to-heaven sign reminds you that the devo is from 1 Kings, Chapter 17.

Week 12, Tuesday

BOOK OF 2 KINGS
Captain Kingaroo the 2nd

Kangaroo begins with the same letter as *Kings*. Captain Kingaroo the 2nd is a picture of all the hopping the kings did in the book of 2 Kings. None of the kings who followed Solomon could fill the kangaroo-size shoes left by David. When you see Captain Kingaroo the 2nd in a picture, you'll know the daily devo is from 2 Kings. Connected to Captain Kingaroo the 2nd are number symbols. (See page 15.) They make the chapter location of the devo click and stick.

The plot of 2 Kings is pretty much the same as 1 Kings, only worse. Of the 40 kings who came after Solomon, only nine even tried to follow God, and many of those still messed up in some way. Their lack of godliness was pitiful. But God never gave up. He lovingly sent prophet after prophet to warn his people and their leaders to turn back from their hip-hopping path, which led to the cliffs that would destroy them. They wouldn't listen, and finally jumped over the edge, one by one. 2 Kings is one sad story after another about the awful ends of those who chose to disobey God.

 MAKE IT STICK

Make a tab to mark the book of 2 Kings in your Bible. (See Week 1, Monday, for directions.)

Did you know that a newborn kangaroo is blind, naked, and only about an inch long? Pretend to be a newborn kangaroo, putting a blindfold over your eyes and letting someone you trust lead you. What could happen to you if you tried to follow your own path without anyone to lead you? The wicked kings who came after Solomon wouldn't let God lead them. They acted like blind newborn kangaroos.

Whenever you see a kangaroo and picture it wearing the number *two*, remember Captain Kingaroo the 2nd and the book of 2 Kings.

JUST FOR FUN

In just a few short verses, you can learn how blind and wicked some of the kings of Israel and Judah were. Check out 2 Kings, Chapter 9 (verses 21-24).

PRAYER

Dear God, I don't want to blindly follow the wrong path. I want to follow you each day and do the things that please you. Help me learn not to be like the wicked kings who would not follow you. Amen.

2 KINGS, CHAPTER 7 (VERSE 9)

Finally, they said to each other, "This is not right. This is a day of good news, and we aren't sharing it with anyone! . . . Come on, let's go back and tell the people at the palace."

DAILY DEVO

I don't play solitaire when there's something good to share.

In the days of Elisha, leprosy was worse than cooties. Most lepers had to live outside the city walls. The four lepers in this story felt they had nothing to lose by giving themselves up to the enemy army. But when they reached the other army's camp, nobody was there. God had caused the enemy soldiers to run and leave everything behind. The four lepers ate and drank like there was no tomorrow. But then they started feeling bad because their friends back home were starving to death. Are you keeping the blessings of God to yourself, when you should be giving them away to your family and friends? Remember the lepers. Don't play alone. Don't play solitaire when you've got something good to share.

MAKE IT STICK

Get out a deck of cards and play a game of solitaire. (Or play any card game alone.) As you play, ask God to bring to your mind someone who needs something you have to share. You'll be surprised to see the wonderful things he'll lead you to do . . . for others.

PRAYER

Thank you, God, for all the good things you do for me. I want to share your blessings with someone. Please show me how to do that. In Jesus' name, amen.

CLICK-ER: CARD GAME OF SOLITAIRE

Whenever you see, play with, or think about a *card game of solitaire*, let this daily devo stack up in your mind as it clicks and sticks. Captain Kingaroo the 2nd with his highway-seven-to-heaven sign reminds you that the devo is from 2 Kings, Chapter 7.

2 KINGS, CHAPTER 21 (VERSES 1–2)

Manasseh was twelve years old when he became king. . . . He did what was evil in the LORD's sight, following the detestable practices of the pagan nations that the LORD had driven from the land ahead of the Israelites.

DAILY DEVO

Every evil practice is like a cactus in my heart.

Manasseh was bad news. At age twelve he became king. But instead of being a good king like his father, Hezekiah, he gave himself over to evil. Whatever God wanted, he did the opposite. He was high on Judah's list of All-Time Worst Kings. The reason is this: He fooled around with the occult and got hooked by Satan. What happened to him then can happen to you today. Stay far, far away from people and things that might get you into the occult: fortune-tellers, palm readers, witches, mediums, psychics, séances, Ouija boards, books, games, and TV shows. If you're ever tempted to dabble in the occult, remember that it punctures whoever touches it, just like a cactus.

 MAKE IT STICK

Find a cactus around your house or in a florist's shop. Gently touch the cactus to feel how sharp it is. Now close your eyes and imagine the pain of really getting stuck by a prickly cactus. That's a picture of the payoff Satan has waiting for all those who follow the occult. So please don't ever touch it at all, for any reason.

PRAYER

Dear God, thank you for including bad examples along with the good ones in the Bible. They help me know not only what I *should* do but what I *shouldn't*. Thanks for keeping me from getting hurt. Amen.

CLICK-ER: CACTUS

Whenever you see, touch, or think about a *cactus*, let this daily devo prick your heart as it clicks and sticks. Captain Kingaroo the 2nd with his two-blue-shoes and one-on-a-bun reminds you that the devo is from 2 Kings, Chapter 21.

2 KINGS, CHAPTER 23 (VERSE 2)

The king went up to the Temple of the LORD with all the people of Judah and Jerusalem, along with the priests and the prophets—all the people from the least to the greatest. There the king read to them the entire Book of the Covenant that had been found in the LORD's Temple.

DAILY DEVO

I eat a bowl of God's scroll every day.

Eight-year-old King Josiah loved God and wanted to do things God's way. When he was about 26 years old and was fixing up the Temple, he found the long-lost scroll of God's Word covered with dust and cobwebs. Now he understood why his dad, King Amon, and his granddad, King Manasseh, had not obeyed God. They had put away God's scroll, the Bible. They didn't care to read it. So Josiah made up his mind to read the scroll to his people. Then everyone would know how to obey God. Doing that helped him become one of the best kings ever. Be like Josiah—read your Bible and learn to do right. Decide today to eat a big bowl of God's scroll every day!

MAKE IT STICK

As you eat a bowl of cereal, read Exodus 20 from your Bible. When you finish "eating" both, repeat this daily devo. Then design a new cover to tape onto your cereal box, and name it "God's Scroll." This will remind you that it's just as important to read God's Word each day as it is to eat your breakfast!

PRAYER

Dear God, thank you for my Bible and for Bible storybooks. Please help me remember to read something from your Word every day. In Jesus' name, amen.

CLICK-ER: BOWL

Whenever you see, eat from, or think about a *bowl*, let this daily devo scroll through your mind as it clicks and sticks. Captain Kingaroo the 2nd with his two-blue-shoes and three-is-the-key reminds you that the devo is from 2 Kings, Chapter 23.

Week 12, Saturday/Sunday

BOOK OF 1 CHRONICLES
Davey Cricket the 1st

Cricket begins with the same sound as *Chronicles*. Like crickets with no heart to hop, God's people needed hope as they struggled to rebuild Jerusalem. When you see Davey Cricket the 1st in a picture, you'll know the daily devo is from 1 Chronicles. Connected to Davey Cricket the 1st are number symbols. (See page 15.) They make the chapter location of the devo click and stick.

Like a kid who levels an anthill with one kick, King Nebuchadnezzar wiped out Jerusalem and hauled God's people off to the country of Babylon for 70 years. Even though they were glad to come home and trust God again, their joy of freedom soon turned to gloom. Jerusalem looked worse than an old junkyard. The city walls were down, Solomon's Temple was gone, and trash littered the streets. First Chronicles was written to jump-start the Jewish people. It was time to remember King David (whose story is also told in 2 Samuel) and rebuild the Temple. God wanted his people to be like chirping crickets, jumping for joy again.

 MAKE IT STICK

Make a tab to mark the book of 1 Chronicles in your Bible. (See Week 1, Monday, for directions.)

Gather some information about crickets. You might even be able to hear their chirping on the Internet. Talk with your family about some things God has done that make you feel like chirping.

Whenever you see a cricket and picture it wearing the number *one*, remember Davey Cricket the 1st and the book of 1 Chronicles.

JUST FOR FUN

God wanted his people to remember the prayer of praise David prayed before Solomon's Temple was first built. You can read it in 1 Chronicles, Chapter 29.

PRAYER

Dear God, I like to remember things that make me feel happy. I love you, God. Thanks for putting a song in my heart. Amen.

WEEKEND ACTIVITY IDEAS

(1) Highlight the verses for Week 12 in your Bible. (2) Find the HoneyWord animal in each picture for this week and identify the chapter-number symbols. (3) Add to your collection of Click-ers. (4) Say the daily devos for Week 12. (5) Check out Saturday/Sunday of Week 19 for a daily devo on sailing thank-you mail to God.

CHIRP 'N DALE

Only boy crickets chirp. Girl crickets don't. Sometimes two boy crickets will have a singing contest for one girl cricket—answering each other chirp for chirp.

1 CHRONICLES, CHAPTER 1 (VERSES 1-4)

The descendants of Adam were Seth, Enosh, Kenan, Mahalalel, Jared, Enoch, Methuselah, Lamech, and Noah. The sons of Noah were Shem, Ham, and Japheth.

DAILY DEVO

I'm a bigwig twig on God's family tree.

Why would God open 1 Chronicles with a phone book of names? It's because he knows every person in his family by name. God began the entire human race with two people. Adam and Eve had babies, who had babies, who had babies, who grew up to be your parents. This huge assembly line of babies is called a "family tree." Adam and Eve are the tree trunk. Their kids are the first big branches. And the rest of us stem from them. Being a small twig on such a large tree can make us feel unimportant. But remember this: God knows your name by heart, and he can spell it right every time. On his tree, you're always a bigwig twig. And that's a big deal!

MAKE IT STICK

Gently hold one of the twigs of a plant in your house or a tree outside. Regardless of how many twigs are on that plant or tree, only one is receiving your care and attention at that moment. That's a picture of how God personally cares for each twig on his big tree, except that he can care for each one at the same time!

PRAYER

Dear God, thank you for letting me be an important part of your family tree. I love belonging to your big family. In Jesus' name, amen.

CLICK-ER: TWIG

Whenever you see, hold, or think about a *twig*, let this daily devo branch out in your mind as it clicks and sticks. Davey Cricket the 1st with his one-on-a-bun in this picture reminds you that the devo is from 1 Chronicles, Chapter 1.

1 CHRONICLES, CHAPTER 14 (VERSE 10)

David asked God, "Should I go out to fight the Philistines? Will you hand them over to me?" The LORD replied, "Yes, go ahead. I will hand them over to you."

DAILY DEVO

I'm not alone when I telephone God.

Isn't it amazing how words come out of your mouth, crawl into your telephone, find their way to the guy you're calling, and then pop out of his phone and jump into his ear—all in a split second? Prayer is even more amazing. At any time we can pick up our "prayer phone" and connect to God instantly at no charge. David called heaven a lot. Even though he was king and had great power, he still talked to God before he went into battle. When do you ask God for help—before you do something, or after it's too late? Be like David. Phone God first. If you do, he'll answer. And you'll never go alone, no matter what you're facing.

**MAKE IT STICK**

Pick up a telephone so you can examine the earpiece and the mouthpiece. While you're thinking about how words get in and out of those places, repeat this daily devo. Now hang up the phone and "call" God to talk about whatever is on your heart.

PRAYER

Hello, God. I'm glad you're always there when I call. I don't need to leave a message, because you hear and answer every prayer. And you help me know how to handle any problem I might have. Thanks, God. Amen.

CLICK-ER: TELEPHONE

Whenever you see, talk on, or think about a *telephone*, let your mind call up this daily devo as it clicks and sticks. Davey Cricket the 1st with his one-on-a-bun and four-on-the-floorboard reminds you that the devo is from 1 Chronicles, Chapter 14.

1 CHRONICLES, CHAPTER 16 (VERSE 33)

Let the trees of the forest rustle with praise, for the Lord is coming to judge the earth.

DAILY DEVO

I'm joining God's chorus like the leaves in the forest.

The Ark of God (also called the Ark of the Covenant) was a very special box. Inside it were the stone tablets on which God had written the Ten Commandments. This ark belonged in the city of Jerusalem. David had a special tent put up to hold the ark. He was so excited that he called the people to a great celebration to worship God. Everybody was singing, shouting, and clapping. Cymbals were crashing! Trumpets were blasting! David even called on the trees to rustle their leaves in praise to God. If trees wore shirts, they'd have leaves of praise up their sleeves. We don't have leaves, but we do have sleeves that cover arms that end in hands that can quietly flutter in praise to God. Be like a tree. Pull some praise out of your sleeves and thank God for being so good to you!

 MAKE IT STICK

Put on a long-sleeve shirt and stuff leaves in both sleeves. As you shake them out, repeat this daily devo. Then praise God for two wonderful things that you know about him. (You'll find some ideas in verses 23-34 of 1 Chronicles 16.)

PRAYER

Lord, you are so great and so good. You're holy and loving. And I praise you for saving me through Jesus, your Son. In his name I pray, with thanksgiving. Amen.

CLICK-ER: LEAVES

Whenever you see, hear, or touch *leaves*, let this daily devo rustle through your mind as it clicks and sticks. Davey Cricket the 1st with his one-on-a-bun and six-pick-up-stix reminds you that the devo is from 1 Chronicles, Chapter 16.

1 CHRONICLES, CHAPTER 21 (VERSE 1)

Satan rose up against Israel and caused David to take a census of the people of Israel.

DAILY DEVO

I keep Mr. Liar in his dryer.

If the Olympics had an event for lying, Satan would win gold every time. Once he whispered something like this to King David: "My, what a big army you have! Count your soldiers so you can trust your own strength!" It was too bad, but David listened. He put his faith in the size of his army and turned his back on God. That upset God, and he punished the whole nation of Israel. We often make the same mistake as David did. Whenever we leave the cool shade of God's protection, we enter the scorching heat of the enemy's lies. Don't listen to Satan. When he invites you to tune in to his spin on the truth, turn up the heat on Mr. Liar. Keep him in the dryer where he belongs.

MAKE IT STICK

Offer to help your dad or mom with the laundry this week, even if that's not one of your regular chores. As you put a load of washed clothes in the dryer, repeat this daily devo. Then tell someone why you don't want to be like David when he listened to Satan and took a senseless census.

PRAYER

Dear God, I want to keep learning from your Word, the Bible, every day. Help me listen to the truth from you, not to any of the lies Satan tries to tell me. In Jesus' name I pray. Amen.

CLICK-ER: DRYER

Whenever you see, use, or think about a *dryer*, let this daily devo heat up your heart as it clicks and sticks. Davey Cricket the 1st with his two-blue-shoes and one-on-a-bun reminds you that the devo is from 1 Chronicles, Chapter 21.

Week 13, Friday

BOOK OF 2 CHRONICLES
Davey Cricket the 2nd

Cricket begins with the same sound as *Chronicles*. Like crickets with no heart to hop, God's people needed hope as they returned to their nation from Babylon. When you see Davey Cricket the 2nd, you'll know the daily devo is from 2 Chronicles. Connected to Davey Cricket the 2nd are number symbols. (See page 15.) They make the chapter location of the devo click and stick.

The books of 1 and 2 Chronicles used to be one super-long story. Years ago somebody divided it into two. Together, both parts tell or chronicle what happens when a nation doesn't listen to God. The people of Israel hadn't cared much about obeying God, so he had let them be taken to another country. The author of 2 Chronicles wrote to those who came back. He reminded them about their life with good kings and with bad kings. Those people learned how to become chirping crickets again—by remembering it's always the right time to listen to God, obey him, and worship him. We can learn that too!

MAKE IT STICK

Make a tab to mark the book of 2 Chronicles in your Bible. (See Week 1, Monday, for directions.)

The people of Israel learned a lot from their past history. What are some things you can learn from the history of your family, your church, your city, or your country? You might like to try writing a simple rhyming song about learning from the past and remembering to do what's right at last.

Whenever you see a cricket and picture it wearing the number *two*, remember Davey Cricket the 2nd and the book of 2 Chronicles.

JUST FOR FUN

A wicked king from Israel's past was King Ahab. You can read about his death in 2 Chronicles, Chapter 18 (verses 28-34). What did that story teach the people of Israel—and what does it teach you—about the sad ending of a king who would not obey God?

PRAYER

Dear God, help me learn the things you want to teach me from the past. I'm glad that you always forgive me for the wrong things I do. When you have done that, I can enjoy worshipping you and obeying you again. In Jesus' name, amen.

2 CHRONICLES, CHAPTER 10 (VERSE 8)

Rehoboam rejected the advice of the older men and instead asked the opinion of the young men who had grown up with him and were now his advisers.

DAILY DEVO

I roll the dice when I listen to bad advice.

When you roll dice, you never know what numbers are going to come up. You can get any number of combinations. Taking a chance is called "rolling the dice" because you can't be sure of anything. When it comes to the game of life, it's never a good thing to take a chance with advice. When Rehoboam became king, he followed the foolish advice of some of his friends, instead of the godly wisdom of some older people. His wrong roll of the dice split his kingdom and caused bad times for everybody. So please don't roll the dice and listen to bad advice. Take the advice of people who want to help you know and please God.

MAKE IT STICK

Get out a board game that uses dice, and ask someone to play with you. See if you can guess what numbers will come up each time you take your turn. How often do you guess right? Remind yourself not to guess wrong when it comes to asking for advice. Ask someone who you know loves God.

PRAYER

Dear God, when I need advice about the right thing to do, help me to find someone who will give good advice. Show me someone who loves you and promises to pray for me. Amen.

CLICK-ER: DICE

Whenever you see, throw, or think about *dice*, let this daily devo roll around in your mind as it clicks and sticks. Davey Cricket the 2nd with his one-on-a-bun and halo-is-a-hero-as-a-zero reminds you that the devo is from 2 Chronicles, Chapter 10.

WEEKEND ACTIVITY IDEAS

(1) Highlight the verses for Week 13 in your Bible. (2) Find the HoneyWord animal in each picture for this week and identify the chapter-number symbols. (3) Add to your collection of Click-ers. (4) Say the daily devos for Week 13. (5) Check out Monday of Week 41 for a related devo on keeping tar out of your mental DVD or VCR.

HOME COMB-ING KING

The singing sound of boy crickets is like the sound of rubbing your fingernail across the teeth of a plastic comb. Try it!

2 CHRONICLES, CHAPTER 16 (VERSE 9)

The eyes of the LORD search the whole earth in order to strengthen those whose hearts are fully committed to him.

DAILY DEVO

It's a blast being found under his magnifying glass.

Early in his reign, King Asa faced an enemy army that outnumbered his own, two to one. What was he to do? The same thing we all must do: call out to God for help. So he did. And God, looking through his magnifying glass from heaven, saw Asa's heart of faith and gave him the strength to win. It was a blast. Sixteen years later, King Asa faced another brick wall, so you'd think he'd trust God again, right? Wrong. This time he trusted himself instead of God. It wasn't a blast. If you've obeyed God in the past, that's great. But what about today? If you hope for God's magnifying glass to find you faithful to him, keep trusting and obeying—today and every day.

MAKE IT STICK

If you have a magnifying glass or can borrow one, try it out and see how it makes small things appear large. Or check an encyclopedia to learn how it works. As you think about God's ability to see even the smallest details of your heart, repeat this daily devo.

PRAYER

Dear God, please search my heart and take away any wrong thoughts or ideas that might keep me from being close to you. I want you to be happy with everything you see. Thank you, God. Amen.

CLICK-ER:
MAGNIFYING GLASS

Whenever you see, use, or think about a *magnifying glass*, let this daily devo enlarge your heart as it clicks and sticks. Davey Cricket the 2nd with his one-on-a-bun and six-pick-up-stix reminds you that the devo is from 2 Chronicles, Chapter 16.

2 CHRONICLES, CHAPTER 34 (VERSE 31)

The king . . . pledged to obey the LORD by keeping all his commands, laws, and decrees with all his heart and soul. He promised to obey all the terms of the covenant that were written in the scroll.

DAILY DEVO

I pledge to build God's hedge around my heart.

Josiah has got to be one of the top cool kid heroes of the Bible, becoming king at the ripe old age of eight. (Remember him from Week 12, Friday—2 Kings, Chapter 23?) When he was in his twenties, he ordered people to clean and fix up the temple. There they found a long-lost copy of the Scriptures. Josiah sat down right away and read the whole scroll. When he saw that he and the other people had not been obeying God, he pledged to rebuild every spiritual hedge his dad and granddad had torn down. A hedge is a row of closely planted bushes that form a protective wall. They keep good things in and bad things out. That's what God's Word does too. When we read and obey God's Word, God keeps evil out. Be like Josiah. Make the pledge to build God's hedge of protection around your heart.

 MAKE IT STICK

The next time you're riding through your neighborhood, keep an eye out for a hedge. The second you see one, repeat this daily devo. From that day forward, every time you pass that hedge, let it help your mind click on this daily devo.

PRAYER

Dear God, thank you for showing me in your Word how to obey you. I pledge to read it and obey it so your hedge will be all around me to protect me. Amen.

CLICK-ER: HEDGE

Whenever you see, walk around, or think about a *hedge*, let this daily devo surround your heart with strength as it clicks and sticks. Davey Cricket the 2nd with his three-is-the-key and four-on-the-floorboard reminds you that this devo is from 2 Chronicles, Chapter 34.

Week 14, Wednesday

BOOK OF EZRA
Ezra-triever

Ezra-triever, a made-up name for a golden retriever, sounds like *Ezra*. The retriever pictures the golden heart of Ezra in the book named after him. Like a golden retriever, Ezra gently retrieved, or brought his people back home, physically and spiritually. When you see Ezra-triever in a picture, you'll know the daily devo is from Ezra. Connected to Ezra-triever are number symbols. (See page 15.) They make the chapter location of the devo click and stick.

Golden retrievers are some of the nicest dogs around. They patiently endure the ear-pulling of tiny kids without biting theirs in return. Retrievers also are good at bringing stuff back to their masters. In fact, *retrieve* means "to bring back to a former place." Like a good retriever, Ezra brought God's people back home. He also helped restore their spiritual hearts. He served them big plates of God's Word. And the best news is this: The people ate what he dished out. Their bodies were back in the land. And even more important, their hearts were back in line with God's.

 MAKE IT STICK

Make a tab to mark the book of Ezra in your Bible. (See Week 1, Monday, for directions.)

Would you like to draw a picture of a golden retriever? You could make him look like Ezra-triever. Or find a photo on your computer by going to "images" on a search engine and typing in "golden retriever." Use the picture to help you draw your own. You can show your retriever bringing a bone or toy back to his owner. Ezra brought *people* back home—God's people.

Whenever you see a golden retriever or think about one, remember Ezra-triever and the book of Ezra.

JUST FOR FUN
You can read the letter a Persian king wrote to Ezra, telling him he could take the people of Israel back home. The letter is in Ezra, Chapter 7 (verses 11-26).

PRAYER
Thank you, God, for leaders like Ezra. Thank you for Sunday school teachers and pastors. I'm glad they help me keep my heart in line with yours. In Jesus' name, amen.

EZRA, CHAPTER 7 (VERSES 8-10)

Ezra . . . had arranged to leave Babylon on April 8, the first day of the new year, and he arrived at Jerusalem on August 4, for the gracious hand of his God was on him. This was because Ezra had determined to study and obey the Law of the LORD and to teach those decrees and regulations to the people of Israel.

DAILY DEVO

I love to dig big in God's Word.

The Bible is like a large field full of buried treasures. Anywhere you dig, you find solid-gold wisdom for living life to the fullest. But you've got to do the digging yourself. No one can do it for you. Not your parents. Not your friends. Not even God. Each of us has to pull out our own shovel and dig big for ourselves. Do you really want to know more about God? Then be like Ezra. Open your Bible, read it, and do what it says. Dig it. Do it. Share it.

 MAKE IT STICK

Ask if you and your family can one day soon empty a plastic jar, such as a jar of peanut butter. Clean the empty jar and place several slips of paper in it, on which you've written favorite Bible verses. Cover the jar with foil and ask if you can bury it in your backyard—or in a box of toys. Then have your dad or mom watch you dig it up with a shovel. When your shovel hits the jar, repeat this daily devo and read the verses you've written down.

PRAYER

Dear God, I know I don't need a real shovel to dig into your Word. But I do need your help to find time to read it every day and discover how to do what the Bible says. In Jesus' name, amen.

CLICK-ER: SHOVEL

Whenever you see, use, or think about a *shovel*, let your mind dig up this daily devo as it clicks and sticks. Ezra-triever with his highway-seven-to-heaven sign reminds you that the devo is from Ezra, Chapter 7.

Week 14, Friday

BOOK OF NEHEMIAH

Nehemiah the Butterfly-ah

Butterfly-ah rhymes with *Nehemiah*. Like a butterfly wanting release from its cocoon, Nehemiah wanted to fly back home and help rebuild the city walls around Jerusalem. When you see Nehemiah the Butterfly-ah in a picture, you'll know the daily devo is from Nehemiah. Connected to Nehemiah the Butterfly-ah are number symbols. (See page 15.) They make the chapter location of the devo click and stick.

Nehemiah's job as cup-bearer to the king of Persia was easy. All he had to do was sample the king's food and drink. If Nehemiah didn't die, everything was poison-free and fit for the king to eat. But Nehemiah wanted to do something much more difficult—return to Jerusalem to rebuild its walls so the city would be safe. After months of prayer, Nehemiah was freed by the king like a butterfly released from its cocoon. God is a transformer. He loves changing caterpillar problems into butterfly opportunities. Things that seem impossible are possible with him.

 MAKE IT STICK

Make a tab to mark the book of Nehemiah in your Bible. (See Week 1, Monday, for directions.)

Politely ask your dad or mom or a librarian to help you find a book that describes the life cycle of a butterfly. You may want to draw your own pictures of the different stages. Nehemiah felt free like a butterfly when God gave him the opportunity to return to Jerusalem.

Whenever you see a butterfly or a picture of one, remember Nehemiah the Butterfly-ah and the book of Nehemiah.

JUST FOR FUN

Nehemiah was stuck in Persia, but the king finally let him leave. Then God gave Nehemiah the freedom to do some great things. To read what he did after he returned to Jerusalem, find Nehemiah, Chapter 2 (verses 11-18) in your Bible.

PRAYER

Dear God, sometimes I feel as if I'm stuck in a cocoon, and I wish I could fly away like a butterfly. Thank you for taking my problems and turning them into opportunities to become as free as a butterfly. I love you, God. Amen.

NEHEMIAH, CHAPTER 2 (VERSES 4-5)

The king asked, "Well, how can I help you?" With a prayer to the God of heaven, I replied, "If it please the king, and if you are pleased with me, your servant, send me to Judah to rebuild the city."

DAILY DEVO

I can shoot arrows of prayer from anywhere.

We can pray anytime, anywhere, because God is always listening and always ready to answer. Nehemiah prayed right in the middle of a conversation, shooting a short prayer to God for help. Like a narrow arrow, it was to the point and hit the target. God heard and answered, helping Nehemiah know what to say to the king. God loves getting showered with short prayers. The key to prayer is faith (trusting God), not the number of words. Whenever you need help, you can shoot short arrows of prayer to God. He'll get the point. And you'll get the power!

MAKE IT STICK

Cut a small slit across the openings of both ends of an empty toilet paper roll. Now stretch and position a rubber band in the slits, making a bow. Find an unsharpened pencil to use as an arrow. On a small piece of paper, write a sentence about the thing you most want God's help on. Tape one end of the paper to the pencil, wrap it around the pencil, and tape it again. Now shoot your "arrow of prayer" into the air and repeat this daily devo.

PRAYER

Whenever I need your help, God, please show me what to do. Amen.

CLICK-ER: ARROW

Whenever you see, shoot, or think about *arrows*, let this daily devo hit the bull's eye of your mind as it clicks and sticks. Nehemiah the Butterfly-ah with his two-blue-shoes reminds you that the devo is from Nehemiah, Chapter 2.

WEEKEND ACTIVITY IDEAS

(1) Highlight the verses for Week 14 in your Bible. (2) Find the HoneyWord animal in each picture for this week and identify the chapter-number symbols. (3) Add to your collection of Click-ers. (4) Say the daily devos for Week 14. (5) Check out Thursday of Week 39 for a related devo that can't explain how prayer can break a chain.

FLYING FLOWERS

Butterflies come in so many bright colors that they
have been described as "flying flowers."

NEHEMIAH, CHAPTER 8 (VERSE 10)

Nehemiah continued, "Go and celebrate with a feast of rich foods and sweet drinks, and share gifts of food with people who have nothing prepared. This is a sacred day before our Lord. Don't be dejected and sad, for the joy of the Lord is your strength!"

DAILY DEVO

It's always great to celebrate with God.

After the walls around Jerusalem were rebuilt and the city was safe, it was time to thank God and celebrate. So everyone got together and did something unusual for a party. They asked Ezra to read God's Word out loud and explain it. As they listened carefully, their eyes filled with tears, and their hearts overflowed with joy. Then they ate great food and drank sweet drinks. It was nonstop fun, food, and fellowship with others. Everyone had a great time, even God. Does that surprise you? It shouldn't. He loves it when his children hoot and holler over what he's done for them. If it's been a while since you've shouted "Yippee!" to God, go ahead and do it now. It's always great to celebrate with God.

MAKE IT STICK

Draw a picture of yourself having fun at a party. Then roll and tape your picture into a cone-shaped party hat. Stick it on your head and repeat this daily devo.

PRAYER

Hooray, God! Thank you for loving me and giving me so many great gifts. You make me feel like shouting with joy. Yippee! And Amen.

CLICK-ER: PARTY HAT

Whenever you see, wear, or think about a *party hat*, let your heart celebrate this daily devo as it clicks and sticks. Nehemiah the Butterfly-ah with his eight-under-skates reminds you that this devo is from Nehemiah, Chapter 8.

NEHEMIAH, CHAPTER 13 (VERSES 30-31)

[Nehemiah said: I] assigned tasks to the priests and Levites, making certain that each knew his work. I also made sure that the supply of wood for the altar and the first portions of the harvest were brought at the proper times.

DAILY DEVO

I won't break out in a rash if I take out the trash.

The job of chopping and stacking wood doesn't sound too spiritual, but it needed to be done to keep the fire burning on the altar. So Nehemiah assigned the job to the priests and Levites who worked at the Temple. Daily chores are just a fact of life. Every day somebody's got to make the bed, pick up the towels, walk the dog, feed the cat, set the table, load the dishwasher, and on and on. It's not a question of *if* the stuff has to be done, just *who* will do it. If your chore is to take out the garbage, then do it every day. You won't break out in a rash taking out the trash. But your parents might break out in the "Hallelujah Chorus" if you do your chores faithfully *and* cheerfully.

MAKE IT STICK

How about shocking your parents by taking out the garbage or bringing in the trash cans without being asked? When they say, "What's gotten into you?" say, "Nehemiah 13," and repeat this daily devo. Then tell them the story about Nehemiah's great leadership.

PRAYER

Dear God, I know you have work for everyone to do. Help me to please you—and my family—by doing my chores without complaining. Amen.

CLICK-ER: TRASH CAN

Whenever you see, take out, or think about a *trash can*, let your mind take in this daily devo as it clicks and sticks. Nehemiah Butterfly-ah with his one-on-a-bun and three-is-the-key reminds you that the devo is from Nehemiah, Chapter 13.

Week 15, Wednesday

BOOK OF ESTHER

Esther the Starfish

The "star" in *starfish* sounds like the last part of the name *Esther*. Esther, whose name meant "star" in the Persian language, became the star queen of Persia. When you see Esther the Starfish in a picture, you'll know the daily devo is from Esther. Connected to Esther the Starfish are number symbols. (See page 15.) They make the chapter location of the devo click and stick.

Starfish live quietly on the ocean floor. It's only when someone brings them to the surface that we see their beauty. That's a picture of Esther's beautiful life. As a teenage orphan living with her people far from her own country, almost no one knew about her. Then overnight, Esther became a star as queen of Persia. But why? God had a plan. Through Esther he saved his people from being killed. God is not named in this little book, but his fingerprints are all over it. Sometimes God seems far away, but he, too, is just under the surface, looking after every detail of our lives.

 MAKE IT STICK

Make a tab to mark the book of Esther in your Bible. (See Week 1, Monday, for directions.)

Draw several starfish with five or six arms. Make them beautiful by coloring them bright red, pink, and orange. Esther was beautiful too, both on the outside and on the inside.

Whenever you see a picture of a starfish or think about one, remember Esther the Starfish and the book of Esther.

JUST FOR FUN

Mordecai was like a father to Esther, both of them living in the land of Persia, far from their own country. You can read about them in the book of Esther, Chapter 2 (verses 5-11). What do you learn in verses 10-11 about how much they cared about each other?

PRAYER

Dear God, thank you for the beauty we can see all around us. But thank you most of all for the beauty inside all those who love and serve you as they love and serve one another. Amen.

ESTHER, CHAPTER 3 (VERSE 6)

[Haman] had learned of Mordecai's nationality, so he decided it was not enough to lay hands on Mordecai alone. Instead, he looked for a way to destroy all the Jews throughout the entire empire of Xerxes.

DAILY DEVO

I sin when I judge on the basis of skin.

In Persia, the Jewish people stood out like zebras in a herd of black horses. Everything about them seemed different—the way they looked, the way they talked, the way they worshipped. Haman, the king's top man, didn't like their differences one bit, so he decided to kill the Jewish people. Isn't that sad? It's always wrong to hurt people for being different. We're *all* beautiful—created in God's image. Don't look down on people because of their skin color, the clothes they wear, or the way they talk. It's a sin. And it makes God really sad.

 **MAKE IT STICK**

Ask God to help you think about anyone you have been unkind to because the person seemed different. If someone comes to mind, repeat this daily devo and confess your sin to God. Then ask God if you need to go to that person and ask for his or her forgiveness too.

PRAYER

Dear God, thank you for creating all people. Thank you for the ways that we are alike, and thank you for all the ways that we are different. Fill us all with your love for one another. In Jesus' name I pray. Amen.

CLICK-ER: SKIN

Whenever you see or think about the color of someone's *skin*, let this picture color your heart as the daily devo clicks and sticks. Esther the Starfish with her three-is-the-key reminds you that the devo is from Esther, Chapter 3.

ESTHER, CHAPTER 4 (VERSE 14)

If you keep quiet at a time like this, deliverance and relief for the Jews will arise from some other place, but you and your relatives will die. Who knows if perhaps you were made queen for just such a time as this?

DAILY DEVO

I'm a major piece of God's master puzzle.

Since the beginning of time, God has been putting his Kingdom together, piece by piece, like a giant jigsaw puzzle. The pieces he uses are not cardboard, but living people who have said they want to be a part of his master plan. When Esther learned of Haman's evil plot to kill her people, the Jews, she had to choose whether or not to be part of God's plan. Happily, she placed herself in God's hands, and he placed her in the big picture at just the right time. God wants to make you a major piece of his master puzzle, just as Esther was. But will you let him? If you put yourself in God's hands, you'll find he has a place just for you, and a perfect part for you to play.

 MAKE IT STICK

Draw a picture of yourself doing what you'd like to do when you grow up. When you're finished, glue the sheet to a piece of stiff paper and make a puzzle by cutting it into eight to ten pieces. As you're putting the pieces back together, repeat this daily devo.

PRAYER

Dear God, I want to be part of your plan. Please show me what you want me to do each day. And lead me to the place where you want me to be when I grow up. Thanks for helping me follow you. In Jesus' name I pray. Amen.

CLICK-ER: PUZZLE

Whenever you see, put together, or think about a *puzzle*, let this daily devo fall into place in your heart as it clicks and sticks. Esther the Starfish with her four-on-the-floorboard reminds you that this devo is from Esther, Chapter 4.

ESTHER, CHAPTER 8 (VERSE 1)

King Xerxes gave the property of Haman, the enemy of the Jews, to Queen Esther. Then Mordecai was brought before the king, for Esther had told the king how they were related.

DAILY DEVO

God is able to turn the tables.

Haman created an evil plan that almost killed Mordecai and the entire Jewish race. But just in the nick of time, God used Esther, the young Jewish queen of Persia, to turn the tables on Haman. He was killed instead of Mordecai, and all the Jewish people were saved. This dramatic turnaround shows how quickly God can change things. God is good at last-minute rescue operations. What are you facing that looks and feels hopeless? If you keep bringing it to God in prayer, in his own time and in his own way, he will turn the tables for you. But between now and then, trust that he has a good plan that he will show you at just the right time.

 **MAKE IT STICK**

Draw a picture of a situation you're worried about. Tape the picture to the top of a card table. Now pick up the card table and turn it around so your picture is facing the opposite way. As you turn the table, repeat this daily devo. Remember that God not only turns pictures around, but he can also change the whole picture!

PRAYER

Dear God, I really enjoy reading about times when you've turned a bad situation into a good one. Help me trust you to take care of my problems in your time and in your way. Amen.

CLICK-ER: TABLE

Whenever you see, sit at, or think about a *table*, let this daily devo turn around in your mind as it clicks and sticks. Esther the Starfish with her eight-under-skates reminds you that the devo is from Esther, Chapter 8.

WEEKEND ACTIVITY IDEAS

(1) Highlight the verses for Week 15 in your Bible. (2) Find the HoneyWord animal in each picture for this week and identify the chapter-number symbols. (3) Add to your collection of Click-ers. (4) Say the daily devos for Week 15. (5) Check out Tuesday of Week 3 for a related devo on slavery and bravery.

THROW UP . . . AND OUT . . . AND BACK

A starfish sends its stomach out of its mouth, surrounds its food with its stomach, digests the food, then sucks it all back in.

Week 16, Monday

BOOK OF JOB

Joe B. Buffalo

Joe B. sounds like *Job*. The buffalo pictures Job's strong, no-budge heart of faith. When you see Joe B. Buffalo in a picture, you'll know the daily devo is from Job. Connected to Joe B. Buffalo are number symbols. (See page 15.) They make the chapter location of the devo click and stick.

Job holds the world record for the worst day ever. One day he lost his home, most of his farm helpers, all of his animals, and all ten of his children. When he didn't think things could get any worse, he lost his health. Job felt sad. But like a strong buffalo, he wouldn't budge from his faith in God. He did ask hard questions, however, and he got more than answers. He got God's presence. Have you ever asked God the question *Why?* Read this book, and let God give you the heart of Job. Over time you, too, can become a no-budge buffalo of the faith.

 MAKE IT STICK

Make a tab to mark the book of Job in your Bible. (See Week 1, Monday, for directions.)

Buffalo is the more common name for the *American bison*. There were millions of these large animals in the American West of the 1800s. Many were killed for their meat and their hides. But today there are still around 150,000 buffalo. And no one is allowed to budge them, just as no one could get Job to budge from his trust in God. Play hide-and-seek with some friends. Take turns pretending to be a buffalo in hiding, but let the buffalo go free when caught.

Whenever you see a picture of a buffalo or think about one, remember Joe B. Buffalo and the book of Job.

JUST FOR FUN

Read what Job said after some terrible things happened to him. You'll find some of his words in Job, Chapter 1 (verses 21-22) and Chapter 2 (verses 9-10). Chapter 19 (verses 25-27) shows that Job believed he would see God after he died. That was real faith, because Job lived long before Jesus came back to life.

PRAYER

Dear God, I pray that my faith will always be strong, no matter what happens. I'm glad you listen to my prayers now, but I look forward to actually seeing you someday! Amen.

JOB, CHAPTER 12 (VERSES 7-8)

Ask the animals, and they will teach you. Ask the birds of the sky, and they will tell you. Speak to the earth, and it will instruct you. Let the fish in the sea speak to you.

DAILY DEVO

Everything at the beach can teach about God.

Pretend that you are holding the written *Word* of God (the Bible) in one hand, and the entire created *world* of God (everything in the universe we see and don't see) in the other. If you could do that, did you know that you'd be holding two books by the same Author? Amazing, isn't it?! But it's true. Job understood this. That's why he told his friends to learn a thing or two from the fish in the sea, the birds at the beach, and even the earth itself. Be like Job. Study and use both books of God. Understand that all things—birds, buffalo, bugs, bees, and, yes, even beaches—can point us to God and teach us about his character and power.

MAKE IT STICK

Look at the index of Click-ers on page 383 in the back of this book of devotions, and see how many things you can include in a fun scene at the beach. Now draw a picture of a beach that includes each Click-er you've chosen. While you're drawing, repeat this daily devo.

PRAYER

Dear God, it's exciting to go outdoors and see the millions of things you've created. Thanks for your wonderful world. You are so absolutely awesome! Amen.

CLICK-ER: BEACH BALL

Whenever you see, touch, or toss a *beach ball*, let this daily devo bounce around in your mind as it clicks and sticks. Joe B. Buffalo with his one-on-a-bun and two-blue-shoes reminds you that this devo is from Job, Chapter 12.

Week 16, Wednesday

BOOK OF PSALMS

Singer the Psalm-Bird

Psalm-Bird, a make-believe songbird, begins with the same sound as *Psalms*. A singing Psalm-Bird pictures the many songs found in the book of Psalms. When you see Singer the Psalm-Bird in a picture, you'll know the daily devo is from Psalms. Connected to Singer the Psalm-Bird are number symbols. (See page 15.) They make the chapter location of the devo click and stick.

We all feel many different emotions every day. But what are we to do with feelings like anger and sadness? Stuff 'em in a drawer inside of us? No. From the book of Psalms we learn that God wants to hear about all our feelings. You name it, he can handle it: awe, anger, love, hate, joy, sorrow, faith, doubt. When we trust God with both our highs and our lows, he touches our hearts and puts a song in our mouths. Pick a psalm to read each day. You'll feel better, and you may even find yourself singing like Singer the Psalm-Bird!

 MAKE IT STICK

Make a tab to mark the book of Psalms in your Bible. (See Week 1, Monday, for directions.)

Make some circles for faces and draw pictures of yourself that show as many different emotions as you can think of. Talk with someone about what might cause each feeling. Then for each face, write —or record yourself singing—a sentence you might say to God when you're feeling that way.

Whenever you hear a bird singing or see a picture of one, think about Singer the Psalm-Bird and the book of Psalms.

JUST FOR FUN

Look up Psalms, Chapter 100. It's a great song of praise. Anytime is a good time to sing songs of praise to God. So listen to some of your favorite praise songs and enjoy singing along.

PRAYER

Thank you, Lord, for letting me talk to you about the way I feel. And thanks for praise music and other worship songs that I can sing along with. Amen.

PSALMS, CHAPTER 1 (VERSES 1-3)

Oh, the joys of those who do not follow the advice of the wicked, or stand around with sinners, or join in with mockers. But they delight in the law of the LORD, meditating on it day and night. They are like trees planted along the riverbank, bearing fruit each season. . . . They prosper in all they do.

DAILY DEVO

I fill my tank on his riverbank.

If trees could pull up their roots and walk to their favorite spots, every riverbank would be backed up for miles. Trees love and need lots of water. You can imagine, then, that hog heaven for a tree is putting down roots by a river where it can get all the water it wants. Such a place keeps a tree's roots and branches alive and well, and full of energy. In Psalm 1 David says that Christians who grow spiritually are like trees that grow by a riverbank. Water to a dry tree is the same as God's Word to a thirsty heart. God's Word keeps us going. If you want power to go God's way, fill your tank on the riverbank of his Word. It's the only way to grow.

 MAKE IT STICK

Ever hear the expression "to tank up"? It might mean to fill up your car with gas, or it might mean to fill yourself up with water! Make a cool water container by molding aluminum foil around a coffee mug. As you carefully fill it to the top from your kitchen faucet, say this daily devo. After you drink from your "water tank," have a spiritual drink from your Bible by reading Psalm 1.

PRAYER

Thanks, God, for giving me everything I need to grow spiritually. And thanks for all 150 psalms, which teach me how to pray and praise and worship you. In Jesus' name, amen.

CLICK-ER: TANK

Whenever you see or think about a *tank*, let this daily devo overflow your mind as it clicks and sticks. Singer the Psalm-Bird and his one-on-a-bun reminds you that this devo is from Psalms, Chapter 1.

PSALMS, CHAPTER 8 (VERSES 4–5)

What are mere mortals that you should think about them, human beings that you should care for them? Yet you made them only a little lower than God and crowned them with glory and honor.

DAILY DEVO

God came down and gave me a crown!

As a shepherd, David had plenty of time to think about life, God, and the universe. This psalm is about one of those moments David had one night while his sheep were sleeping. As he looked up into the heavens, he started thinking about how big and awesome God is, and how small and unimportant people seem to be. Then he thought about the place of high honor God has given his people in the world he created. You see, we're not some unimportant pieces of dust floating in space. We are the most important part of God's entire creation. That's why he crowned us with glory and honor. Doesn't that make you feel special? It should, because God created people—including you—to rule over the rest of his creation.

MAKE IT STICK

Politely ask your dad or mom to help you make a crown out of paper or cardboard. Before you staple it together, write this daily devo on it. Then put it on your head and look at yourself in the mirror. As you take it off and put it back on, say the daily devo.

PRAYER

Dear God, thank you for making people the greatest creation of all. You made us to be like you, and you want us to be your friends. That makes me feel very special. Thanks again, God. Amen.

CLICK-ER: CROWN

Whenever you see, wear, or think about a *crown*, let this daily devo rule in your heart as it clicks and sticks. Singer the Psalm-Bird with his eight-under-skates reminds you that this devo is from the book of Psalms, Chapter 8.

PSALMS, CHAPTER 18 (VERSE 30)

*God's way is perfect. All the L*ORD'*s promises prove true. He is a shield for all who look to him for protection.*

DAILY DEVO

God is my shield on every battlefield.

Life can sometimes feel a lot like being out in a bad storm. The howling wind and the pouring rain make us feel wet, cold, and scared. What are we to do? God wants us to be like David. Again and again, he found God to be his protective shield during stormy battles. At times we all need to be sheltered so we're safe from the storms of life. Are you going through a hard time right now that makes you wonder how much more you can take? If so, turn to God. Ask him to be your shield on this battlefield. If you do, he'll come through in a way you never dreamed possible.

MAKE IT STICK

Draw a picture of your family inside your car or van. Show the windshield protecting you from something that's coming against you: rain, snow, bugs, or wind. Then think of some different kinds of storms you are facing. Maybe it's a stormy relationship with a parent, a teacher, or a neighborhood bully. Maybe it's an illness in your family. Or maybe one of your parents needs a job. Ask God to be your personal shield, protecting you from every stormy battlefield.

PRAYER

Dear God, thank you for being my shield that protects me from every kind of storm in my life. In Jesus' name, amen.

CLICK-ER: WINDSHIELD

Whenever you see, ride behind, or think about a car's *windshield*, let this daily devo protect your heart as it clicks and sticks. Singer the Psalm-Bird with his one-on-a-bun and eight-under-skates reminds you that the devo is from Psalms, Chapter 18.

WEEKEND ACTIVITY IDEAS

(1) Highlight the verses for Week 16 in your Bible. (2) Find the HoneyWord
animal in each picture for this week and identify the chapter-number symbols.
(3) Add to your collection of Click-ers. (4) Say the daily devos for Week 16.
(5) Check out Thursday of Week 30 for a related devo on how to be waterproof
under God's roof.

JUST SINGING IN THE RAIN

If there were such a thing as a Psalm-Bird, it would
sing happy or sad, rain or shine, day or night.

PSALMS, CHAPTER 19 (VERSES 9-10)

Reverence for the LORD is pure, lasting forever. The laws of the LORD are true; each one is fair. They are more desirable than gold, even the finest gold. They are sweeter than honey, even honey dripping from the comb.

DAILY DEVO

I love God's honey more than money.

In Psalm 19 David made a big list of good things that come from obeying God's Word: protection, joy, wisdom, light, and insight. Then he said two amazing things: God's Word is way better than tons of money, and it's so sweet to the soul that it tastes better than honey. You might not believe that now, but one day you will. As you choose to follow God, you'll find that his honey (the Bible) is the sweetest thing in life. You'll want to taste more and more of it. It will be a greater help than any amount of money.

 MAKE IT STICK

Politely ask your dad or mom if you can do this activity. Get some round crackers and pretend they are large coins. Now place the crackers on a plate and pour a little honey over them. Then say this daily devo as you hold each "coin" between your fingers and lick it clean. The sweet taste should remind you of the sweeter-than-honey, better-than-money taste of God's Word as you learn to obey it.

PRAYER

Dear God, the more I learn about you, the more I want to know. Your words are sweet and make me want to follow you. Thanks for the honey of your Word. In Jesus' name, amen.

CLICK-ER: HONEY

Whenever you see, taste, or think about *honey*, let your heart enjoy the sweetness of this daily devo as it clicks and sticks. Singer the Psalm-Bird with his one-on-a-bun and nine-foot-pine reminds you that the devo is from the book of Psalms, Chapter 19.

Week 17, Tuesday

PSALMS, CHAPTER 23 (VERSES 1–4)

The LORD is my shepherd; I have all that I need. He lets me rest in green meadows; he leads me beside peaceful streams. He renews my strength. He guides me along right paths, bringing honor to his name. Even when I walk through the darkest valley, I will not be afraid, for you are close beside me. Your rod and your staff protect and comfort me.

DAILY DEVO
God is the guide by my side.

Psalm 23 pictures God as a kind shepherd to people, for we're like sheep in need of help. Since few of us know much about sheep and shepherds, let's just think about God taking care of us the way a Seeing Eye dog cares for a person who is blind. Without a loyal guide dog always by their side, there are many things blind people couldn't do. And without God as our guide, we wouldn't be able to get around the many problems that could trip us up. That's good to know, isn't it? No matter what you're going through, God is the guide by your side forever.

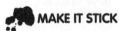 **MAKE IT STICK**

Check encyclopedias and Web sites for information about guide dogs. Talk with your family about the parallel between what guide dogs do for people who are blind and what God does for you. Politely ask your dad, mom, or teacher if someone in your church or town has a guide dog. Ask to meet that person and learn what his or her dog does.

PRAYER
Thank you, Lord, for being my guide and taking me to peaceful places. You help me choose the right paths. And I never need to be afraid, because you are always close by. Thanks, God! Amen.

CLICK-ER: GUIDE DOG
Whenever you see, pet, or read about a *guide dog*, let the eyes of your heart see this daily devo as it clicks and sticks. Singer the Psalm-Bird with his two-blue-shoes and three-is-the-key reminds you that the devo is from the book of Psalms, Chapter 23.

PSALMS, CHAPTER 27 (VERSE 10)

Even if my father and mother abandon me, the LORD will hold me close.

DAILY DEVO

God never sweeps my need for a hug under the rug.

Do you need a hug because your parents aren't getting along too well these days? Perhaps your parents are divorced. Or do you find yourself in a blended family because your dad or mom got married to someone else? You might be adopted and wonder why your biological parents couldn't keep you and raise you. Maybe you live in a foster home or an orphanage. If any of these things are true for you or for a friend, this psalm is for you or that friend. God understands how you're feeling, even though it may not seem like it sometimes. And he wants you to know that he's always there for you, even if your parents can't or won't always be. God promises that he will always hold you close. He never sweeps under the rug your need for a hug.

 ### MAKE IT STICK

On a slip of paper write the words "I need a hug" and place the paper under a rug in your house. When you take it out, imagine being held in the arms of Jesus. As you do that, thank him for never sweeping your need for a hug under the rug.

PRAYER

Dear God, I'm so happy you didn't walk away from the world after you made it. But what really makes me happy is that you'll never walk away from *me*! Thanks for your hugs. In Jesus' name, amen.

CLICK-ER: RUG

Whenever you see, walk on, or think about a *rug*, let this daily devo hug your heart as it clicks and sticks. Singer the Psalm-Bird with his two-blue-shoes and highway-seven-to-heaven sign reminds you that the devo is from Psalms, Chapter 27.

PSALMS, CHAPTER 37 (VERSE 23)

The LORD directs the steps of the godly. He delights in every detail of their lives.

DAILY DEVO

God plans my plot, dot to dot.

Everybody's life is a story with a lot of day-to-day details. Every story has a plot—that's the story line. Have you ever wondered how much God knows and remembers about your plot? Did he see those bumps you got as you learned how to walk? Did he see when you first rode a bike? Was he around when you first tied your shoes? What about the times when you were alone? The answer is YES! YES! YES! God always follows your life plot, dot to dot, day by day, in every way. He sees and cares about everything you do. Even though you can't see him, God is always with you. In fact, your plot is his daily delight.

MAKE IT STICK

Draw a picture of yourself doing something you know makes God happy. Now lay a clean sheet of paper over your drawing. Outline your drawing with numbered dots to create a dot-to-dot picture on the clean paper. Politely ask your dad or mom to connect the dots and see if he or she can guess what it is you're doing in that picture. Then say this daily devo and talk about what it means.

PRAYER

Dear God, thanks for caring about all the little details of my life. You not only care, but you also give me directions every day. That makes me feel very secure, God. I love you. In Jesus' name, amen.

CLICK-ER:
DOT-TO-DOT PICTURE

Whenever you see, complete, or think about a *dot-to-dot picture*, let your mind connect the dots on this daily devo as it clicks and sticks. Singer the Psalm-Bird with his three-is-the-key and highway-seven-to-heaven sign reminds you that the devo is from the book of Psalms, Chapter 37.

PSALMS, CHAPTER 42 (VERSES 5-6)

Why am I discouraged? Why is my heart so sad? I will put my hope in God! I will praise him again—my Savior and my God!

DAILY DEVO

When life's lemon-sour, I lean on God's power.

God wants us to be honest with him about our feelings. He wants us to tell him if we feel like shouting or crying; if we feel like jumping up and down or curling up alone in a corner. This psalm is proof that God wants us to speak openly with him about the ups and downs of life. As you go through times when life feels and tastes lemon-sour, bring your emotions to God. He wants to hear from you. And he wants you to know that he alone has the strength you need to make it through.

MAKE IT STICK

Politely ask your dad or mom for permission to make fresh lemonade. Squeeze lemons to get their juice, and add water. Is your lemonade sweet or sour? Sometimes life is lemon-sour, but God's power can change that—just like you can change your sour lemonade. Try adding sugar until the lemonade becomes sweet. As you enjoy your lemonade, remember this daily devo. It may take time to sweeten up a difficult situation, but God's power can do it!

PRAYER

Dear God, when I'm sad or discouraged, remind me to talk to you about it and put my hope in you. Then I'll soon be praising you again for your power and love. In Jesus' name I pray. Amen.

CLICK-ER: LEMON

Whenever you see, taste, or squeeze a *lemon*, let your mind lean on this daily devo as it clicks and sticks. Singer the Psalm-Bird with his four-on-the-floorboard and two-blue-shoes reminds you that the devo is from the book of Psalms, Chapter 42.

PSALMS, CHAPTER 50 (VERSE 10)

For all the animals of the forest are mine, and I own the cattle on a thousand hills.

DAILY DEVO

Wow! God owns every cow from here to Moscow.

Did you know that God is the major pet owner in the world? He not only owns every cow, but all of the dogs, cats, birds, and every other living thing. If you have a pet, you may think you're the owner. But really, you're just the caretaker. God is the owner. Know why? God is the only One who can keep something alive. Yeah, you can give a pet some food and water. But can you make its body turn food into energy so it's able to grow and be active? Farmers can feed green grass to brown cows. But can they make green grass turn into white milk? No way. God is the One who gives life and keeps life going. That's why he's the real owner of everything, from here to Moscow and everywhere else. That's pretty amazing, isn't it?

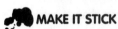 **MAKE IT STICK**

Politely ask your dad or mom to help you pinpoint your town and the city of Moscow on a world map or globe. Then, while holding a finger on each, think about all the millions and zillions of cows between them. That's a lot of cows. And God owns them all.

PRAYER

You are amazing, God. You create life, and you keep it going. Wow! No one else can do that. I praise you for being the owner of all Creation. Amen.

CLICK-ER: COW

Whenever you see, touch, or think about a *cow*, let this daily devo milk your mind as it clicks and sticks. Singer the Psalm-Bird with his five-on-a-hive-hat and halo-is-a-hero-as-a-zero reminds you that the devo is from the book of Psalms, Chapter 50.

WEEKEND ACTIVITY IDEAS

(1) Highlight the verses for Week 17 in your Bible. (2) Find Singer the Psalm-Bird in each picture for this week and identify the chapter-number symbols. (3) Add to your collection of Click-ers. (4) Say the daily devos for Week 17. (5) Check out Thursday of Week 49 for a related devo on how to know the milky way to grow.

AMERICA'S BEST-KNOWN SINGER

While the name Singer the Psalm-Bird is made-up, there is a real songbird called the Song Sparrow. This little brown bird is found all across America. It sings as many as 20 tunes and can come up with about 1,000 different ways to sing those songs.

PSALMS, CHAPTER 56 (VERSE 8)

You keep track of all my sorrows. You have collected all my tears in your bottle. You have recorded each one in your book.

DAILY DEVO

God knows my fears and bottles all my tears.

God made the whole universe. He's concerned about wars and governments and other big stuff. Do you think he cares about your tears? Well, he does! He keeps track of every detail of your life, including every tear you cry and every fear you feel. It's good to cry, especially when life hurts. But it's also good to remember that God is very near to you and collects your tears in his bottle. What have you cried about lately? Whatever it is, God understands. And when you get to heaven, there will be no more tears for God to collect. Instead, he'll offer you an eternal bucket of joy.

MAKE IT STICK

For this fun activity you'll need a water bottle, a bowl, and an eyedropper. Fill the bowl with water and suction the eyedropper full of water. Pretending that the average good cry has 10 teardrops, drip 10 drops into your bottle. See how many cries you can drip into the bottle before you get bored. One bottle holds a lot of tears, but God's "heavenly bottle" holds everyone's tears. He cares about you—he cares about all of his children!

PRAYER

Dear God, it really helps to know that you care about my tears. When I'm sad, you understand. And you're right beside me to comfort me. Thanks for being there, God. Amen.

CLICK-ER: TEARS

Whenever you see, wipe away, or think about *tears*, let your heart bottle this daily devo as it clicks and sticks. Singer the Psalm-Bird with his five-on-a-hive-hat and six-pick-up-stix reminds you that the devo is from the book of Psalms, Chapter 56.

PSALMS, CHAPTER 62 (VERSES 6-7)

He alone is my rock and my salvation, my fortress where I will not be shaken. My victory and honor come from God alone. He is my refuge, a rock where no enemy can reach me.

DAILY DEVO

God is my rock around the clock.

If you've ever played hide-and-seek around big rocks, you know how great they are for hiding behind. Not only are they too thick to see through, but they can keep you safe from the sun, wind, or rain. And big rocks won't move. David, who wrote this psalm, had learned over the years that God is like a rock that is too big to shake. God was his hide-and-seek place of safety. Many times David ran to God, who protected him day and night. God wants to be your safe place too. When you're scared, or not sure about what to do next, run to God. Talk to him and trust him. He's your rock, and he will keep you safe around the clock.

MAKE IT STICK

Put a rock about the size of your hand beside your alarm clock. Each morning this week when you wake up, say this daily devo. Then thank God that he, just like that rock, was there all through the night while you were sleeping. Also thank him for his promise to be with you through the day ahead of you.

PRAYER

Dear God, I'm so glad I can talk to you when I need a safe place. Thanks for being with me and protecting me day and night. In Jesus' name, amen.

CLICK-ER: ROCK

Whenever you see, touch, or think about a *rock*, let this daily devo stand firm in your mind as it clicks and sticks. Singer the Psalm-Bird with his six-pick-up-stix and two-blue-shoes reminds you that this devo is from the book of Psalms, Chapter 62.

PSALMS, CHAPTER 78 (VERSES 5-6)

[The Lord] issued his laws to Jacob; he gave his instructions to Israel. He commanded our ancestors to teach them to their children, so the next generation might know them—even the children not yet born—and they in turn will teach their own children.

DAILY DEVO

I promise to pass on the baton of faith.

God wants all of his children to read, understand, and obey all of his Word—and pass it on to friends and family, who will then pass it on to others. If you love God, it's because someone loved God before you did and took the time to teach you. As in a relay race, that person received the "baton of faith" and passed it on to you. Someday it will be your turn to pass your faith on to someone. You probably haven't thought too much yet about having children who may give you grandchildren, but what you believe today will be passed on tomorrow. What will your children and other children in your church family learn about God from you? Think about it. They will learn from your example, whether good or bad.

 MAKE IT STICK

Ask one of your parents if you may have the cardboard tube from an empty roll of paper towels. Write the words "baton of faith" on its side. When your dad or mom has a minute, hand it to one of them, and then politely ask for it back. As you take it, say this daily devo.

PRAYER

Thank you, Lord, for every grown-up who has taught me to trust and obey you. As I grow up, teach me how to pass my faith on to the children around me. Amen.

CLICK-ER: BATON

Whenever you see, twirl, or think about a *baton*, let your mind pass this daily devo along to your heart as it clicks and sticks. Singer the Psalm-Bird with his highway-seven-to-heaven sign and eight-under-skates reminds you that the devo is from Psalms, Chapter 78.

PSALMS, CHAPTER 91 (VERSE 1)

Those who live in the shelter of the Most High will find rest in the shadow of the Almighty.

DAILY DEVO

I've got it made in the shade of God's shadow.

When the sun is hotter than an oven, what do you do? You probably try to get some relief in the shade. God is like that shade. Like a big umbrella, his shadow shelters us from whatever "heat" we face in this life. Are you afraid about something that's happening at school? Well, come under God's umbrella and rest for a while as you talk to him. Is something going on at home that's got you down? Come sit in God's shadow—under his umbrella. Tell him all about everything. As you trust him, you'll feel his protection. And before long, being under God's umbrella will be the only place you want to be.

 MAKE IT STICK

Have fun making an umbrella! Trace around a cereal bowl on a piece of colored paper. Now cut out the circle, write this daily devo on it, and decorate your umbrella any way you like. In the center of your umbrella, punch a small hole with a pen or pencil. Then carefully push the top of a soda straw into the hole you've punched. Presto! You've got it made in the shade with a homemade umbrella.

PRAYER

Dear God, I love being able to rest in the shade of your shadow. It's like being under a heavenly umbrella. Thank you for keeping me safe as I sit here and talk with you. Amen.

CLICK-ER: UMBRELLA

Whenever you see, open, or think about an *umbrella* and its *shadow*, let this daily devo shade and shelter your heart as it clicks and sticks. Singer the Psalm-Bird with his nine-foot-pine and one-on-a-bun reminds you that the devo is from Psalms, Chapter 91.

PSALMS, CHAPTER 95 (VERSE 8)

The LORD says, "Don't harden your hearts."

DAILY DEVO

I'm not meant to harden like cement.

If you place your hand on wet cement, you'll leave a handprint. But after cement gets hard, you can't change it anymore. Someone has said that children are like "wet cement." They have soft hearts and are able to change as they learn new things. We're all born with soft hearts that can learn to please God more and more. But over time, some hearts get hard like cement. Is your heart still soft? It is if you like learning how to please God. And it is if you ask God to help you change when you're not pleasing him. You're not meant to harden like cement. So stay soft.

 MAKE IT STICK

Politely ask for permission to put some water and dirt in a shallow cake pan. Pretend this is "wet cement" and place it beside some hard cement—a sidewalk, driveway, or road curb. Feel how hard the dry cement is and how soft the wet "cement" is. Then say this daily devo.

PRAYER

Dear God, please help my heart stay soft so I'll keep wanting to learn and grow and change to be more like you. Help me today to please you in every way. In Jesus' name, amen.

CLICK-ER:
CEMENT SIDEWALK

Whenever you see or walk on a *cement sidewalk*, let this daily devo soften your heart as it clicks and sticks. Singer the Psalm-Bird with his nine-foot-pine and five-on-a-hive-hat reminds you that the devo is from the book of Psalms, Chapter 95.

PSALMS, CHAPTER 101 (VERSES 2-3)

I will lead a life of integrity in my own home. I will refuse to look at anything vile and vulgar.

DAILY DEVO

I only watch top-notch TV.

TVs are everywhere. There's both bad and good stuff on TV, but sometimes you have to look hard to find the good. It would be interesting to ask King David, who wrote this psalm, about today's TV programs. We know he would "refuse to look at anything *vile* and *vulgar*." Without going into a lot of detail about what these two *V* words mean, it's safe to say these words could take their place: *evil* and *disgusting*. Would David have watched anything like that? Psalm 101 tells us no way! Be like David. Watch only what's top-notch.

MAKE IT STICK

Using a large cardboard box, make a play TV with a friend. Out of one side, cut a square for your TV screen. Cut out the entire back side of the box—the side opposite the TV screen. Now place your TV box so that the back of it is on the edge of a table. Take turns sitting behind your TV so you can get "into" it and act out some fun, top-notch programs together. The person across the table will see only the upper body of whoever is "on TV."

PRAYER

Dear God, I don't want to watch anything on TV that's evil or disgusting. Thank you for the good programs that my parents and I do enjoy. I'll stick with them. In Jesus' name, amen.

CLICK-ER: TELEVISION

Whenever you see or think about a *TV*, let your mind picture this daily devo as it clicks and sticks. Singer the Psalm-Bird with a one-on-a-bun on each side of his halo-is-a-hero-as-a-zero reminds you that the devo is from Psalms, Chapter 101.

WEEKEND ACTIVITY IDEAS

(1) Highlight the verses for Week 18 in your Bible. (2) Find Singer the Psalm-Bird in each of the pictures for this week and identify the chapter-number symbols. (3) Add to your collection of Click-ers. (4) Say the daily devos for Week 18. (5) Check out Monday of Week 41 for a related devo on keeping tar out of your mental DVD or VCR.

IT MUST BE SPRING!

Every spring, robins leave their southern winter homes and fly north. They sing a cheerful song that may sound like a whistle during the day and like the whinny of a tiny horse in the evening. What a great way to praise God all day long and be a real Psalm-Bird!

PSALMS, CHAPTER 104 (VERSE 14)

You cause grass to grow for the livestock and plants for people to use. You allow them to produce food from the earth.

DAILY DEVO

Only God can grow the grass I mow.

Some kind of grass can be found almost everywhere in the world: backyards, parks, playgrounds, swamps, deserts, polar regions, tropical forests, rocky ground, and even snowy mountains. But have you ever thought about what makes grass grow? A scientist will tell you that all it takes is the right mixture of good grass seed and good soil, along with just the right amount of water and light. But even then, if all these things didn't do what God made them to do, nothing would happen. We can try to help grass grow by giving it extra plant food and water, but nothing we do actually makes it grow. Think about it. Only God can grow the grass you mow.

 MAKE IT STICK

If you can, grab a freshly cut clump of grass, put it in an envelope, and keep it by your bed overnight. Or draw a picture of grass. If you have some cut grass, how will it look the next morning? It will probably be brown, because it stopped growing. If you drew some green grass, now draw some dried-up grass. What you see will remind you of this daily devo.

PRAYER

Thank you, God, for giving every living thing everything it needs to grow. I'm glad you care for animals that eat grass and for people like me, who love eating food from plants, like corn, apples, rice, and beans. Amen.

CLICK-ER: GRASS

Whenever you see, mow, or think about *grass*, let this daily devo cut through your mind as it clicks and sticks. Singer the Psalm-Bird with his one-on-a-bun, halo-is-a-hero-as-a-zero, and four-on-the-floorboard reminds you that the devo is from Psalms, Chapter 104.

PSALMS, CHAPTER 119 (VERSE 11)

I have hidden your word in my heart, that I might not sin against you.

DAILY DEVO

I've swallowed the Book—hook, line, and sinker.

Sometimes when people go fishing, a fish bites so hard that it takes the bait "hook, line, and sinker." That means the fish not only swallows the bait and hook, but it swallows even the line and the little metal sinker that keeps the hook below the water. That's one hungry fish! When we say that a person swallows something "hook, line, and sinker," it means the person believes everything about it. That's how God wants us to believe his Word, the Bible. He wants us to take it in "hook, line, and sinker" so we understand it, believe it, and obey it. God's Book keeps us away from sin and hooked on the right stuff.

MAKE IT STICK

The next time you eat spaghetti, ask if you may put six strands of spaghetti on a separate dish. Shape the first one into a fishhook, the second one into a fishing line, and the third one into a sinker. As you eat them one by one, say this daily devo. Then, as you eat the other three strands, name three ways to "swallow" the Bible: understand it, believe it, and obey it.

PRAYER

Dear God, please help me get hooked on your Word, and not hooked by sin. I believe in your Word, and with all my heart I want to do what it says. Thank you for helping me understand it and obey it. Amen.

CLICK-ER: FISHHOOK

Whenever you see, fish with, or think about a *fishhook*, let this daily devo sink deeply into your mind as it clicks and sticks. Singer the Psalm-Bird, who has caught two one-on-a-bun meals and a nine-foot-pine, reminds you that the devo is from the book of Psalms, Chapter 119.

PSALMS, CHAPTER 119 (VERSE 99)

Yes, I have more insight than my teachers, for I am always thinking of your laws.

DAILY DEVO

I'm glad I wear God's glasses.

Is it important to get a good education? Of course! But it's even more important to know and live God's Word. In fact, knowing and living the Bible, even at your age, can give you more insight than your teachers can! *Insight* is simply the ability to see into something. When we have insight into the Word of God, we understand what it means through the lens of God's point of view. We see clearly into the things that really matter—how to get along with God and with other people. So how about deciding right now to wear God's glasses every day? The more you wear them, the more insight for living you'll get.

 MAKE IT STICK

Make a pair of eyeglass frames from play dough or politely ask your dad or mom if you can borrow an old pair of eyeglasses. Now close your eyes and put them on. As you open your eyes, say this daily devo. Each time you read your Bible, pretend to put on God's glasses. As you do, ask God to help you see and understand what you read.

PRAYER

Dear God, when I read my Bible, I need your wisdom to understand it. Teach me to see everything the way you see it, and help me to love other people the way you love them. In Jesus' name I pray. Amen.

CLICK-ER: EYEGLASSES

Whenever you see, wear, or think about *eyeglasses*, let your mind see through this daily devo as it clicks and sticks. Singer the Psalm-Bird with a one-on-the-bun on each side of his head and a nine-foot-pine next to him reminds you that the devo is from Psalms, Chapter 119.

PSALMS, CHAPTER 121 (VERSES 5-6)

The LORD himself watches over you! The LORD stands beside you as your protective shade. The sun will not harm you by day, nor the moon at night.

DAILY DEVO

God is my unseen sunscreen.

Did you ever get a sunburn because you forgot to put on sunscreen? Ouch! The neat thing about sunscreen is how it protects us from sunburn without slowing us down. We just put it on and forget about it while we play and have fun in the sun. God is a lot like sunscreen in the way he protects us. He's always as close as our skin. And he protects us from all kinds of harm, even when we don't know he's doing it. But how does God protect each one of his children all over the world? Only God knows, but we do know this: He never needs to sleep, which means he's always on the job doing whatever it takes to protect you and keep you safe.

 **MAKE IT STICK**

No matter what time of year it is, rub a dab of sunscreen (or hand lotion, if that's all you've got) onto your arm. See how it disappears? Your unseen sunscreen protects you from getting burned by harmful, unseen, ultraviolet sun rays. That's how God protects us from things that might harm us. As you dab on more sunscreen or lotion, say this daily devo.

PRAYER

Dear God, thanks for being everywhere and for never being too busy or too sleepy to watch over me. Thank you for all the times you have protected me and I didn't even know it. Amen.

CLICK-ER: SUNSCREEN

Whenever you see, put on, or think about *sunscreen*, let this daily devo protect your mind as it clicks and sticks. Singer the Psalm-Bird with a one-on-a-bun on each side of his two-blue-shoes reminds you that this devo is from Psalms, Chapter 121.

PSALMS, CHAPTER 127 (VERSE 3)

Children are a gift from the LORD; they are a reward from him.

DAILY DEVO

I'm a trophy award from the Lord.

People get trophies when they compete against one another and do a great job, especially in sports. The Heisman Trophy, for example, is awarded each year to the most outstanding college football player in the United States. The idea of giving people rewards is God's. Every person is presented to his or her parents at birth as a heaven-sent reward from the Lord! You are one of your parents' most outstanding achievements. Have you thanked them for giving you life? You should. And have you thanked God for making you one of his trophies? Remember, he's put you here for a purpose. You are a reward from the Lord, and he loves you.

 MAKE IT STICK

Draw a picture of yourself in the shape of a trophy, like the one pictured in this daily devo. Show your hands on your hips looking like the two handles. Let the lower part of the cup be your entire lower body. Now show your picture to your dad or mom. Your parent will probably ask, "What's this?" Then just say, "Me! I'm a trophy award from the Lord." And look up today's verse in your Bible.

PRAYER

Dear God, thanks for letting me know that I am a reward from you. And thanks for giving me life through my parents. Show me how to live for you today. Amen.

CLICK-ER: **TROPHY**

Whenever you see, win, or think about a *trophy*, let your heart give this daily devo a standing ovation as it clicks and sticks. Singer the Psalm-Bird with a one-on-a-bun, two-blue-shoes, and highway-seven-to-heaven sign reminds you that this devo is from the book of Psalms, Chapter 127.

PSALMS, CHAPTER 136 (VERSE 1)

Give thanks to the LORD, for he is good! His faithful love endures forever.

DAILY DEVO

I love to sail thank-you mail to God.

Think about this. Did you create and give yourself the sun so you could see during the day? Did you make your own legs so you could walk, skip, and jump? Did you make your own eyes so you could read this page? No, none of us did any of these things. But God did. He's the only one who could. And believe it or not, these are all gifts from God to you. God likes to hear your thanks. Why don't you sail some thank-you mail to him right now? It'll warm your heart and his.

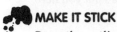 **MAKE IT STICK**

Draw the outline of a postcard on a piece of paper. Think of something you're really thankful to God for, and draw a picture of it on your postcard. Now draw a sail (a triangle shape) on a separate piece of paper and add a rectangle shape below it for a tab. Cut out the sail with the tab, fold the tab back, and glue the tab to one end of your postcard so the sail is upright. Imagine this thank-you mail sailing itself up into heaven. See God catching it and smiling when he reads it.

PRAYER

Lord, thanks for being so good to me. You help me do all the things I need to do. And your love for me will never end. Thank you, God. In Jesus' name, amen.

CLICK-ER:

MAIL (POSTCARD)

Whenever you send or receive a postcard in the *mail*, let this daily devo sail through your mind as it clicks and sticks. Singer the Psalm-Bird with his one-on-a-bun, three-is-the-key, and six-pick-up-stix reminds you that this devo is from Psalms, Chapter 136.

WEEKEND ACTIVITY IDEAS

(1) Highlight the verses for Week 19 in your Bible. (2) Find Singer the Psalm-Bird in each picture for this week and identify the chapter-number symbols. (3) Add to your collection of Click-ers. (4) Say the daily devos for Week 19. (5) Check out Thursday of Week 36 for a related devo on lone-leper pepper praise.

CAW, CAW, CAW

Big, black crows like shiny objects and can count. They can even mimic the human voice. Usually they make a loud cawing sound. The caw of a crow isn't beautiful, but crows use the voice God gave them to sing praises to him. The crow—another real Psalm-Bird!

PSALMS, CHAPTER 139 (VERSES 13-14)

You made all the delicate, inner parts of my body and knit me together in my mother's womb. Thank you for making me so wonderfully complex! Your workmanship is marvelous—how well I know it.

DAILY DEVO

I'm knit to fit for life.

Have you ever thought about how God forms a baby inside his or her mother? King David thought about it too. He realized that he didn't know how to explain it. So he compared it to knitting, which was something he did understand. He knew that when someone knits a scarf or a sweater, the person does it by hand. It's a personal gift that takes lots of time, skill, and attention to detail. In the same personal, careful way, God forms every baby. Only God can make a baby. And only God could have made you. He lovingly made you stitch by stitch. You're not a mistake. You're a wonderful miracle. We know it's true because God says so!

MAKE IT STICK

Look at a sweater to see how it is knitted. Gently stretch a section of it so you can see the pattern of the stitches, and try to draw that pattern on a piece of paper. Then look in an encyclopedia or on the Internet to find a picture of the human skeleton. Think about how God knit all of your bones together. He added a heart, lungs, stomach, kidneys, and intestines, along with muscles, joints, and blood vessels. And he covered everything with skin and hair.

PRAYER

Wow! It's amazing, God, to think about how complex my body is. Thank you for knitting me together. Please help me to keep my body strong and healthy. In Jesus' name, amen.

CLICK-ER:
KNITTING NEEDLES

Whenever you see or use *knitting needles*, let this daily devo knit your heart and mind together as it clicks and sticks. Singer the Psalm-Bird with his one-on-a-bun, three-is-the-key, and nine-foot-pine reminds you that the devo is from Psalms, Chapter 139.

PSALMS, CHAPTER 141 (VERSE 3)

Take control of what I say, O LORD, and guard my lips.

DAILY DEVO

I'm learning to zip my lip.

Keeping our mouths shut at the right times may sometimes feel like one of the hardest things we need to do. King David knew this from experience. He found that his tongue was so slippery sometimes that he could barely hold it back from saying hurtful things to people. In the New Testament, the book of James even says that the tongue can be like a fire. It can set off sparks that do a lot of damage. Learning to zip our lip takes the power of God. Have you said something lately that made someone feel really bad? If so, ask God to forgive you. Then go to that person, admit that you were wrong, and ask for forgiveness. This will take a lot of courage, but you can do it.

 MAKE IT STICK

Draw a picture of yourself with your lips zipped shut. Then ask God to remind you of hurtful words you've let out that you should have held in. If you've not yet said you're sorry to God and to the person you hurt, don't let this day go by without doing it.

PRAYER

Dear God, please don't let my words make anyone feel bad. If I have said something that hurt someone, give me the courage to ask you and that person for forgiveness. In Jesus' name I pray. Amen.

CLICK-ER: ZIPPER

Whenever you see, zip up, or think about a *zipper*, let this daily devo zip through your mind as it clicks and sticks. Singer the Psalm-Bird with a one-on-a-bun on each side of his four-on-the-floorboard reminds you that the devo is from Psalms, Chapter 141.

Week 20, Wednesday

BOOK OF PROVERBS

Professor Wowl

Professor begins with the same sound as *Proverbs*. The owl is often thought of as being very wise. King David's son Solomon, who wrote most of the book of Proverbs, was much wiser than any owl. When you see Professor Wowl in a picture, you'll know the daily devo is from Proverbs. Connected to Professor Wowl are number symbols. (See page 15.) They make the chapter location of the devo click and stick.

The makers of vitamin pills pack a little of this and a little of that into a small pill that's easy to swallow. Once it gets into your stomach, it dissolves, giving energy and strength to your entire body. The book of Proverbs is like a bottle of spiritual vitamins. It is filled with bite-size proverbs or wise sayings that are easy to understand and remember—to swallow and digest. They strengthen your relationship with God, family, friends, and neighbors. Join the Proverbs One-a-Day Club! Each day read just one of these chunks of wisdom, and watch yourself grow wiser than an owl.

 MAKE IT STICK

Make a tab to mark the book of Proverbs in your Bible. (See Week 1, Monday, for directions.)

People think owls are wise for several reasons: (1) They can see at night. (2) Their big eyes make them look wise. (3) Their big head feathers make them look like they've got a big brain. Politely ask someone to help you find a book with pictures of owls. Why do owls look wise to you?

Whenever you see a picture of an owl or think about one, remember Professor Wowl and the book of Proverbs.

JUST FOR FUN

Wise King Solomon wrote about someone who is wiser than owls, wiser than himself, and wiser than anyone else. You can read about him in your Bible by looking up Proverbs, Chapter 3 (verses 5-6).

PRAYER

Dear Lord, thank you for being the wisest of all. And thank you for the wisdom you gave Solomon to write short proverbs so I, too, can become wise. In Jesus' name, amen.

PROVERBS, CHAPTER 1 (VERSES 1-3)

These are the proverbs of Solomon, David's son, king of Israel. Their purpose is to teach people wisdom and discipline, to help them understand the insights of the wise. Their purpose is to teach people to live disciplined and successful lives, to help them do what is right, just, and fair.

DAILY DEVO

I need spiritual speed bumps.

When drivers see a sign that says "Speed Bump Ahead," they slow their cars way, way down. Why? At normal speed, the bottom of a car will bang the bump so hard that everyone inside will feel it in a big way! Speed bumps are good warnings for drivers to slow down for people. Without speed bumps near playgrounds, in parking lots, and even in some neighborhoods, drivers might hurt someone. God's Word, like a good speed bump, makes us slow down and learn how God wants us to act so we don't hurt other people or ourselves. When we slow down to read God's Word—our spiritual speed bump—we become safe, thoughtful people.

MAKE IT STICK

Look for a speed bump in your neighborhood and think about why it was placed there. Is it to protect children playing nearby? Is it to keep people safe as they get out of parked cars in a parking lot? Whatever it is, thank God for his Word, which is like a spiritual speed bump. Slow down to read it every day, and it will protect you from doing things that might hurt someone and make God sad.

PRAYER

Dear God, thank you for teaching me to slow down and pay attention to what you want me to do. Please show me every day how to do what is right and just and fair. In Jesus' name I pray. Amen.

CLICK-ER: SPEED BUMP

Whenever you see, ride over, or think about a *speed bump*, let this daily devo jolt your memory as it clicks and sticks. Professor Wowl riding in his one-on-a-bun car reminds you that the devo is from Proverbs, Chapter 1.

PROVERBS, CHAPTER 2 (VERSES 2–4)

Tune your ears to wisdom, and concentrate on understanding. Cry out for insight, and ask for understanding. Search for them as you would for silver; seek them like hidden treasures.

DAILY DEVO
I'm diving deep for treasure to keep.

Many years ago, a treasure hunter named Mel Fisher began looking for a Spanish ship full of gold and silver treasures. He believed it had sunk somewhere off the coast of Florida. For sixteen years he searched for it. One day he found it. It's now on record as the single largest treasure ever found, worth hundreds of millions of dollars. But even that treasure is nothing compared to the value of God's Word! If you search for wisdom in the Bible, you'll find a super rich life of walking with God. Dive deep for God's treasure. It's the only treasure you can keep in this life *and* the next!

MAKE IT STICK

With a friend or two, play "Hide 'n Go HoneyWord" with your Bible. Take turns being the one who hides God's Word somewhere in your home. As your friends try to find it, coach them by saying "warm" or "cold." Whoever finds it first must shout out this daily devo and its location. If the first person can't remember both the daily devo and the location, whoever can say them first gets to be "it."

PRAYER

Dear God, with all my heart I want to find the treasure of your wisdom. Thank you for placing it in your Word, where I can find it as I read it every day. In Jesus' name, amen.

CLICK-ER:
TREASURE CHEST

Whenever you see, read about, or think about a *treasure chest*, let your heart dive deep for this daily devo as it clicks and sticks. Professor Wowl with his two-blue-shoes reminds you that the devo is from Proverbs, Chapter 2.

PROVERBS, CHAPTER 6 (VERSES 20–21)

My son, obey your father's commands, and don't neglect your mother's instruction. Keep their words always in your heart. Tie them around your neck.

DAILY DEVO

I tie and apply his commands to my heart.

We may not often think about it, but our hands help us every day in a thousand ways. We use them to eat our food, wave hello, play sports, tie knots, scratch our noses, write notes, play musical instruments, and type on our computers. People who are deaf use them to speak. People who are blind use them to feel and "see." But most important of all, everyone can use them to open God's Word to see what God has written. It sounds simple, but the first step in tying and applying God's commands to your heart is using your hands to open his Book, the Bible. Read God's Word! And listen to your parents. Why? Because that's one of God's commands. He knows they can help you obey him. If you don't obey, you'll be like a man who looks at his tie in the closet but never ties it on or wears it out.

 MAKE IT STICK

Politely ask your dad or granddad if you may borrow an old necktie. Now ask him to please help you tie it. As he does, repeat this daily devo.

PRAYER

Dear God, one of your commands is for me to obey my father's commands and my mother's instructions. I know how wise you are, God. So help me always to listen both to you and to my parents. Amen.

CLICK-ER: NECKTIE

Whenever you see, wear, or think about a *necktie*, let your mind tie this daily devo around your heart as it clicks and sticks. Professor Wowl with his six-pick-up-stix reminds you that the devo is from Proverbs, Chapter 6.

WEEKEND ACTIVITY IDEAS

(1) Highlight the verses for Week 20 in your Bible. (2) Find the HoneyWord animal in each picture for this week and identify the chapter-number symbols. (3) Add to your collection of Click-ers. (4) Say the daily devos for Week 20. (5) Check out Saturday/Sunday of Week 46 for a related devo on slicing and dicing the Word.

OWL ABOUT THAT?

When surprised and afraid, many owls flatten their feathers and lengthen their bodies to look like a tree branch.

PROVERBS, CHAPTER 8 (VERSE 1)
Listen as Wisdom calls out! Hear as understanding raises her voice!

DAILY DEVO
I follow the truthful tone of God's microphone.

A microphone can make a person's voice loud enough to be heard by a large group. In Proverbs, Chapter 8, Solomon talks about wisdom as if it's a lady using an outdoor microphone. We are all in her audience. At the top of her lungs, she's asking us to listen closely to God's wisdom. If we do, she promises we will receive all the wonderful things that come with wisdom—things like truth, understanding, good advice, and common sense. Wouldn't you like to latch onto those things? You can! Just make it a habit to listen when Lady Wisdom speaks, and God will give you all those good gifts.

 MAKE IT STICK

Politely ask your dad or mom to please help you make a paper microphone. You can use poster board, flexible cardboard, or even an old plastic place mat, if that's okay with your parents. Roll this into the shape of a mike and tape it together. Once you're ready to roll, ask a family member to quiz you on your favorite daily devos. Show them the list of Click-ers at the back of this book and identify five to ten that you've learned. When they name a Click-er, shout the daily devo and location through your microphone.

PRAYER
Dear God, I hear all kinds of advice from friends, TV shows, and Web sites. Help me listen first to the truth in your Word. Then you'll give me the common sense to know when advice is good and when it's not. Thanks, God. Amen.

CLICK-ER: MICROPHONE
Whenever you see, use, or think about a *microphone*, let this daily devo echo through your mind as it clicks and sticks. Professor Wowl with his eight-under-skates reminds you that the devo is from Proverbs, Chapter 8.

PROVERBS, CHAPTER 11 (VERSE 1)

The Lord detests the use of dishonest scales, but he delights in accurate weights.

DAILY DEVO

I won't cheat on any receipt.

Most of us struggle with cheating. For example, what if you buy candy that weighs a pound, but the checkout clerk gives you too much change back, charging you for only a half pound? What will you do? Will you just pay for the half pound or tell the clerk you think there is a mistake and ask to have the candy weighed again? God hates cheating. That's what *detest* means. *Hate* is a strong word, but it's the first one that comes to God's mind when he thinks about cheating. And it must become the first word that comes to your mind if you want God to bless you. Cheating your way through life is not the way to get rich—and it's not the way to be happy. If you're honest, God will be happy with you and you'll be happy with yourself.

MAKE IT STICK

See if your dad or mom will help you practice making change. You might set out cans of food for your parent to "buy" at twenty-five cents each. When you get the money, give back the correct change. Explain that you're working on a daily devo from Proverbs 11. It's important to know how to make change. If you do, you'll be able to be honest because you'll know if a clerk gives you back too much money.

PRAYER

Dear God, I want to be honest in everything I say and do. Please help me learn how to watch carefully to be sure I never accept too much or too little change from a checkout clerk. Amen.

CLICK-ER: RECEIPT

Whenever you see, receive, or think about a *receipt*, let this daily devo register in your mind as it clicks and sticks. Professor Wowl with a one-on-a-bun in each claw reminds you that this devo is from Proverbs, Chapter 11.

PROVERBS, CHAPTER 12 (VERSE 18)

Some people make cutting remarks, but the words of the wise bring healing.

DAILY DEVO

My words give life or cut like a knife.

Have you ever looked closely at your tongue in the mirror? It's kind of gross and funny looking, don't you think? It's attached to the bottom of your mouth by a shiny, tissue-thin piece of skin. And the top is a grainy-looking field of bumps called taste buds. Somehow, when food rubs next to these bumps or liquid sloshes all over them, the brain is able to send us signals like "yum, ice cream," or "yuck, medicine." But that's not all the tongue can do. It shapes the sounds of words that make people feel good—or make them feel bad. Kind words make people happy to be alive. Unkind words make people hurt inside. Don't use your tongue to cut people down. Use it to build them up. God can help you do it!

MAKE IT STICK

Politely ask your dad or mom to let you watch them use a sharp knife to cut up some meat or vegetables. Talk about what kinds of words can cut like a knife and hurt people. Then think of words that can give life and help people feel good.

PRAYER

Dear God, I don't like it when people say unkind words to me. So please keep me from cutting others down. Let my words be wise and help others feel good. In Jesus' name I pray. Amen.

CLICK-ER: KNIFE

Whenever you see, touch, or think about a *knife*, let this daily devo sharpen your mind as it clicks and sticks. Professor Wowl with a one-on-a-bun and two-blue-shoes reminds you that the devo is from Proverbs, Chapter 12.

PROVERBS, CHAPTER 16 (VERSE 28)

A troublemaker plants seeds of strife; gossip separates the best of friends.

DAILY DEVO

I don't dish dirt.

A gossip is a person who "dishes dirt" on other people's names by saying bad things about them behind their backs. Gossips don't care if what they're saying is true or not. They simply pass on the bad words they've heard or made up. All gossip is bad. But it's really bad when it's about a friend. If you hear gossip about a friend, don't just sit there and believe it. Go to your friend and tell what you've heard to see if it's true. You'll probably find out that it's not. Most gossip isn't. But even if it is, your friend will be glad you came to ask about it. To keep good friends, don't believe gossip or pass it along.

 **MAKE IT STICK**

Use a marker to write the names of your best friends on a piece of paper. Then place the paper on a clean dish. With permission from a parent, scrape the leftovers from your dirty dinner dishes onto the paper. Watch how this dirties your friends' names. That's how gossip works. God doesn't want you to gossip or believe gossip. He wants you to keep your friends.

PRAYER

Dear God, sometimes I hear gossip that sounds exciting and I pass it along. Forgive me for that, and help me to stop doing it. I don't want to lose or upset any of my friends. In Jesus' name, amen.

CLICK-ER: DIRTY DISH

Whenever you see, clean, or think about a *dirty dish*, let this daily devo make your words clean as it clicks and sticks. Professor Wowl with his one-on-a-bun car and six-pick-up-stix steering wheel reminds you that this devo is from Proverbs, Chapter 16.

PROVERBS, CHAPTER 18 (VERSE 24)

There are "friends" who destroy each other, but a real friend sticks closer than a brother.

DAILY DEVO

I paper-clip **friendship to my heart.**

Let's pretend that two pieces of paper are a picture of two people trying to be friends. Sometimes one friend holds on so tightly that the other person feels stapled to the first one. Stapled friendships don't work because we can't force someone to stay close to us. Good friendships are different. It's as if paper clips hold them close but give them the freedom to come and go without getting torn or crumpled. If God has blessed you with good friends, carefully and prayerfully paper-clip them to your heart. Don't try to staple them down. Time will tell if you and they will stay.

MAKE IT STICK

Get two sheets of paper. Draw a picture of yourself on one of them. On the other one, draw a good friend. Now paper-clip these pictures together and pray that God will help you stick close to each other. For the next week, put a paper clip in your pocket. Each time you feel it, thank God for this friendship.

PRAYER

Thank you, God, for my Christian friends. I pray that we will stick close together. But when we need to be apart, help us still care about one another and pray for each other. In Jesus' name, amen.

CLICK-ER: **PAPER CLIP**

Whenever you see, use, or think about a *paper clip*, let your heart hold your friends close as this daily devo clicks and sticks. Professor Wowl with his one-on-a-bun and eight-under-skates reminds you that this devo is from Proverbs, Chapter 18.

PROVERBS, CHAPTER 20 (VERSE 1)

Wine produces mockers; alcohol leads to brawls. Those led astray by drink cannot be wise.

DAILY DEVO

Alcohol can make me trip and fall.

Good, safe drinking water is just a fact of life in America today. We either get it from the kitchen faucet, or we buy bottled water and keep it in the fridge. But in the long-ago world of Bible times, the water in many of the wells and springs was not clean. It often caused people to get sick. So people would sometimes drink grape juice that had turned into wine. Solomon, in his great wisdom, knew that too much alcohol could make people do unwise things. They would say things they didn't mean to say or get into fights they didn't mean to start. The same is true today. As you grow up, learn to walk away from alcohol. You don't need it. It can make you trip and fall.

MAKE IT STICK

On a sheet of paper, draw the alcohol bottle you see here in this daily devo. Then draw the "do not do" red circle around it with the red diagonal line through it. Ask your dad or mom what he or she thinks this verse means.

PRAYER

Dear God, please make me wise when it comes to alcohol. As I grow up, I don't want to get drunk and get into fights. I'll trust you to make me strong and help me avoid any drink that makes me do stupid things. Amen.

CLICK-ER:

ALCOHOL BOTTLE

Whenever you see or think about any kind of *alcohol bottle*, let this daily devo sober your heart as it clicks and sticks. Professor Wowl with his two-blue-shoes and halo-is-a-hero-as-a-zero reminds you that this devo is from Proverbs, Chapter 20.

WEEKEND ACTIVITY IDEAS

(1) Highlight the verses for Week 21 in your Bible. (2) Find Professor Wowl in each of the pictures for this week and identify the chapter-number symbols. (3) Add to your collection of Click-ers. (4) Say the daily devos for Week 21. (5) Check out Friday of Week 32 for a related devo on how to zap a trap.

WISE NIGHT OWLS

Owls look wise because they have large eyes on the front of their head. They look like teachers who always seem to know just what to do. Owls are not really wise, but they do use their ability to see at night to hunt for food while other birds and animals sleep.

PROVERBS, CHAPTER 22 (VERSE 6)

Direct your children onto the right path, and when they are older, they will not leave it.

DAILY DEVO

I keep my training on track.

Parents who love God want only God's best for their children. You've probably never thought about this, but there's nothing easy about raising a kid like you. Your dad and mom have to work hard at learning how to help you follow the wisdom of God. That takes a lot of time and patience, for them and for you. Please receive their training as if it was coming from God himself, because it probably is. When you do that, you keep your train on track. And you'll enjoy a smooth ride into the future.

MAKE IT STICK

If you have a model train, send it for a trip around the tracks. Every now and then have it "jump the tracks." If you don't have one, find a picture of a train engine to copy from a book or the Internet. Hold your picture up and ride it along pretend tracks on the edge of your kitchen table. Then let your train crash over the side to the ground. That's a picture of how important it is to let your parents help you keep your life on the right track.

PRAYER

Dear God, sometimes I wish I didn't have to follow all the directions I get from my mom and dad. But if I learn now to do what's right, I know my life will be much easier as I grow up. So thanks for all the training I am getting. Amen.

CLICK-ER: TRAIN TRACK

Whenever you see, play with, ride on, or think about a *train track*, let this daily devo choo-choo through your heart as it clicks and sticks. Professor Wowl with his two pairs of two-blue-shoes reminds you that this devo is from Proverbs, Chapter 22.

PROVERBS, CHAPTER 24 (VERSE 16)

The godly may trip seven times, but they will get up again. But one disaster is enough to overthrow the wicked.

DAILY DEVO

Like a bowling pin, I get back up again and again.

Bowling is a fun sport. Machines gather up scattered bowling pins and reset them in the right places. However, before there were machines, every time somebody bowled and knocked down pins, someone had to be at the end of the lane to set the bowling pins back up again. When people hurt us by being unkind, we sometimes feel like we've been knocked down by a big, speeding bowling ball. And just like those people who used to set the bowling pins back up again, God is there to set things right so we can get back up. God isn't a machine. He wants us to talk to him and ask for his help. When we do, we find God is soon helping us get back up on our feet and ready for another round of life.

MAKE IT STICK

Lie down on the floor and get up again seven times. Then think of one way in which you've felt "knocked down" by someone. Pray about it silently to God. Ask him for help to forgive and strength to get back up again.

PRAYER

Thank you, God, for being with me when I feel like I've been knocked down. I'm so glad you help me get back up and face another day. In Jesus' name, amen.

CLICK-ER: BOWLING PIN

Whenever you see, play with, or think about a *bowling pin*, let this daily devo roll through your mind as it clicks and sticks. Professor Wowl with his two-blue-shoes and four-on-the-floorboard reminds you that the devo is from Proverbs, Chapter 24.

PROVERBS, CHAPTER 24 (VERSES 30-34)

I walked by the field of a lazy person, the vineyard of one with no common sense. I saw that it was . . . covered with weeds, and its walls were broken down. Then, as I looked and thought about it, I learned this lesson: A little extra sleep, a little more slumber, a little folding of the hands to rest—then poverty will pounce on you like a bandit.

DAILY DEVO

Laziness leads to a garden of weeds.

Weeds got their start way back in the Garden of Eden, after Adam and Eve sinned against God. Since then, weeds have done a lot of bad things. They steal light, water, and food from good plants. They often provide a home for the insects and diseases that kill the good plants. Weeds also mess up beautiful lawns and flower beds. But they're here to stay, so we have to work hard to get rid of them. The same is true about your heart. When something bad like laziness crops up in your life, you have to do something to stop it. Don't let it grow—pull it out by the roots as often as you need to. Laziness, if allowed to grow, leads to a life that looks like a garden of weeds.

MAKE IT STICK

Find some weeds in your yard or some patches of grass that might be growing out of cracks in the sidewalk. Say this daily devo as you pull the weeds out by the roots. It's not easy, is it? Pulling out the bad things in our lives takes a lot of work too. And no one else can do that for us.

PRAYER

Dear God, there are so many things to learn. And there is always work to be done. Help me to eat well, exercise, and get the sleep I need. Then I'll have the energy to study and do what you want me to do. Amen.

CLICK-ER: WEEDS

Whenever you see or pull up *weeds*, let this daily devo take root in your heart as it clicks and sticks. Professor Wowl with his two-blue-shoes and four-on-the-floorboard reminds you that the devo is from Proverbs, Chapter 24.

PROVERBS, CHAPTER 26 (VERSES 13-14)

The lazy person claims, "There's a lion on the road! Yes, I'm sure there's a lion out there!" As a door swings back and forth on its hinges, so the lazy person turns over in bed.

DAILY DEVO

I get ahead when I get out of bed.

It's weird, but the less you do, the less you *want* to do and the more you just want to sit around and do nothing. God has created each one of us to be busy and do helpful things. The bodies God has given us are so strong that they can do tons of cool things, even if parts of them are disabled. Solomon knew that what it really comes down to is that laziness is saying no to God. It's looking him in the face and saying, "No, I won't get out of bed and live like you want me to." If you've been sitting curbside on "Lazybone Lane," ask God to forgive you. Then get out of bed and do something. Start small. Pick a daisy. Pick anything. And over time, you'll find your strength picking up, making you stronger and stronger.

 **MAKE IT STICK**

Tonight before you go to bed, write out this daily devo and location. Put it where you'll see it as soon as you wake up. Tomorrow morning when you roll out of bed, say the daily devo to yourself. And then have a great day doing lots of things with God!

PRAYER

Dear God, thank you for creating me to do thoughtful things for others. And thanks for making me strong enough to do whatever you ask. Show me at least one way today to be helpful to someone. Amen.

CLICK-ER: BED

Whenever you see, get out of, or think about your *bed*, let this daily devo make up your mind as it clicks and sticks. Professor Wowl with his two-blue-shoes and six-pick-up-stix reminds you that the devo is from Proverbs, Chapter 26.

PROVERBS, CHAPTER 27 (VERSE 2)

Let someone else praise you, not your own mouth—a stranger, not your own lips.

DAILY DEVO

My self-praise smells like spoiled mayonnaise.

Have you ever been told, "Don't toot your own horn"? It means you shouldn't run around telling everybody about all the great things you've done. God knows that people who toot their own horns won't have friends for long. People like that are kind of like mayonnaise that's been left outside the refrigerator and has spoiled. Before you know it, everything around it smells terrible! It's okay to tell your friends about some of the things you've done. But not all the time. It's better to spend more time talking about the good things your friends have done. If you only talk about yourself, you've got a self-praise, spoiled-mayonnaise problem. And people can smell that from a mile away.

MAKE IT STICK

Ask if it's okay to leave a small amount of mayonnaise on a paper plate on your kitchen counter or outside in the sun. See how many days it takes to spoil. Once it spoils (and your nose will tell you when), say this daily devo. Whew! Now that you know how bad spoiled mayonnaise smells, ask God for help to praise others more, and yourself less.

PRAYER

Dear God, I'm really thankful for all my friends. Help me to talk more about the cool things they do than the things I do. But most of all, help me to talk about you, God. You are the greatest of all. In Jesus' name, amen.

CLICK-ER: MAYONNAISE

Whenever you see, eat, or think about *mayonnaise*, let this daily devo spread through your mind as it clicks and sticks. Professor Wowl with his two-blue-shoes and highway-seven-to-heaven sign reminds you that the devo is from Proverbs, Chapter 27.

Week 22, Saturday/ Sunday

BOOK OF ECCLESIASTES
Eagle-easy-astes

Eagle begins with the same letter as *Ecclesiastes*. Like an eagle has, Solomon wants us to have a bird's-eye view of life—a view from God's perspective. When you see Eagle-easy-astes in a picture, you'll know the daily devo is from Ecclesiastes. Connected to Eagle-easy-astes are number symbols. (See page 15.) They make the chapter location of the devo click and stick.

King Solomon had everything: brains, money, power, fame, wisdom, and lots of time to have fun. Most of his days were spent getting whatever he wanted, whenever he wanted it. Sounds great, right? Well, that's not what Solomon says. After spending his life enjoying all this world has to offer, he finally learned the secret of real happiness: to love God and obey his Word. This so changed his life that he wrote Ecclesiastes so you can see life from a bird's-eye view—God's wise view. If you do, you'll stay focused on him and avoid a lot of dead-end roads.

 MAKE IT STICK

Make a tab to mark the book of Ecclesiastes in your Bible. (See Week 1, Monday, for directions.)

Pretend you are an eagle flying over the area where you live. Take turns with a friend or family member describing what you see. Or, if you prefer, just draw a picture. How is a bird's eye view different from what we usually see? How do you think God's view is different from ours?

Whenever you see an eagle or a picture of one, think about Eagle-easy-astes and the book of Ecclesiastes.

JUST FOR FUN
Read a few verses that name some of the things Solomon learned. In the book of Ecclesiastes, look up Chapter 5 (verses 18-20) and Chapter 12 (verse 13).

PRAYER
Dear God, teach me to look at life from your point of view. Please keep me busy every day, loving you, enjoying your world, and obeying your Word. In Jesus' name, amen.

WEEKEND ACTIVITY IDEAS

(1) Highlight the verses for Week 22 in your Bible. (2) Find the HoneyWord animal in each picture for this week and identify the chapter-number symbols. (3) Add to your collection of Click-ers. (4) Say the daily devos for Week 22. (5) Look back at Wednesday of Week 19 for a related devo on being glad about wearing God's glasses.

EASY RIDER

An eagle's bones are hollow and filled with air, making them extremely light.

ECCLESIASTES, CHAPTER 4 (VERSE 9)
Two people are better off than one, for they can help each other succeed.

DAILY DEVO

Two can do a canoe better than one.

Paddling around in a canoe all by yourself isn't much fun—it's just plain hard work! The point Solomon is making in this verse is that everything goes better with a friend. Work is easier. And play is more fun. Even falling down is better, because someone's there to help you get up. God understands our need for friends; in fact, he built us to need them. We really can't make it through life without them. But to get friends, you have to be a friend. And part of being a friend is taking the first step, again and again. If you don't learn this now, you might find yourself paddling through life all alone.

 MAKE IT STICK

Make a canoe from aluminum foil so it looks like a picture from a magazine or an encyclopedia. Then draw pictures of yourself and a friend, and cut the figures out. Fold them at the waist, tape toothpick oars to each one, and set them inside your canoe. Now float your canoe in a sink full of water. Ask your dad or mom—and God—to help you think of more ways you and your friend can work together.

PRAYER
Thank you, God, for all the fun things I do with my friends. Please show me how to be a really good friend by doing first for them what I'd like them to do for me. In Jesus' name, amen.

CLICK-ER: CANOE
Whenever you see, paddle, or think about a *canoe*, let this daily devo float quietly through your mind as it clicks and sticks. Eagle-easy-astes with his four-on-the-floorboard reminds you that the devo is from Ecclesiastes, Chapter 4.

ECCLESIASTES, CHAPTER 11 (VERSE 1)

Send your grain across the seas, and in time, profits will flow back to you.

DAILY DEVO

I'm in the gang throwing God's boomerang.

There are many places in the Bible where God tells us that what we give has everything to do with what we get back. It's like using a boomerang. Invented thousands of years ago, the boomerang is a flat, curved piece of wood that can be thrown so it returns to the person who threw it. Isn't that amazing? But even more amazing is how giving to others follows the same flight plan. Whatever we give will circle around and someday come back to us. Are you in the gang throwing God's boomerang? If so, get ready to receive. Whatever you throw, good or bad, God will one day boomerang back to you.

 MAKE IT STICK

Find this Web site and read about boomerangs: www.howstuffworks.com. Then draw a boomerang on a piece of cardboard and cut it out. On one side write a one-sentence note of thanks to your dad or mom, naming one special thing he or she always does for you. After you give this to one or both of them, watch how God boomerangs back the great attitude you just sent out.

PRAYER

Dear God, when I smile, smiles come back to me. When I'm kind, people are kind back to me. When I give, I get back thanks and joy and much, much more. Thank you, God, for helping me to smile, be kind, and give to others! Amen.

CLICK-ER: BOOMERANG

Whenever you see, throw, or think about a *boomerang*, let this daily devo circle through your mind as it clicks and sticks. Eagle-easy-astes with a one-on-a-bun under each wing reminds you that the devo is from Ecclesiastes, Chapter 11.

ECCLESIASTES, CHAPTER 12 (VERSE 1)

Don't let the excitement of youth cause you to forget your Creator. Honor him in your youth before you grow old and say, "Life is not pleasant anymore."

DAILY DEVO

His guardrail keeps me on the trail.

When you walk up a flight of stairs or look out from a balcony, what makes you feel safe? The railing, right? It holds you in and protects you from falling. In the same way, God, through his Word, is like a rail that keeps us on the right trail and protects us from falling off into things that hurt us. But you can't just place your Bible by your bed and expect big things to happen. You've got to pick it up, read it, and think about its truths deep within your heart, rail by rail, over a period of years. Start today. God is the one who created you. Don't forget that he is your best guardrail. He alone keeps you on the right trail.

MAKE IT STICK

See how many places you can find guardrails on staircases at home, church, and school. Hold on to them and see how they protect you from falling as you walk up and down the steps. Notice how safe you feel. Say this daily devo as you hold on to a rail, and thank God for keeping you safe from anything that might hurt you or take you away from him.

PRAYER

Dear God, please help me learn all I can from your Word while I'm young. Learning to do what's right protects me from evil, and that makes me feel very safe. Thanks! In Jesus' name, amen.

CLICK-ER: GUARDRAIL

Whenever you see, hold on to, or think about a *guardrail*, let this daily devo hold firm in your mind as it clicks and sticks. Eagle-easy-astes with his one-on-a-bun and two-blue-shoes reminds you that the devo is from Ecclesiastes, Chapter 12.

Week 23, Thursday

BOOK OF SONG OF SONGS

Swans-a-Swimming

Swan begins with the same letter as *Song*. Two beautiful swans gracefully swimming together remind us of the love written about in the Song of Songs. Like swans, a married man and woman are created to pair for life. When you see Swans-a-Swimming in a picture, you'll know the daily devo is from Song of Songs. Connected to Swans-a-Swimming are number symbols. (See page 15.) They make the chapter location of the devo click and stick.

People who read the Song of Songs are usually in love and ready to get married. Marriage is probably the last thing on your mind, but the message of this little love story is good to know. God made marriage to be a wonderful lifelong promise that one man and one woman make to each other. Years from now when the time is right, God may give you a desire to find the right mate. If that's his plan for you, he will bring you and this person together. And you can trust him to help you be like swans that pair for life.

MAKE IT STICK

Make a tab to mark the book of Song of Songs in your Bible. (See Week 1, Monday, for directions.)

Draw two swans with their beaks together by making a forward *S* and a backward *S*. Do you see the heart shape between the two necks? That's one of the reasons why people think about love and marriage when they see two swans.

Whenever you see a swan or a picture of one, think about two Swans-a-Swimming and the book of Song of Songs.

JUST FOR FUN

When people are in love, they say or write sweet things to each other. You might think their words sound silly. But it's God who puts feelings of love into people's hearts and minds. To find one thing the young man said and one thing the young woman said in Song of Songs, find Chapter 2 (verses 2-3).

PRAYER

Thank you, God, for your gift of love between a man and a woman. If there is someone you want me to marry, I trust that you'll show me someday who that is. But right now, thank you for your love and the love of my family. In Jesus' name, amen.

SONG OF SONGS, CHAPTER 8 (VERSE 4)

Promise me, O women of Jerusalem, not to awaken love until the time is right.

DAILY DEVO

When it comes to marriage, I'm keeping the horse in front of the carriage.

Wrong messages about people living and sleeping together are everywhere: TV, movies, billboards, and even magazine covers at grocery-store checkout counters. So what can you do about the wrong messages you see or hear? Well, one thing is for sure. You can decide right now to agree with God's view on marriage. God planned for a man to live with one woman, and for a woman to live with one man *after* they get married. And his perfect plan is for them to stay married to each other as long as they live. When it comes to love, stay pure until you're married. You'll never ever regret it.

 MAKE IT STICK

On one sheet of paper draw a picture of a horse. On another sheet draw a carriage. Then cut out both pictures. Put the carriage in front of your horse and imagine how far the horse would get pushing the carriage. Nowhere, right? Now put the horse in front of the carriage as it should be, and repeat this daily devo.

PRAYER

Dear God, when I grow up, I pray that I'll follow your teachings about love and marriage. Please protect me so I'll always enjoy your perfect plan for my life. In Jesus' name, amen.

CLICK-ER:

HORSE CARRIAGE

Whenever you see, ride in, or think about a *horse carriage*, let this daily devo gallop through your mind as it clicks and sticks. The two Swans-a-Swimming with their eight-under-skates remind you that the devo is from Song of Songs, Chapter 8.

Week 23, Saturday/Sunday

BOOK OF ISAIAH

Isaiah the Irish Setter

Irish begins with the same letter as *Isaiah*. The Irish setter, a hunting dog, points out the animal being hunted. In the same way, Isaiah pointed out the sins God wanted his people to give up. When you see Isaiah the Irish Setter in a picture, you'll know the daily devo is from Isaiah. Connected to Isaiah the Irish Setter are number symbols. (See page 15.) They make the chapter location of the devo click and stick.

Irish setters are good at pointing—freezing like a statue after spotting a hunted animal. By pointing their noses forward and their tails backward, Irish setters look like big arrows. God is a special kind of hunter who looks for his people, not to catch them, but to help them obey. He told Isaiah to point out sins his people needed to give up. But God doesn't force people to change. He lets us choose whether to follow him. And we alone are responsible for what happens because of our choices. The Israelites discovered this the hard way.

 MAKE IT STICK

Make a tab to mark the book of Isaiah in your Bible. (See Week 1, Monday, for directions.)

You may also want to make an arrow from cardboard or poster board. Find newspaper or magazine pictures of people arguing or doing unkind things. Point your arrow toward those who need to give up their bad ways and choose to obey God. What actions might God want you to give up? What might he want you to do instead?

Whenever you see an Irish setter or a picture of one, think about Isaiah the Irish Setter and the book of Isaiah.

JUST FOR FUN

Read in Isaiah, Chapter 53 (verses 2-6) about God's Son, Jesus. These words about Jesus were written 700 years before he was born! Isn't it great how God revealed what he was going to do before he did it?

PRAYER

Dear God, I know you can see and point out the bad things I sometimes do. But you also sent Jesus to help me. Thank you, Jesus, for dying on the cross so God can forgive my sins. Amen.

WEEKEND ACTIVITY IDEAS

(1) Highlight the verses for Week 23 in your Bible. (2) Find the HoneyWord
animal in each picture for this week and identify the chapter-number symbols.
(3) Add to your collection of Click-ers. (4) Say the daily devos for Week 23.
(5) Check out Friday of Week 41 for a related devo on looking to the Lamb
when you're in a jam.

RUN, DOG, RUN

Irish Setters need a lot of exercise. Running one to two
hours every day will help to keep them from getting
into trouble. They get both mental and physical
exercise by retrieving objects just like a retriever does.

ISAIAH, CHAPTER 1 (VERSE 18)

"Come now, let's settle this," says the LORD. "Though your sins are like scarlet, I will make them as white as snow. Though they are red like crimson, I will make them as white as wool."

DAILY DEVO

God turns all my dirty rotten into pure white cotton.

Car mechanics get their hands, clothes, and faces full of oily, greasy dirt. Can you imagine those mechanics trying to make you believe their clothes are clean? That's what God's people were doing when Isaiah started bringing them messages from God. The people were covered from head to toe with the stains of their sins, but they kept saying they were clean. Through Isaiah, God invited them to let him clean up their dirty rotten sins. But they wouldn't listen. What about you? Will you let God clean up all your sins, including the ones you feel the worst about? Don't be like the people Isaiah knew. Admit your need for forgiveness, ask for it, and watch God make you as pure as clean, white cotton—or white wool or snow!

MAKE IT STICK

On a piece of paper draw the outline of a heart—your heart. Scribble inside the lines with dark markers or crayons. Then glue cotton balls all over this picture of your heart, until all you can see is clean white cotton. Show it to your dad or mom and repeat this daily devo.

PRAYER

Dear God, I'm sorry about the wrong things I've done. My sins make me feel dirty inside. Please forgive me, and make me pure and clean. Thank you! In Jesus' name I pray. Amen.

CLICK-ER: COTTON BALL

Whenever you see, use, or think about a white *cotton ball*, let this daily devo clean out your heart as it clicks and sticks. Isaiah the Irish Setter with his one-on-a-bun reminds you that the devo is from Isaiah, Chapter 1.

ISAIAH, CHAPTER 10 (VERSE 15)

Can the ax boast greater power than the person who uses it? Is the saw greater than the person who saws? Can a rod strike unless a hand moves it? Can a wooden cane walk by itself?

DAILY DEVO

I see that I'm just a saw.

Sometimes when we feel proud, our pride crawls into our tongues and comes out in words that boast and brag. Pride is as kooky as an ax claiming, "I can cut down trees without the strength of a lumberjack." Boasting is as silly as a saw saying, "I can saw wood without the help of a carpenter," or a rod saying, "I can hit a snake without a hand holding on to me." And bragging is as wacky as a cane whispering, "I can walk all by myself, thank you very much." Each of us is like a tool—an ax, a saw, a rod, or a cane—in God's hands. There's not one thing you can do without him. But when God makes you strong enough to do something—great or small—let everyone know you did it in his strength, not yours.

 MAKE IT STICK

Politely ask your dad or mom to teach you how to use a saw. Write this daily devo on a piece of wood. Then saw the wood in half. Notice how the saw moves back and forth only if you help to make it move. As you saw the wood, repeat this daily devo. Talk with your family about ways God works with you to do things, just like you worked with the saw.

PRAYER

Dear God, forgive me for bragging about all the things I'm able to do. I know I couldn't do anything without your help and strength. Thanks for working with me. Amen.

CLICK-ER: SAW

Whenever you see, use, or think about a *saw*, let this daily devo cut back and forth through your mind as it clicks and sticks. Isaiah the Irish Setter with his one-on-a-bun and halo-is-a-hero-as-a-zero reminds you that the devo is from Isaiah, Chapter 10.

ISAIAH, CHAPTER 14 (VERSE 12)

How you are fallen from heaven, O shining star, son of the morning! You have been thrown down to the earth, you who destroyed the nations of the world.

DAILY DEVO

Satan fell far, like a shooting star.

Did you know that shooting stars are really chunks of metal or stone called meteoroids? They enter the earth's atmosphere from outer space, usually breaking apart and burning up before they hit the ground. So don't worry about one hitting you! But there is one fallen star you do need to be aware of. Satan was as beautiful as a star. He began to believe that he was as great as God. Satan led a rebellion against God, who threw him out of heaven. This verse may be talking about that time. You can read what Jesus said about Satan in Luke, Chapter 10 (verse 18). As he fell to earth like a shooting star, Satan's glory was burned up, leaving only an evil heart that wants to turn people away from God. Steer clear of his lies and traps by staying close to God.

MAKE IT STICK

Look up *shooting star* in an encyclopedia and see how it refers you to *meteor*. Read all about meteoroids and meteorites. As many as 200 million visible meteors may hit the earth's atmosphere every day! Remember that a shooting star looks beautiful but is only dust and bits of rock. Satan may also appear beautiful, but we can see how ugly he really is if we stay close to God.

PRAYER

Dear God, no one is as great as you, and no one loves me as much as you do. Keep me close to you so I'll stay far away from Satan. In Jesus' name, amen.

CLICK-ER: **SHOOTING STAR**

Whenever you see, draw, or think about a *shooting star*, let this daily devo shoot through your mind as it clicks and sticks. Isaiah the Irish Setter with his one-on-a-bun and four-on-the-floorboard reminds you that the devo is from Isaiah, Chapter 14.

ISAIAH, CHAPTER 40 (VERSE 31)

Those who trust in the Lord will find new strength. They will soar high on wings like eagles. They will run and not grow weary. They will walk and not faint.

DAILY DEVO

I love riding and gliding with God.

At first glance, gliders look just like airplanes. But there's one major difference: They don't have engines. So how do gliders fly? Having no strength of their own, they're towed into the air by engine-powered airplanes. When they get high enough, they're let go to soar on their own. Then, like birds, they glide through the air, letting the power of the wind keep them up. We're all just like gliders. We have no power of our own and never will. But we do have a choice. We can spend our Christian life on the ground, or we can sign up for heaven's team of riders and gliders. God wants to be the wind that gives you the power to glide through life like an eagle. Become a member today! The only fee is faith.

 ### MAKE IT STICK

Politely ask if your dad or mom would take you to a hobby store so you can buy a small wooden glider with your own money. Or simply make a paper airplane. Carefully use a pen to write this daily devo on its side. Then go outside and enjoy watching it use the power of the wind to glide through the air just like an eagle. And think about one way you can trust God to be your strength so you can glide with him.

PRAYER

When I trust you, God, you give me the strength I need to glide through life with you. Thank you that when I have problems, you keep me from getting tired and giving up. In Jesus' name. Amen.

CLICK-ER: GLIDER

Whenever you see, play with, or think about a *glider*, let this daily devo glide through your mind as it clicks and sticks. Isaiah the Irish Setter with his four-on-the-floorboard and halo-is-a-hero-as-a-zero reminds you that the devo is from Isaiah, Chapter 40.

ISAIAH, CHAPTER 42 (VERSE 3)

He will not crush the weakest reed or put out a flickering candle. He will bring justice to all who have been wronged.

DAILY DEVO

God loves to heed a bruised reed like me.

If you were a blade of grass—a reed—you could get stepped on and be crushed or bruised. People can get crushed too—by others who try to hurt them. Long before God's Son, Jesus, was born, Isaiah the prophet gave a super summary of how Jesus would live. Jesus wouldn't be a bully. He wouldn't even think of crushing the weakest person or snuffing out the smallest hope. Are you like a bruised reed, hurt by someone who's wronged you? If you've lost hope and don't think things are going to turn out well, cry out to God for help right now! God heeds (stops to notice) bruised reeds like you. That's his specialty.

MAKE IT STICK

Try to find a long, dried-up blade of grass. Carefully pull it out of the ground and bend it at the top. Look at how easily it breaks. That's a picture of how our souls feel when they've been hurt, beaten down, or broken. As you think deeply about this daily devo, ask God for extra strength to trust him for a hard time you might be facing. Pray that God will help make things right.

PRAYER

Dear God, thank you for caring about me when I feel hurt and bruised. Thank you for giving me hope when I face hard times. And thank you for being loving, kind, and fair. In Jesus' name, amen.

CLICK-ER: REED

Whenever you see, handle, or think about a broken *reed*, let your heart feel hope from this daily devo as it clicks and sticks. Isaiah the Irish Setter with his four-on-the-floorboard and two-blue-shoes reminds you that the devo is from Isaiah, Chapter 42.

ISAIAH, CHAPTER 43 (VERSE 1)

O Israel, the one who formed you says: "Do not be afraid, for I have ransomed you. I have called you by name; you are mine."

DAILY DEVO

My ID tag is in the bag.

When you meet someone new, you say, "Hi!" and give your name. Your name tells who you are. God loves to call you by your correct name. In fact, he loves you so much that he paid a big price to get rid of your sins so you could be close to him. Then he called you his own. It's as if God put an ID tag on you so everyone would know that you belong to him. So if you think God might be too busy for you, remember: He's just waiting to call you by name. Your ID tag is in the bag!

MAKE IT STICK

Make a square ID tag from aluminum foil, using as many layers as needed to give it that thick metal-plate look. With the prong of a fork, engrave your name and the book and chapter location of this daily devo in small letters on one side of the tag. Now politely ask your dad or mom to help you poke a small hole through one end of it. Put a string or a small chain through the hole so you can wear the tag around your neck. Be ready to talk about your ID tag if someone asks you about it!

PRAYER

Dear God, I'm glad you know my name. And I'm thankful that your Son gave his life for me. That was a big price to pay to get rid of my sins. I'm proud to belong to you. In Jesus' name, amen.

CLICK-ER: ID TAG

Whenever you see, wear, or think about any kind of *ID tag*, let your mind identify this daily devo as it clicks and sticks. Isaiah the Irish Setter with his four-on-the-floorboard and three-is-the-key reminds you that the devo is from Isaiah, Chapter 43.

WEEKEND ACTIVITY IDEAS

(1) Highlight the verses for Week 24 in your Bible. (2) Find Isaiah the Irish Setter in each of the pictures for this week and identify the chapter-number symbols. (3) Add to your collection of Click-ers. (4) Say the daily devos for Week 24. (5) Check out Friday of Week 3 for a related devo on why God keeps your name in a special picture frame.

BETTER SETTER

Most hunters agree—it's hard to find a better go-getter than an Irish Setter.

ISAIAH, CHAPTER 43 (VERSE 25)

I—yes, I alone—will blot out your sins for my own sake and will never think of them again.

DAILY DEVO

It's pretty neat how God hits delete.

Only God can forgive sins. He forgives because he loves us and doesn't want to think about the wrong things we've done. About 700 years after Isaiah wrote this book, Jesus came to earth. He said he could forgive sins, which means that he is God. We can't see if a sin is forgiven, but we can see when someone is healed. So Jesus did both. Then he died on a cross to delete our sins forever. The word *delete* comes from the old Latin word *deletus*, which means "to wipe out totally." Now that old word appears on computer keyboards everywhere. It's the button that deletes millions of words every day. And the old cross on which Jesus died is what God uses to delete all our sins, totally wiping them out forever. Need forgiveness? Just tell God, and he will hit delete.

 MAKE IT STICK

Type this daily devo on a computer. Underneath it, write a sentence about something wrong you did that still bothers you. Now highlight your sentence, and with one hit to the delete button, erase it forever. God forgives all your sins just like that. Isn't he great?

PRAYER

Dear God, I'm so glad that you love me and forgive my sins. When I tell you I'm sorry, you delete the wrong things I've done and never think about them again. Thank you. In Jesus' name, amen.

CLICK-ER:
DELETE BUTTON

Whenever you see, hit, or think about a *delete button*, let this picture appear and disappear in your mind as the daily devo clicks and sticks. Isaiah the Irish Setter with his four-on-the-floorboard and three-is-the-key reminds you that the devo is from Isaiah, Chapter 43.

ISAIAH, CHAPTER 49 (VERSE 1)

Listen to me, all you in distant lands! Pay attention, you who are far away! The LORD called me before my birth; from within the womb he called me by name.

DAILY DEVO

Hooray! God always remembers my birthday.

For most people, birthdays mean special attention from family and friends. We all hope someone will bake us a cake, send us a card, or give us a special present (maybe even two or three), just because it's our birthday. But every once in a while, someone we think should remember us ends up forgetting. When that happens, it hurts, doesn't it? But no matter who remembers and who forgets, always keep this in mind: God never ever forgets your birthday. After all, he was the One who decided when and why you'd be born anyway. How could he forget? He won't. He can't, because you're always on his heart. From now on, for the rest of your life, listen for his "Hooray!" as you celebrate your special day.

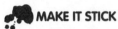 **MAKE IT STICK**

Politely ask your dad or mom if one of them would help you bake a Happy Un-birthday cake, since today is probably not your birthday. Put on the right number of candles for your age today. As you blow out the candles, say this daily devo.

PRAYER

Hooray, God! Thank you for knowing all about me—even before I was born! And thanks for remembering me today and every day, but especially on my birthday. I'm so glad you'll never forget me. Amen.

CLICK-ER:
BIRTHDAY CAKE

Whenever you see, cut, or eat *birthday cake*, let your heart enjoy a big piece of this daily devo as it clicks and sticks. The three candles that look like Isaiah the Irish Setter, a four-on-the-floorboard, and a nine-foot-pine remind you that the devo is from Isaiah, Chapter 49.

ISAIAH, CHAPTER 50 (VERSE 7)

Because the Sovereign LORD helps me, I will not be disgraced. Therefore, I have set my face like a stone, determined to do his will. And I know that I will not be put to shame.

DAILY DEVO

I have the iron will to follow God over any hill.

There are so many ups and downs in life that we all feel like quitting sometimes. How about you? Are you facing something that feels so hard you don't think you can follow God over that next hill? Please don't quit. But do think about Jesus. As he followed God to the Cross to die for our sins, he could have quit. But he didn't. He kept on trusting God for the strength to take one more step and climb one more hill. And God ironed out the way before him. God also made Jesus strong like iron. (Iron is a sturdy, heavy metal used to make many machines and nails.) Nothing could keep Jesus from following God's plan. Such "iron-will" strength is supernatural. It comes only from God. He gave it to Jesus. And he wants to give it to you. Don't quit. Trust God. He has a wonderful surprise for you, just over that next hill.

 MAKE IT STICK

Politely ask your dad or mom to show you how to use an iron. Notice how a hot iron in a strong hand can smooth out any wrinkle. In the same way, God irons out some of the bumps in the road ahead. And he makes us strong like iron, the metal, so nothing can keep us from following him.

PRAYER

Lord, please make me strong like iron so I can follow you over every hill. Thank you for walking with me. I need you, and I trust you. In Jesus' name, amen.

CLICK-ER: IRON

Whenever you see, use, or think about an *iron*, let this daily devo smooth any wrinkles in your mind as it clicks and sticks. Isaiah the Irish Setter with his five-on-a-hive-hat and halo-is-a-hero-as-a-zero reminds you that the devo is from Isaiah, Chapter 50.

ISAIAH, CHAPTER 61 (VERSE 1)

The Spirit of the Sovereign LORD is upon me, for the LORD has anointed me to bring good news to the poor. He has sent me to comfort the brokenhearted and to proclaim that captives will be released and prisoners will be freed.

DAILY DEVO

The Good News is enough to break any handcuff.

Even though handcuffs are mostly used on prisoners, they stop whoever wears them from doing almost anything with their hands, bad or good. With handcuffs, it is hard to fight a police officer, but it is just as hard to play basketball. Wearing handcuffs makes it difficult not only to steal but also to swim and keep your head above water. Sin in our hearts is like handcuffs on our hands: It holds us back from living the life God has called us to live. The Good News is that Jesus died on the cross for our sins and made it possible for every "heart-cuff" in the world to be broken off. So come to God and get free!

MAKE IT STICK

Politely ask your dad or mom to "handcuff" you by tying your wrists together with an old towel or pillowcase. Then go into your room alone, close your eyes, and talk to God about one sin in your life that feels like handcuffs on your heart. Thank God for the Good News about Jesus, and ask him to break that sin off and out of your life. Then have one of your parents remove your "handcuff."

PRAYER

Dear God, I don't want any sin to make me feel like I'm handcuffed and not able to obey you. Please take away any wrong thoughts or actions so that I'll be free to follow you every day. Amen.

CLICK-ER: HANDCUFFS

Whenever you see or think about *handcuffs*, let this daily devo unlock your heart as it clicks and sticks. Isaiah the Irish Setter with his six-pick-up-stix and one-on-a-bun reminds you that the devo is from Isaiah, Chapter 61.

Week 25, Friday

BOOK OF JEREMIAH
Jerry the Jackrabbit

Jackrabbit begins with the same letter as *Jeremiah*. Instead of running to God for safety, the people of God in the book of Jeremiah darted away as a jackrabbit runs from a hunter. When you see Jerry the Jackrabbit in a picture, you'll know the daily devo is from Jeremiah. Connected to Jerry the Jackrabbit are number symbols. (See page 15.) They make the chapter location of the devo click and stick.

When Jeremiah the prophet arrived on the scene, the little kingdom of Judah was coming to an end. The people had stopped obeying the Word of the Lord for so long that God finally decided to use another nation, Babylon, to discipline them. For over 40 years, Jeremiah begged the people to obey God and give themselves up to Babylon. If they would, God promised to help them. But instead of running to their heavenly Father, they darted here and there like a jackrabbit. Babylon finally took over their land and took the people away in 586 BC. Jeremiah is a good book from which to learn what a bad idea it is to try to run from God.

 MAKE IT STICK

Make a tab to mark the book of Jeremiah in your Bible. (See Week 1, Monday, for directions.)

Find a friend who will dart around with you like a jackrabbit in your yard or at a neighborhood playground. Enjoy playing hide-and-seek as you hop along and look for the hiding "jackrabbit." Remember how important it is to run *to* God instead of running away and trying to hide *from* him.

Whenever you see a jackrabbit or a picture of one, think about Jerry the Jackrabbit and the book of Jeremiah.

JUST FOR FUN

In Jeremiah, Chapter 5 (verses 20-23), you can read some of the things God said to the people of Judah. Remember, they could have stopped disobeying God, but they didn't.

PRAYER

Dear God, when I don't know what to do, please help me run to you in prayer instead of running away from you in fear. In Jesus' name I pray. Amen.

JEREMIAH, CHAPTER 1 (VERSE 5)

I knew you before I formed you in your mother's womb. Before you were born I set you apart and appointed you as my prophet to the nations.

DAILY DEVO

God made me bloom in my mother's womb.

Sooner or later you'll hear people ask questions like these: When does a baby become a real person? Is it during the first month inside its mother? How about after the sixth month? Or maybe only after it's born? Questions like these are silly to God, because he feels the same way about you as he did about Jeremiah. God knew all about you and loved you even before he made you bloom in your mother's womb. And he will remain your best friend throughout your entire life. After that, he wants to spend all of eternity with you. Always remember that God knows and loves everything about you, from womb to tomb, and beyond.

MAKE IT STICK

Ask your dad or mom if you may please drop by the florist's shop in a grocery store. Pick up a rose and carefully examine the strong stem, the beautiful color, and the soft petals. Remember that God enjoys admiring you even more than you enjoy admiring that rose. As you put the rose back, thank God for making you special, and say this daily devo.

PRAYER

Dear God, thank you for knowing me and loving me even before I started growing inside my mother. You really make me feel special, and I love you very much. In Jesus' name, amen.

CLICK-ER: ROSE BLOOM

Whenever you see, smell, or think about a *rose bloom*, let the beauty of this daily devo fill your heart as it clicks and sticks. Jerry the Jackrabbit with his one-on-a-bun reminds you that the devo is from Jeremiah, Chapter 1.

WEEKEND ACTIVITY IDEAS

(1) Highlight the verses for Week 25 in your Bible. (2) Find the HoneyWord animal in each of the pictures for this week and identify the chapter-number symbols. (3) Add to your collection of Click-ers. (4) Say the daily devos for Week 25. (5) Check out Monday of Week 20 for a related devo on how you're knit to fit for life.

WASHCLOTH WABBIT

After it eats, a rabbit washes every part of its body—ears, sides, nose, even between its toes. It wets its paws, then uses them like a washcloth.

JEREMIAH, CHAPTER 10 (VERSE 2)

This is what the LORD says: "Do not act like the other nations, who try to read their future in the stars. Do not be afraid of their predictions, even though other nations are terrified by them."

DAILY DEVO

I always say NOPE! to horoscopes.

Horoscopes are man-made charts of the stars that pretend to show a person's future. Of course they never work—even if they sometimes seem to. So why do some people (even some of God's people) read them? One reason is that when we ask God about our future, he often stays silent. Another reason is that he may tell us something we'd rather not hear. Then we have a choice to make. We can choose to trust God or trust man-made, phony-baloney solutions. Make a good choice: Trust God. Always say NOPE! to reading a horoscope and to all the other false ways of trying to look into the future. God will guide you. You have his Word on it.

MAKE IT STICK

Politely ask your dad or mom to help you look up and read the definition of the word *horoscope* in a dictionary. After reading it, ask one of them to explain what it means. Once you think you understand, repeat this daily devo. Then make a commitment to never fall into the trap of trying to learn about the future through horoscopes.

PRAYER

Dear God, help me to put my trust in you, not in the stars you created. I know you hear my prayers, so please give me patience as I wait for your answers. Thank you! In Jesus' name, amen.

CLICK-ER: HOROSCOPE

Whenever you hear people speak about their *horoscope* or the signs of the zodiac, let this daily devo be a signal to your mind as it clicks and sticks. Jerry the Jackrabbit and his one-on-a-bun and halo-is-a-hero-as-a-zero reminds you that the devo is from Jeremiah, Chapter 10.

JEREMIAH, CHAPTER 18 (VERSES 5-6)

*Then the L*ORD *gave me this message: "O Israel, can I not do to you as this potter has done to his clay? As the clay is in the potter's hand, so are you in my hand."*

DAILY DEVO

I'm clay, letting God have his way.

To make a clay pot, the potter must first press and squeeze the clay with his hands until it becomes soft, smooth, and free of air bubbles. When it's just right, he puts it on a spinning table called a potter's wheel. Using his hands, he shapes the clay into whatever he wants it to be. Can you imagine the clay saying to the potter, "Hey, wait a minute! You can't make me like that"? As silly as it sounds, that's often what we say to God. He's lovingly molding each of us into a beautiful and useful person, but sometimes we say no. Don't try to be your own potter. Be good clay that lets God have his way.

 **MAKE IT STICK**

Find a little clay gardening pot and hold it in your hands. Turn it all around and examine it. Look at the thickness of its upper rim, the size of the hole in the bottom, and the way it's narrow at the base and wider at the top. Now pretend that you are this clay pot and God is holding you in his hands. After you hug the pot to your chest, gently set it down. That's a picture of the way God carefully handles you.

PRAYER

It's so special, God, to be shaped by your very own hands! I promise to keep my heart soft as you mold me to become the person you've created me to be. In Jesus' name I pray. Amen.

CLICK-ER: **CLAY POT**

Whenever you see, touch, or think about a *clay pot*, let this daily devo mold your mind as it clicks and sticks. Jerry the Jackrabbit with his one-on-a-bun and eight-under-skates reminds you that the devo is from Jeremiah, Chapter 18.

JEREMIAH, CHAPTER 20 (VERSE 9)

If I say I'll never mention the LORD or speak in his name, his word burns in my heart like a fire. It's like a fire in my bones! I am worn out trying to hold it in! I can't do it!

DAILY DEVO

I admire hearts on fire.

Have you ever gotten your feelings hurt so badly that you wanted to quit and go home? Well, join the club. Jeremiah did everything God wanted him to do, and what did he get for it? Nothing, it seemed, but put-downs, hateful words, and beatings. So he let God know he was ready to quit. But the minute he tried to stop doing what God had called him to do, it was as if a fire broke out in his heart and spread into his bones. God's calling is like that. One day God will let you know what he is calling you to do. And if you get excited about it and stay on fire for God, you'll find it's the only way to live. God admires a heart that's on fire. Let him find one in you.

MAKE IT STICK

Draw a picture of a campfire giving off heart-shaped flames. Below your fire write this daily devo. What you've drawn is a picture of how total commitment, or a heart on fire, affects those around you. Like folks gathering around a campfire, people will be attracted to your fiery desire to live for God.

PRAYER

I love you, God, and I'm excited about helping others love you too. Make this desire so great that it burns like a fire inside of me. In Jesus' name, amen.

CLICK-ER: CAMPFIRE

Whenever you see, sit by, or think about a *campfire*, let this daily devo warm your heart as it clicks and sticks. Jerry the Jackrabbit with his two-blue-shoes and halo-is-a-hero-as-a-zero reminds you that the devo is from Jeremiah, Chapter 20.

JEREMIAH, CHAPTER 29 (VERSE 11)

"I know the plans I have for you," says the LORD. "They are plans for good and not for disaster, to give you a future and a hope."

DAILY DEVO

I carry God's map in my thinking cap.

When Jeremiah mailed this letter to God's people in Babylon, Daniel was already there. As a young man, Daniel prayed. And he studied God's Word—he followed it like a map, so that it directed all his thinking and helped him make wise decisions. One day as an old man, Daniel just happened to be studying this chapter of Jeremiah. You can read about it in Daniel, Chapter 9 (verses 1-2). Daniel learned about God's plan to bring his people home after 70 years of having to live in another country. Like Daniel, you, too, can learn about God's plans for you. But you've got to first stick God's Word—his map—inside your thinking cap, or it will never happen.

MAKE IT STICK

On an old city or state map, cut out a circle a little bit bigger than the round part of one of your baseball caps. Carefully shape and flatten the map against the inside walls of your cap. Holding the map in place, put on your new "thinking cap," letting the edges of the map stick out. Now think about this: How is truth in your heart like a map in your cap?

PRAYER

Dear God, I believe you created me for a purpose. Having your Word in my mind is like having your plans—your map—in my thinking cap. Thank you for the good plans you have for me. Amen.

CLICK-ER: MAP

Whenever you see, use, or think about a *map*, let your mind follow this daily devo as it clicks and sticks. Jerry the Jackrabbit with his two-blue-shoes and nine-foot-pine reminds you that the devo is from Jeremiah, Chapter 29.

Week 26, Friday

BOOK OF LAMENTATIONS
Mama Llama

Llama begins with the same letter as *Lamentations*. The llama is a pack animal that is a picture of the captured children of Israel in the book of Lamentations. When you see Mama Llama in a picture, you'll know the daily devo is from Lamentations. Connected to Mama Llama are number symbols. (See page 15.) They make the chapter location of the devo click and stick.

Shattered walls and burning buildings were everywhere. For over 40 years Jeremiah had told the people that Jerusalem would be destroyed if they did not obey God. Now that the city was in ruins, Jeremiah cried. He cried for the city. He cried for all the people who had died. And he cried for those who had to leave. They looked like a long line of llamas, carrying their few possessions on their backs as they were forced to walk across the desert to Babylon. This sad book reminds us that the payoff for sin is like our worst nightmare come true. It's a crying shame if we don't learn from the boo-hoo heartache in this book.

MAKE IT STICK

Make a tab to mark the book of Lamentations in your Bible. (See Week 1, Monday, for directions.)

Ask your dad or mom to help you find places (at a library or on the Internet) where people have had to pack up and leave because of war, fire, an earthquake, a hurricane, or a terrorist attack.

Whenever you see a picture of a pack animal called a llama or think about one, remember Mama Llama and the book of Lamentations.

JUST FOR FUN

To see how Jeremiah learned to trust God even when sad things were happening, open your Bible and read Lamentations, Chapter 3 (verses 22-24).

PRAYER

Dear God, I don't like reading about the sad things people have had to go through. But I do like reading about your love, which never ends. Thank you for understanding my sadness and for bringing me new hope every morning. Amen.

LAMENTATIONS, CHAPTER 4 (VERSE 2)

See how the precious children of Jerusalem, worth their weight in fine gold, are now treated like pots of clay made by a common potter.

DAILY DEVO

Behold, I'm worth my weight in gold.

Gold is mentioned over 500 times in the Bible. Pure gold is shiny and beautiful. But what really makes it valuable is the fact that there's not much of it and it's hard to find. That's why the discovery of gold is called a "gold rush." People *rush* to the site and try to get their fair share. When you were born, many angels rushed to see the new baby that was like solid gold. Maybe they even playfully fought over who would get to be your golden guardian angel! But this is for certain: You're worth everything to God.

 MAKE IT STICK

Step on a scale to see how much you weigh. Since there are 16 ounces in every pound, multiply your pounds by 16 to get your total weight in ounces. Now ask your dad or mom if they would please help you check out the current price of an ounce of gold. (Look on the Internet or find a gold dealer in the yellow pages.) Multiply the price times your total number of ounces, and that's what your weight in gold is worth today. But just for the record, remember that in God's eyes you're priceless.

PRAYER

Thank you, God, for teaching me that I'm worth my weight in gold. Knowing that you love me makes it easy for me to love you back! In Jesus' name, amen.

CLICK-ER: GOLD

Whenever you see, touch, or think about *gold*, let this daily devo weigh heavily but happily on your mind as it clicks and sticks. Mama Llama on her four-on-the-floorboard reminds you that the devo is from Lamentations, Chapter 4.

WEEKEND ACTIVITY IDEAS

(1) Highlight the verses for Week 26 in your Bible. (2) Find the HoneyWord animal in each of the pictures for this week and identify the chapter-number symbols. (3) Add to your collection of Click-ers. (4) Say the daily devos for Week 26. (5) Check out Monday of Week 34 for a related devo on golden guardian angels.

LOADS ON ROCKY ROADS

In the high mountains of South America, sure-footed llamas are great at carrying heavy loads up rocky roads.

Week 27, Monday

BOOK OF EZEKIEL
E. Zeek Eel

E. Zeek Eel sounds like *Ezekiel*. Like an eel, the hearts of God's people stayed slippery and slimy as they slithered away from God into sin. When you see E. Zeek Eel in a picture, you'll know the daily devo is from Ezekiel. Connected to E. Zeek Eel are number symbols. (See page 15.) They make the chapter location of the devo click and stick.

Ezekiel and Jeremiah were tag-team prophets to God's people. They brought the same message from God at the same time. Jeremiah lovingly used words to pound on the people from within Jerusalem, while Ezekiel pounded on them from without. But no matter what they said or did, the people were like slippery, slimy eels—they wiggled away from God again and again. Because they were God's chosen people, they thought they could get away with murder. Well, not real murder, but almost everything else. Of course they were dead wrong. God let King Nebuchadnezzar sack the city and haul the people off to Babylon. Once there, they came to their senses, and God promised to one day bring them home again.

MAKE IT STICK

Make a tab to mark the book of Ezekiel in your Bible. (See Week 1, Monday, for directions.)

An eel is a fish that's long and smooth like a snake. Its skin gets slippery when wet. That's why people who try to get away with doing things they shouldn't are often called "slippery as an eel." Make an eel from play dough. Then drip some drops of liquid soap on it to make it slippery all over. Ask God to help you not slip away when you've done something wrong.

Whenever you see a picture of an eel or think about one, remember E. Zeek Eel and the book of Ezekiel.

JUST FOR FUN
Learn about God's promise to bring his slippery people back home from Babylon. Read Ezekiel, Chapter 36 (verses 24-26).

PRAYER
Dear God, I'm sorry about the times I've tried to get away with doing things I knew I shouldn't do. I'm turning to you. Thanks for welcoming me back. In Jesus' name, amen.

EZEKIEL, CHAPTER 3 (VERSE 3)

"Fill your stomach with this," he said. And when I ate it, it tasted as sweet as honey in my mouth.

DAILY DEVO

I savor the sweet flavor of the Word.

In a vision, Ezekiel was told to receive the word of God and eat it all. The word God sent was about sins. Because God's message told how he would punish his people for their sins, Ezekiel probably thought it would taste pretty yucky. But by faith, he opened up his mouth, gobbled it down, and found it to be as sweet as honey. Today God doesn't want us to tear out pages of the Bible and make Scripture sandwiches, but he does want us to develop a taste for his Word. There's only one way to do it. You've got to choose to read it, remember it, and obey it. Over the next few years, if you "fill your stomach" with God's Word by reading all of the Bible, you'll find you savor or enjoy the taste of it more than the sweetest sugary treat in the whole world. It's that good.

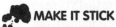 **MAKE IT STICK**

The next time you're in a restaurant and waiting for your food to arrive, grab a packet of sugar and write this daily devo on both sides of the little bag. Someone's bound to ask what you're doing. When someone does, tell him or her about Ezekiel's sweet experience with the Word.

PRAYER

Dear God, thank you for the sweet times we have when I read your Word and obey what you say. Thank you also for feeding me spiritually and keeping me strong. In Jesus' name I pray. Amen.

CLICK-ER: SUGAR

Whenever you see, touch, or taste *sugar*, let this daily devo sweeten your heart as it clicks and sticks. E. Zeek Eel with his three-is-the-key reminds you that the devo is from Ezekiel, Chapter 3.

Week 27, Wednesday

BOOK OF DANIEL

Dan O. Saur

Dinosaur begins with the same letter as *Daniel*. Daniel left dinosaur-sized faith-prints in the Babylonian landscape. When you see Dan O. Saur in a picture, you'll know the daily devo is from Daniel. Connected to Dan O. Saur are number symbols. (See page 15.) They make the chapter location of the devo click and stick.

Dinosaurs fascinate everyone. The apatosaurus, for example, was so big it could have seen over a three-story building, and it would have shaken the earth when it moved. We know a little about what dinosaurs were like, because they left bones behind. In the same way, the book of Daniel is a record of one man whose faith is as easy to see as dinosaur bones. Like an apatosaurus, he stood out among those around him. He was strong, bright, gifted, and good looking. But it was his faith in God that shook the earth. Dinosaurs are extinct, but Daniel's example of faith will live forever.

 MAKE IT STICK

Make a tab to mark the book of Daniel in your Bible. (See Week 1, Monday, for directions.)

What do you know about the apatosaurus? Find pictures of these dinosaurs if you can. Then draw a picture of one with its head as high as the top of a tall palm tree. Maybe you'll want to show it eating the palm branches. If Daniel's faith was as big as that dinosaur, he had a lot of faith, didn't he?

Whenever you see a picture of a dinosaur or think about one, remember Dan O. Saur and the book of Daniel.

JUST FOR FUN

To see how Daniel responded with dinosaur-sized faith to a wicked law, read Daniel, Chapter 6 (verses 6-10). If you don't know what happened next, you can read about Daniel and the lions in Chapter 6 (verses 16-23).

PRAYER

Dear God, I want to be like Daniel and never be afraid of standing out in a crowd because of my faith. In Jesus' name I pray. Amen.

DANIEL, CHAPTER 1 (VERSE 12)

"Please test us for ten days on a diet of vegetables and water," Daniel said.

DAILY DEVO

Maybe I should eat my green beans after all.

The Babylonian king, Nebuchadnezzar, picked the brightest Jewish teenagers to serve in his court. Daniel was one of them. The king's goal was to turn these teenagers into real Babylonians who would think like he did and believe as he did. But he didn't have a clue about the strength of Daniel's character. When told to eat the rich, royal food of the king, Daniel said no. He knew that much of the king's food was not allowed by the law of Moses. Because Daniel wanted to obey God, he chose to eat good, clean, fresh vegetables. And guess what—he grew stronger and wiser than those eating the king's food! Maybe you should eat your green beans. Besides being good for your health, they'll remind you to be like Daniel.

MAKE IT STICK

The next time you order macaroni and cheese, ask if you can have a side dish of green beans, just for fun. Try them. You might like them! When your folks give you that shocked look, remind them of what happened to those Old Testament guys who obeyed God and ate their veggies.

PRAYER

Dear God, I want to please you in everything I do. Help me to eat good food. Help me to obey my parents. And help me to learn from my teachers so I'll be able to do the work you give me to do. Amen.

CLICK-ER: GREEN BEANS

Whenever you see, eat, or think about *green beans*, let your mind take a bite of this daily devo as it clicks and sticks. Dan O. Saur with his one-on-a-bun reminds you that the devo is from Daniel, Chapter 1.

DANIEL, CHAPTER 3 (VERSE 17)

If we are thrown into the blazing furnace, the God whom we serve is able to save us. He will rescue us from your power, Your Majesty.

DAILY DEVO

When things get hot, I trust God a lot.

Have you ever felt like you were in big trouble and would need a miracle to get out of it? That's how Shadrach, Meshach, and Abednego must have felt when King Nebuchadnezzar was about to throw them into the fiery furnace. But they were in trouble for the right reason: They had refused to worship the king's statue even though he had commanded everyone to do that. They would only worship the one true God. As the showdown heated up, Daniel's three friends weren't about to trust old Nebuchadnezzar for help. They kept their trust in God—and he kept them safe even when things were at their hottest. When things get hot around you, remember these three teenagers, and trust God a lot. Keep looking up to him, and he won't let you down.

 MAKE IT STICK

Spend some time with your dad or mom in the kitchen. When the oven is on, politely ask if you can take a peek by pulling the oven door open a bit. When you feel the heat, remember the faith of Daniel's friends and say this daily devo.

PRAYER

Dear God, I'm glad I can trust you no matter how hot or scary things get. I love you, God. You are the only one I ever want to worship. In Jesus' name I pray. Amen.

CLICK-ER: **HOT OVEN**

Whenever you see, use, or feel the heat from a *hot oven*, let this daily devo bake in your mind as it clicks and sticks. Dan O. Saur and his three-is-the-key reminds you that the devo is from Daniel, Chapter 3.

DANIEL, CHAPTER 6 (VERSE 4)

High officers began searching for some fault in the way Daniel was handling government affairs, but they couldn't find anything to criticize or condemn. He was faithful, always responsible, and completely trustworthy.

DAILY DEVO

I'm a fan of Dan the man of God.

If someone had started a fan club for Daniel, most of God's people would have been members. Wouldn't you? Listen to some of Daniel's qualities: honest to the core, hardworking, brave, disciplined, prayerful, godly, full of faith; he was a lion tamer, a handwriting-on-the-wall reader, and a royal-dream interpreter. God was awesome as he worked through Daniel. But that was then, and your life is now. If you want to be a fan, and live like the man, do what Dan did at your age. Follow God, no matter where he takes you or what he asks you to do.

MAKE IT STICK

To make a fan-club banner, place a sheet of paper horizontally on a table. Draw lines from the top and bottom corners of the left side to the middle point of the right side. Cut along these lines to make a banner. Now write this daily devo on each side of your banner and color it. Politely get permission to use tape or string to attach it to the outside center of an electric fan. (Be sure the fan is turned off when you fasten it.) Now turn on the fan and imagine feeling the cool wind of Daniel's faith blowing into your heart.

PRAYER

Dear God, thank you for my Sunday school teacher and others who are showing me how to follow you. And thanks for the amazing Bible stories about Daniel's faith in you. Amen.

CLICK-ER: FAN

Whenever you see, feel the breeze from, or think about a *fan*, let this cool daily devo warm your heart as it clicks and sticks. Dan O. Saur and his six-pick-up-stix reminds you that the devo is from Daniel, Chapter 6.

WEEKEND ACTIVITY IDEAS

(1) Highlight the verses for Week 27 in your Bible. (2) Find the HoneyWord animal in each of the pictures for this week and identify the chapter-number symbols. (3) Add to your collection of Click-ers. (4) Say the daily devos for Week 27. (5) Check out Thursday of Week 46 for a related devo on standing out like a steeple among God's people.

RAGING THUNDER LIZARDS

The sauropod dinosaur, or "thunder lizard," was as long as a tennis court, weighing over 150,000 pounds. Its head was 40 feet above the ground, as high as a four-story building.

Week 28, Monday

BOOK OF HOSEA

Hosea the Horse

Horse begins with the same sound as *Hosea*. Hosea tells how God's people, like a beautiful runaway horse, ran from him again and again. But he always took them back no matter what they'd done or how far they'd run. When you see Hosea the Horse in a picture, you'll know the daily devo is from Hosea. Connected to Hosea the Horse are number symbols. (See page 15.) They make the chapter location of the devo click and stick.

Imagine that you owned a beautiful horse. You fed her, groomed her, and patiently trained her. But again and again she jumped the fence and ran away for weeks, sometimes months. Would you feel like calling it quits and getting rid of her? The book of Hosea tells how God's people, like your imaginary horse, often ran away from God. But he never gave up on them. He never gives up on us either. He takes us back, no matter what we've done or how far we've run.

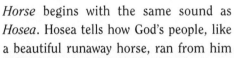

MAKE IT STICK

Make a tab to mark the book of Hosea in your Bible. (See Week 1, Monday, for directions.)

Play a game of tag with a family member or friend, with one of you pretending to be a runaway horse, and the other the trainer. Give the "horse" a high five or a big hug each time he or she is caught. That's a reminder of God's love for everyone who runs from him, and then comes back.

Whenever you see a horse or a picture of one, remember Hosea the Horse and the book of Hosea.

JUST FOR FUN

Read about how God loves us when we're sorry about running away from him. In your Bible, look up Hosea, Chapter 6 (verses 1-3).

PRAYER

Dear God, I'm sorry about the times I've tried to run away from you. But thanks for loving me every time I come back. In Jesus' name, amen.

HOSEA, CHAPTER 11 (VERSE 4)

I led Israel along with my ropes of kindness and love. I lifted the yoke from his neck, and I myself stooped to feed him.

DAILY DEVO

God is my strong rope of hope.

A good kindergarten teacher sometimes uses a line rope to guide a class down the hall. You've seen these ropes, haven't you? Maybe you've held on to one. The teacher helps each child grab the rope, creating a human rope train. The rope keeps the kids in line as the teacher heads out with the hope of leading them from point A to point B. God is like that rope. He knows where you need to go and what it will take to get you there. But will you grab on, and stay holding on, as he leads you down his path for your life? Nobody can answer that question but you. And it's not a onetime decision. You might hold on today but let go tomorrow. What are you really going to do with God's rope of hope?

MAKE IT STICK

Get a short piece of string and pretend it's a strong rope. Keep it in one of your pockets for a week. Each time you touch the "rope" as you reach into your pocket, let it remind you to hope in God at that very moment. Then repeat this daily devo.

PRAYER

Dear God, even though I can't see you, I believe you're holding my hand and leading me step by step. Please keep me from falling. Thank you. Amen.

CLICK-ER: ROPE

Whenever you see, use, or think about a *rope*, let this daily devo lasso your heart as it clicks and sticks. Hosea the horse with his one-on-a-bun on each side reminds you that the devo is from Hosea, Chapter 11.

Week 28, Wednesday

BOOK OF JOEL
Joel the Mole

Mole rhymes with *Joel*. Like a blind mole burrowing through the dirt, the people in the book of Joel dug a hole to get away from God as fast as they could. When you see Joel the Mole in a picture, you'll know the daily devo is from Joel. Connected to Joel the Mole are number symbols. (See page 15.) They make the chapter location of the devo click and stick.

Joel brought the people of Judah a message from God. He said that if they weren't sorry for their sins, a swarm of locusts would eat everything in sight. Do you think the people thanked God for his warning? No. Like a blind mole, they nose-dived into the dirt and dug a hole to get away from God. Their lives are an example of what not to do. The more we try to run from God, the more we find ourselves in empty holes, surrounded by dirt. God has a much better plan for our lives. He wants to clean up the messes we make and fill our empty hearts.

MAKE IT STICK

Make a tab to mark the book of Joel in your Bible. (See Week 1, Monday, for directions.)

Blind moles make underground tunnels that mess up nice green lawns. Act like a mole by putting on old clothes and a blindfold, and crawling from one end of your backyard to the other. Then see how much more fun it is to run through your yard without being blindfolded. That's a picture of your friendship with God. Running with God in the light is better than digging a hole in the dark.

Whenever you see a picture of a mole or think about one, remember Joel the Mole and the book of Joel.

JUST FOR FUN
Do you know the difference between a locust and a grasshopper? Check out Joel, Chapter 2 (verses 25-27) in your Bible and read about the kinds of locusts God said he would send.

PRAYER
Lord, please help me remember a mess I made by not obeying you. And please give me the wisdom and the courage to make it right. In Jesus' name I pray. Amen.

JOEL, CHAPTER 2 (VERSE 12)

*The L*ORD *says, "Turn to me now, while there is time. Give me your hearts. Come with fasting, weeping, and mourning."*

DAILY DEVO

I don't dillydally in the valley of decision.

Don't you think *dillydally* is a funny-sounding word? *Dilly* is just *silly* with a *D*. And *dally* is like the word *delay*, which means to put something off. So *dillydally* means "to be silly and delay." Joel saw thousands of people wasting their lives in the valley of decision. He must have wondered why they would dillydally there when God had offered to take them to high ground. There he would forgive them and be the guide by their sides every day. If you're in the valley and not sure about following God, don't dillydally another second. Take God's hand while you can, and follow his lead to higher ground today!

MAKE IT STICK

Politely ask permission to create a valley between two mountains of laundry or pillows. Then lie down between them. When you decide to roll out of your valley onto one of the mountains, do it right away. Remember to have fun, but don't dillydally in the valley of decision. Each time you roll out and up, shout this daily devo.

PRAYER

When it comes to loving and obeying you, God, I know that *right now* is the right time. Help me not to be silly and delay. Help me live for you *today*! In Jesus' name, amen.

CLICK-ER: VALLEY

Whenever you see, travel through, or think about a *valley*, let this daily devo dally in your mind as it clicks and sticks. In the picture, Joel the Mole with his two-blue-shoes reminds you that the devo is from Joel, Chapter 2.

Week 28, Friday

BOOK OF AMOS

Amos the Moose

Moose sounds like *Amos*. A moose has powerful, flat antlers that stick out like huge fingers. Amos warned that the mooselike nation of Assyria would lock horns with God's people if they didn't change their ways. When you see Amos the Moose in a picture, you'll know the daily devo is from Amos. Connected to Amos the Moose are number symbols. (See page 15.) They make the chapter location of the devo click and stick.

Amos spoke out boldly about the importance of sticking up for the poor and treating everyone as equals. (In the 1960s, Dr. Martin Luther King Jr. followed his example.) A hardworking farmer, Amos knew the poor did all the planting and got little or nothing in return, while the rich didn't plant anything and got almost everything. To right this wrong, Amos commanded God's people to let justice flow like a river through their lives—taking away evil and making everything it touched fresh and clean. When nobody listened, Amos announced that Assyria would lock horns with God's people and drive them out of the land.

 MAKE IT STICK

Make a tab to mark the book of Amos in your Bible. (See Week 1, Monday, for directions.)

Ask your librarian for a book about Martin Luther King Jr. After reading it, talk with your family about how he was like Amos. Then look for ways that your family can help people in your community who don't have as much food or clothing as you do. How does a moose remind you of the way God punished his people when they didn't care about those who were poor?

Whenever you see a picture of a moose or think about one, remember Amos the Moose and the book of Amos.

JUST FOR FUN

To learn about some of the wicked things God's people were doing, look up Amos, Chapter 3 (verses 10-12). Read what God did to get their attention and help them change their ways.

PRAYER

Dear God, help me be kind to those who don't have as much as I do. Show me what I can do to share food and clothing with them. In Jesus' name, amen.

AMOS, CHAPTER 3 (VERSE 7)

Indeed, the Sovereign Lord never does anything until he reveals his plans to his servants the prophets.

DAILY DEVO

Prophets are born to honk the horn.

God's people in the Old Testament were often like cars going the wrong way down a one-way street. Every now and then, God sent prophets to honk their horns and warn everyone to turn around. But most of the time, the prophets got run over. Then God's people were hurt very badly in major head-on crashes. Everybody knows the prophets were a strange bunch that went against the flow of traffic, but their messages were on target and backed by the love of God. Each prophet showed how kind and willing God was to warn his people before he disciplined them. Don't turn a deaf ear to the honks of God's Word. When you hear his warning, it's time to make a U-turn.

MAKE IT STICK

Politely ask your dad or mom to help you find the horn under the hood of your family car. Look near the engine while someone inside the car gives a short honk. The sound will lead you straight to the horn. In the same way, the words of true prophets are like car horns that lead you straight to God.

PRAYER

Dear God, thank you for the prophets who warn your people to do what's right. Help me to listen to their warnings in your Word. In Jesus' name, amen.

CLICK-ER: CAR HORN

Whenever you see, hear, or think about a *car horn*, let this daily devo honk loud and clear as it clicks and sticks. Amos the Moose with his three-is-the-key reminds you that the devo is from Amos, Chapter 3.

WEEKEND ACTIVITY IDEAS

(1) Highlight the verses for Week 28 in your Bible. (2) Find the HoneyWord animal in each of the pictures for this week and identify the chapter-number symbols. (3) Add to your collection of Click-ers. (4) Say the daily devos for Week 28. (5) Check out Thursday of Week 38 for a related devo on the only complete one-way street.

USEFUL MOOSE

Some Native Americans named this animal *mooswa*. It means "twig-eater." Early explorers heard the word and in time it became *moose*. The Native Americans ate moose meat. They made clothes and tents from moose hides. They also used moose bones and antlers to make tools.

AMOS, CHAPTER 5 (VERSE 24)

I want to see a mighty flood of justice, an endless river of righteous living.

DAILY DEVO

I desire to be a fair umpire.

Millions of people play baseball, and tens of millions watch it. Every major-league game has umpires at each of the three bases and at home plate. These four umpires make sure everyone follows the rules. They also settle differences between players who don't agree. No team could play baseball without umpires. God needs umpires too—young and old—who will take a stand and bring justice into messed-up situations. It's good to admire a fair umpire, but it's even better to be one yourself. When you see someone doing something right, call it "safe on base." But if it's wrong, ask God for the courage to call it "out." Call 'em like you see 'em, but call 'em fair.

 MAKE IT STICK

Draw a picture of yourself in an umpire's uniform. Think about the way every umpire has to learn all the rules of a game in order to make fair calls. Then think about what you need to do to tell the difference between right and wrong, truth and lies, and say this daily devo. The next time you see a baseball game, tell the person you're with all about your desire to be a fair umpire for God.

PRAYER

Dear God, teach me what is right and wrong as I read my Bible, go to church, and learn from grown-ups who love you. Help me to be fair in everything I say and do with my friends. In Jesus' name, amen.

CLICK-ER: UMPIRE

Whenever you see, watch, or think about an *umpire*, let your heart make the call on this daily devo as it clicks and sticks. Amos the Moose with his five-on-a-hive-hat reminds you that the devo is from Amos, Chapter 5.

Week 29, Tuesday

BOOK OF OBADIAH
O-bad-eye-ah the Ostrich

Ostrich begins with the same letter as *Obadiah*.

Like an ostrich with its head in the sand, the people from the country of Edom looked the other way when Judah was attacked. When you see O-bad-eye-ah the Ostrich in a picture, you'll know the daily devo is from Obadiah. Connected to O-bad-eye-ah are number symbols. (See page 15.) They make the chapter location of the devo click and stick.

Does an ostrich really bury its head in the sand when it doesn't want to know what's going on? No, it just looks like it does when it puts its long neck down. But that's a perfect picture of Edom—Judah's bully neighbor to the south. The two nations, started by twin brothers (Jacob and Esau), should have looked out for each other. But in 586 BC, when Babylon took over Judah, Edom buried its head in the sand and wouldn't help its brother. Instead, the Edomites helped the enemy win. God notices those who turn a blind eye to the needs of others. So he gave Obadiah a message for the Edomites. By closing their eyes, they'd end up losing their lives.

 MAKE IT STICK

Make a tab to mark the book of Obadiah in your Bible. (See Week 1, Monday, for directions.)

Draw a picture of an ostrich looking like its head is in the sand. If you have a sandbox or can go to a playground that has one, make an ostrich from play dough and place its head in the sand. Can your ostrich see anything? The people of Edom wouldn't help the people of Judah and didn't even try to see how they could help.

Whenever you see a picture of an ostrich or think about one, remember O-bad-eye-ah the Ostrich and the book of Obadiah.

JUST FOR FUN
Find Obadiah, Chapter 1 (verse 15), in your Bible and read what God said to the Edomites about getting what they deserved for looking the other way.

PRAYER
Dear God, whenever my family or my friends need me, please help me to see what I can do. I want to be helpful and not look the other way. Amen.

OBADIAH, CHAPTER 1 (VERSES 3-4)

"You have been deceived by your own pride because you live in a rock fortress and make your home high in the mountains. 'Who can ever reach us way up here?' you ask boastfully. But even if you soar as high as eagles and build your nest among the stars, I would bring you crashing down," says the LORD.

DAILY DEVO

My pride is a roller-coaster ride downhill.

The Edomites built a city high up on a rocky ridge. None of their enemies could reach them. Over time, they became so proud of what they had built, they began to trust in themselves instead of in God. But pride is always the beginning of the end. When we start patting ourselves on the back and giving ourselves credit for the good things we receive, we're headed for a fall. Don't put your trust in anything but God. He alone is the source of your strength and abilities. So whenever pride offers to give you a ride, run the other way. Like a roller-coaster ride downhill, it'll take you nowhere but down and off the side of a cliff. Ask the Edomites. They know.

 MAKE IT STICK

Draw a roller coaster going straight downhill. Draw yourself in the front seat. In the seats behind you, draw things that might make you proud, like nice clothes, good grades, money, or athletic or musical talent. Thank God for these things, remembering that each good gift comes from him.

PRAYER

Dear God, I'm happy about all the things I can do, and I'm glad I have some nice stuff. But don't let me brag about these things. Keep reminding me that they are gifts from you. Thanks, God. In Jesus' name I pray. Amen.

CLICK-ER:
ROLLER COASTER

Whenever you see, ride on, or think about a *roller coaster*, let this daily devo scream through your mind as it clicks and sticks. O-bad-eye-ah the Ostrich with his one-on-a-bun reminds you that the devo is from Obadiah, Chapter 1.

Week 29, Thursday

BOOK OF JONAH

Jonah the Moan-ah Fish

Moan-ah sounds like *Jonah*. God sent a big fish to do an inside job on Jonah—the man who liked to moan-ah. When you see Jonah the Moan-ah Fish in a picture, you'll know the daily devo is from Jonah. Connected to Jonah the Moan-ah Fish are number symbols. (See page 15.) They make the chapter location of the devo click and stick.

Jonah was a runaway prophet. If God wanted him here, Jonah went there. That's what happened when God gave him a special message for the people of Nineveh. Instead of going there, Jonah went in the opposite direction, hopping on a slow boat to nowhere. So God sent a great fish. Three days after being swallowed whole, Jonah begged God to burp him up on the nearest beach. So God did. And from then on, when God said, "Go there today," Jonah never again said, "No way."

 MAKE IT STICK

Make a tab to mark the book of Jonah in your Bible. (See Week 1, Monday, for directions.)

To make a large fish with a big belly, cut out and tape a paper tail, fins, and a head to an empty tub of margarine or whipped topping. Inside the tub, place a small plastic figure, or a paper cutout person. What do you think Jonah did while he was inside that big fish? What would you have done? Would you still have moaned and groaned after God made the fish spit you out?

Whenever you see a picture of a big, sad fish or think about one, remember Jonah the Moan-ah Fish and the book of Jonah.

JUST FOR FUN

You and another family member can take turns reading what Jonah said to God while he was in that great big fish. You will find it in Jonah, Chapter 2.

PRAYER

Dear God, I pray that I'll always go where you want me to go, do what you want me to do, and say what you want me to say. In Jesus' name, amen.

JONAH, CHAPTER 1 (VERSE 3)

Jonah got up and went in the opposite direction to get away from the LORD. He went down to the port of Joppa, where he found a ship leaving for Tarshish. He bought a ticket and went on board, hoping to escape from the LORD by sailing to Tarshish.

DAILY DEVO

I've got a ticket to ride on God's side.

Jonah was upset. Very upset. He couldn't believe what he'd just heard about the people of Nineveh, Israel's greatest enemy. God wanted them to know how much he loved them. God even wanted them to learn how to be sorry for their sins and be saved from the coming judgment. And he wanted Jonah to tell them how to do it! For years Jonah had been hoping to hear the exact opposite message from God. He wanted Nineveh nuked now. So he bought a one-way ticket to ride and hide from God. Well, you know the rest of the story. But what about you? Are you running away from something God has asked you to do? If so, think twice. God will get your attention, even if he has to go deep-sea fishing.

MAKE IT STICK

The next time you go to a movie, or any other activity needing a ticket, save your ticket stub and tape it to your bedroom or bathroom mirror for one week. Each day you see it, remember Jonah's one-way, wrong-way ticket to ride and hide. Then pray that God will help you obey and ride on his side.

PRAYER

Dear God, I admit I don't always want to do what you want me to do. But I know I need to trust you for what's best. So please help me obey you and do it right away. In Jesus' name I pray. Amen.

CLICK-ER: TICKET

Whenever you see, buy, or grab a *ticket* of any kind, let this daily devo ride and hide in your heart as it clicks and sticks. Jonah the Moan-ah Fish with his one-on-a-bun reminds you that the devo is from Jonah, Chapter 1.

JONAH, CHAPTER 4 (VERSES 1-2)

[God's] change of plans greatly upset Jonah, and he became very angry. So he complained to the LORD. . . . "I knew that you are a merciful and compassionate God, slow to get angry."

DAILY DEVO

God isn't fickle when I'm in a pickle.

Jonah was in a pickle—he had a problem. He was so mad at God he couldn't see straight. So he said that he didn't want to be friends anymore unless God would see things his way. If God wouldn't do that, Jonah was ready to die. Aren't you glad God isn't fickle like that when we find ourselves in a pickle? God listened kindly to Jonah and let him blow off a little leftover steam. That's the way God is with you. He loves you—period. And he's never fickle. He doesn't change his feelings toward you just because you've had a bad day, or even a bad month. God loves you, and nothing you do will ever change his feelings.

MAKE IT STICK

Put a pickle on your dinner plate. But before you eat, talk with your dad or mom about what it means to be "in a pickle." Also discuss what "fickle" people are like and how they make you feel. Is God fickle? Does he change his mind a lot? Say this daily devo as you get ready to pop your pickle into your mouth.

PRAYER

Dear God, I'm glad your love for me never changes. It's really great to know you won't leave me, even when I get angry, sad, or upset. Thanks for sticking with me. Amen.

CLICK-ER: PICKLE

Whenever you see or eat a *pickle*, let this daily devo tickle your mind as it clicks and sticks. Jonah the Moan-ah Fish on his four-on-the-floorboard reminds you that the devo is from Jonah, Chapter 4.

WEEKEND ACTIVITY IDEAS

(1) Highlight the verses for Week 29 in your Bible. (2) Find the HoneyWord animal in each of the pictures for this week and identify the chapter-number symbols. (3) Add to your collection of Click-ers. (4) Say the daily devos for Week 29. (5) Check out Friday of Week 41 for a related devo on looking to the Lamb when you get in a jam.

SAY AHH!

God sent a huge fish to rescue Jonah. It may have been the size of a blue whale, which has a tongue that weighs as much as an elephant. A baby blue whale is 23 feet long at birth and drinks more than 150 gallons of Mama's milk every day.

Week 30, Monday

BOOK OF MICAH
Micah the Cat

Cat begins with the same letter as the second part of *Micah's* name. A cat can become so independent it won't come when called. Micah warned God's catlike people that they should listen to God's call. When you see Micah the Cat in a picture, you'll know the daily devo is from Micah. Connected to Micah the Cat are number symbols. (See page 15.) They make the chapter location of the devo click and stick.

Micah told God's catty, independent people to be sorry for their sins. He told them they should think about others, not just themselves. He said if the people wouldn't change their ways, they'd be sent to live in other countries. But only a few listened, so God let his people be taken away. He promised he would one day help them land on their feet and return to live in the Promised Land. Many years later God would send his Son, Jesus, to earth. Micah said he would be born in Bethlehem. Jesus would grow up and die for our sins. He would be kind and fair and would always listen when God called.

 MAKE IT STICK

Make a tab to mark the book of Micah in your Bible. (See Week 1, Monday, for directions.)

If you or a friend has a cat, try calling it to see if it comes to you. If it does, great. If it doesn't, it's like a lot of other cats—and people—who are too independent to come when called. Have fun with your friend by making up a silly story about a cat. Take turns saying one sentence, going back and forth until you're both laughing out loud. Use words like *purr*, *meow*, *hiss*, *claws*, *rub*, *tail*, and *hungry*.

Whenever you see a cat or a picture of one, remember Micah the Cat and the book of Micah.

JUST FOR FUN

Look up Micah, Chapter 5 (verse 2), and read about the town where Jesus would be born. What's amazing about this verse is the fact that it was written about 700 years before Jesus' birth!

PRAYER

Dear God, teach me to listen and to come right away when you call, just like your Son, Jesus, did when he lived on the earth. In his name I pray. Amen.

MICAH, CHAPTER 4 (VERSE 3)

The LORD will mediate between peoples and will settle disputes between strong nations far away. They will hammer their swords into plowshares and their spears into pruning hooks. Nation will no longer fight against nation, nor train for war anymore.

DAILY DEVO

One day we'll be done with every gun.

In a famous prophecy, Micah spoke of a day coming when nations will stop fighting each other. And military training for war will come to an end. Can you imagine? He went on to say that God himself will personally settle the differences between nations. People will stop making weapons and start living in peace and prosperity as they plow their fields and prune their trees. Doesn't that sound great? Nobody in their right mind likes the evil of war and terrorism. But Micah's words from God can give you hope. Someday God will see to it that we'll all be done with every kind of gun—and every other tool that destroys—once and for all.

 MAKE IT STICK

On one side of a sheet of paper, draw any weapon of war you can think of. On the other side, draw a new, peaceful use for the same tool of war. For example, swords could be pounded down in the ground around your yard for a fancy new fence. Show your ideas to your dad or mom, and fill your parents in on this hopeful daily devo.

PRAYER

Lord, I'm looking forward to the day when no one will be hurt by anyone anymore. It'll be so cool to feel totally safe at all times. Until then, give me your peace and help me stay close to you. In Jesus' name, amen.

CLICK-ER: GUN

Whenever you see, hear, or think about a *gun*, let this daily devo comfort your heart as it clicks and sticks. Micah the Cat on his four-on-the-floorboard reminds you that the devo is from Micah, Chapter 4.

Week 30, Wednesday

BOOK OF NAHUM
Na-hum-ing-bird

Hummingbird sounds like the last part of *Nahum's* name. The hummingbird is a picture of the speed of Assyria in the days of Nahum the prophet. But this nation would not flap its wings backward and back off from sin, so God destroyed it. When you see Na-hum-ing-bird in a picture, you'll know the daily devo is from Nahum. Connected to Na-hum-ing-bird are number symbols. (See page 15.) They make the chapter location of the devo click and stick.

The people of Assyria darted in and out like hummingbirds, attacking enemies with lightning speed. Just their humming presence struck terror in the hearts of other nations, including the nation of Judah. But this would soon change. The people of Nineveh, Assyria's capital city, had listened to Jonah 100 years earlier. They had told God they were sorry for their sins, and he had kept them safe. But now they had become more evil than ever. Because they would not back away from sin, God finally destroyed them. It's important to change direction before the cost of sin catches up with us.

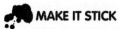 **MAKE IT STICK**

Make a tab to mark the book of Nahum in your Bible. (See Week 1, Monday, for directions.)

See how many facts you can learn about hummingbirds from a book about birds. Or enter the words *hummingbird facts* in a search engine on the Internet. How fast can they fly? How fast do their wings beat? In how many different directions can they fly? How big are their nests? How much do they weigh?

Whenever you see a hummingbird or a picture of one, remember Na-hum-ing-bird and the book of Nahum.

JUST FOR FUN

When the people of Nineveh would not turn back from their sin, God told Nahum to give them a very strong message. Read some of his hard words to them in Nahum, Chapter 1 (verse 3).

PRAYER

Lord, thank you for the personal warnings you give, which keep me away from sin. Please teach me how to turn to you when I feel tempted to do anything that's wrong. In Jesus' name I pray. Amen.

NAHUM, CHAPTER 1 (VERSE 7)

The LORD is good, a strong refuge when trouble comes. He is close to those who trust in him.

DAILY DEVO

Under God's roof I'm waterproof.

Have you ever been caught in a cold, rainy storm and been totally soaked? That's probably not a good memory. But it pictures the downpour of fear God's people felt when they thought about the Assyrians. After all, those people had forcefully taken over Judah's sister nation, Israel, just north of them. So God sent the prophet Nahum to remind his people that he is the world's best refuge for people in trouble and needing help. God is still in the refuge business today. He loves to shelter his people, and he stands ready to shelter you. Are you being blown away by some stormy situation that's beating against your life? If so, come in out of the rain. Get under the roof of God's waterproof protection. Nothing can get you there.

 MAKE IT STICK

Draw a picture of your home in the middle of a storm. The next time there is a real storm, think about how awesome God's protection is. God is like a waterproof roof in all the stormy situations in your life.

PRAYER

Dear God, the weather brings all kinds of storms—wind, rain, snow, and hail. But sometimes I feel like I have storms inside me that make me afraid of what may happen next. Thanks for keeping me safe through all my ups and downs. Amen.

CLICK-ER: ROOF

Whenever you see, stand under, or think about a *roof*, let this daily devo keep you warm and dry as it clicks and sticks. Nahum-ing-bird with his one-on-a-bun reminds you that the devo is from Nahum, Chapter 1.

Week 30, Friday

BOOK OF HABAKKUK
Habakkuk the Hawk

Hawk begins and ends with the same letters as *Habakkuk*. The prophet Habakkuk watched God like a hawk. But Habakkuk didn't understand what God was doing until he made it clear. When you see Habakkuk the Hawk in a picture, you'll know the daily devo is from Habakkuk. Connected to Habakkuk the Hawk are number symbols. (See page 15.) They make the chapter location of the devo click and stick.

Habakkuk watched God like a hawk. But as sharp as his prophetic eyes were, they couldn't see what God was up to. And what Habakkuk could see troubled him. Why did bad guys always seem to win? Why did good people suffer? And why would God use a wicked nation like Babylon to punish his people? God let Habakkuk know that when it comes to sin, nobody gets away with anything. But God alone chooses how and when to give loving discipline. Listening in on Habakkuk's doubts and questions should encourage you. If he could question God, so can you. Just be ready to act when God answers.

MAKE IT STICK

Make a tab to mark the book of Habakkuk in your Bible. (See Week 1, Monday, for directions.)

Did you know that a hawk can see four times farther than a human? Ask your mom or dad if you may please look through a pair of binoculars or a magnifying glass. When you do, you'll get a better feel for how easily a high-flying hawk can spot a tiny mouse for dinner. What are some things you wish you could see more easily?

Whenever you see a picture of a hawk or think about one, remember Habakkuk the Hawk and the book of Habakkuk.

JUST FOR FUN

Habakkuk was so upset that he couldn't see what God was planning. Read all about the reasons behind his feelings by turning to Habakkuk, Chapter 1 (verses 2-3). Then read Chapter 2 (verse 1) about Habakkuk's plan to watch God like a hawk

PRAYER

God, I don't get it. Why do some people always seem to get away with doing really bad things? I may never get it, but I'm still going to trust you. Please keep me watching you like a hawk, waiting for your answers. Amen.

HABAKKUK, CHAPTER 3 (VERSES 17-18)

Even though the fig trees have no blossoms, and there are no grapes on the vines; even though the olive crop fails, and the fields lie empty and barren . . . yet I will rejoice in the LORD! I will be joyful in the God of my salvation!

DAILY DEVO

I'm a God-pleaser, even with an empty freezer.

Habakkuk's heart began to pound, and his knees began to knock. God was showing him that when the Babylonians came, fig trees would no longer blossom. Grapes wouldn't grow. And fields wouldn't produce crops. That's sort of like you opening your refrigerator freezer only to find frosted ice. But Habakkuk's heart of faith never dreamed of screaming, "There's nothing to eat!" Instead, it broke out in the "Hallelujah Chorus." As he remembered God's goodness, his heart moved away from fear, toward faith and joy. Be like Habakkuk. Whatever is in the freezer, decide now to be a God-pleaser and live by faith.

 MAKE IT STICK

Draw a picture of Habakkuk the Hawk with the words of this daily devo coming out of his mouth. After you cut him out, place him on your refrigerator freezer door. For the next few days, when you open the freezer, remember how important good attitudes are, especially when you don't find what you want to eat.

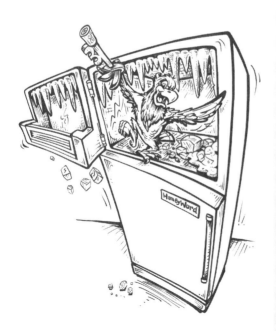

PRAYER

Lord, you already know how cranky I can be. Sometimes just not having my favorite ice cream in the freezer can get me going. Please help me to believe that you really will provide what I need. Thanks, God. Amen.

CLICK-ER: FREEZER

Whenever you see, open, or think about a *freezer*, let this daily devo freeze-proof your heart as it clicks and sticks. Habakkuk the Hawk with his three-is-the-key reminds you that the devo is from Habakkuk, Chapter 3.

WEEKEND ACTIVITY IDEAS

(1) Highlight the verses for Week 30 in your Bible. (2) Find the HoneyWord animal in each of the pictures for this week and identify the chapter-number symbols. (3) Add to your collection of Click-ers. (4) Say the daily devos for Week 30. (5) Check out Friday of Week 18 for a related devo on why you're not meant to harden like cement.

EYE IN THE SKY

Seeing four times farther than a person can see, a high-flying hawk can spot a ground squirrel from a thousand feet away.

Week 31, Monday

BOOK OF ZEPHANIAH
Zeph the Zebra

Zebra begins with the same letter as *Zephaniah*. Like a zebra, Zephaniah alternated his stripes as he explained what happens when God's people zig when they should have zagged. When you see Zeph the Zebra in a picture, you'll know the daily devo is from Zephaniah. Connected to Zeph the Zebra are number symbols. (See page 15.) They make the chapter location of the devo click and stick.

It's an age-old question: Is a zebra a black horse with white stripes or a white horse with black stripes? Along those same lines, does a true prophet bring messages from God about darkness and anger? Or are the messages about light and hope? Actually, the answer is both. On the one hand, Zephaniah let people know that God would zap sin. On the other hand, if God's people would just be sorry and admit they zigged when they should have zagged, God would forgive and save. As you zip through this short, power-packed book, remember that it wasn't written just for the people of Judah. It's for people of all stripes, even you.

 MAKE IT STICK

Make a tab to mark the book of Zephaniah in your Bible. (See Week 1, Monday, for directions.)

Draw a striped zebra like the one shown on this page. From each dark stripe, draw a line that ends in a message of anger from God. (Example: *I will punish sin.*) From each white stripe, draw a line that ends in a message of hope from God. (Example: *I will forgive you.*)

Whenever you see a zebra or a picture of one, think about Zeph the Zebra and the book of Zephaniah.

JUST FOR FUN
Find a message of anger from God in Zephaniah, Chapter 1 (verse 14). Find a message of hope from God in Zephaniah, Chapter 3 (verse 17).

PRAYER
Because you are holy, dear God, you must punish sin. But because you are also kind, you will forgive sin. Thank you for always doing what's right. In Jesus' name, amen.

ZEPHANIAH, CHAPTER 1 (VERSE 2)

"I will sweep away everything from the face of the earth," says the LORD.

DAILY DEVO

God's broom sweeps every room.

King Josiah was one of Judah's best kings. He became king at age eight. But most important, he loved God and wanted to make sure he and his people did things God's way. As a young man, he had the Temple fixed up and found the long-lost scroll of God's Word. After dusting it off and reading it all, he realized God wanted to sweep sin away from the nation. So he and his prophet buddy Zephaniah rolled up their sleeves and got out their dustpans. But they couldn't clean the entire nation. They found out that God cleans up only those who invite him in. Don't be like the people of Judah. When God knocks on the door of your life with the handle of his broom, let him in.

MAKE IT STICK

Just for fun, shock your dad or mom by sweeping the kitchen floor without being asked. As you sweep, think about this daily devo. Ask God to speak to you about something in your life that needs a little sweeping. Then ask him to clean up that part of your life. Let God know that you'll do whatever you can to keep your life clean from sin.

PRAYER

I'm trusting you, Lord, to sweep every wrong thought and every wrong action out of my life. Thank you for sending Jesus to make me pure and clean. Amen.

CLICK-ER: BROOM

Whenever you see, use, or think about a *broom*, let this daily devo sweep through your mind as it clicks and sticks. Zeph the Zebra with his one-on-a-bun reminds you that the devo is from Zephaniah, Chapter 1.

Week 31, Wednesday

BOOK OF HAGGAI

Haggai the Hedgehog

Hedgehog begins with the same letter as *Haggai*. Like a hedgehog, the people of Judah rolled themselves into a ball to keep God at a safe distance, refusing to complete God's Temple—until Haggai came along. When you see Haggai the Hedgehog in a picture, you'll know the daily devo is from Haggai. Connected to Haggai the Hedgehog are number symbols. (See page 15.) They make the chapter location of the devo click and stick.

With their 70-year Babylonian jail sentence behind them, the people of Judah were back in the land, just as God had promised. They were ready to rebuild Solomon's Temple, but their excitement cooled when people from the area tried to stop them. Instead of trusting God, they rolled themselves into a ball and let their do-not-disturb spines keep God away for 16 years. When Haggai showed up and told the people to put God first, they listened and finally finished the Temple. God has plans for you to complete too. But these will be finished only if you let God be first in your life.

 MAKE IT STICK

Make a tab to mark the book of Haggai in your Bible. (See Week 1, Monday, for directions.)

Take turns with a friend rolling up like a hedgehog. First find a place to hide. Then roll yourself into a ball. When your friend finds you and taps you, you must get up and pretend to work on the Temple. Do one thing he tells you to do, like hammering pretend nails, sawing a piece of imaginary wood, or sweeping a dirty floor. Just remember not to roll into a ball when there is work to do!

Whenever you see a hedgehog or a picture of one, think about Haggai the Hedgehog and the book of Haggai.

JUST FOR FUN

The people of Judah built their own homes but would not rebuild God's house, the Temple. You can read about it in your Bible by looking up Haggai, Chapter 1 (verses 2-4).

PRAYER

Dear God, when there is work to be done, help me to get busy. And please teach me how to finish what I start. Thanks, God. Amen.

HAGGAI, CHAPTER 1 (VERSE 6)

You have planted much but harvest little. You eat but are not satisfied. You drink but are still thirsty. You put on clothes but cannot keep warm. Your wages disappear as though you were putting them in pockets filled with holes!

DAILY DEVO

I get holes in my purse when I don't put God first.

When the Jews returned to their homeland in 538 BC, rebuilding the Temple was their number one job. God's blessings flowed as they worked. But things changed when the people quit working on God's house and started working on their own homes. Without God's blessing, they had food but never enough to feel full. They had clothes but couldn't stay warm. They made money but lost it as if they were putting it into pockets filled with holes. Why couldn't they see what was happening? They had stopped putting God first. Have any of these things been happening to you? Always put God first, and he will provide what you need.

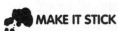

MAKE IT STICK

Write the words "Hole-y Purse" on a paper bag. Carefully cut two holes a little bigger than a quarter in its bottom. Now fill it with a handful of coins. Walk around your house while holding the bag. Pretend you don't know what's going to happen. As you go back and pick up the coins that fell out, think about this daily devo. Ask God for the strength to keep him first in your life, as he wants to be.

PRAYER

Lord, please show me what it means to put you first in my life. I want to know your voice and follow your ways because I love you. In Jesus' name, amen.

CLICK-ER: PURSE

Whenever you see, draw, or think about a lady's *purse*, let your heart cash in on this daily devo as it clicks and sticks. Haggai the Hedgehog with his one-on-a-bun reminds you that the devo is from Haggai, Chapter 1.

Week 31, Friday

BOOK OF ZECHARIAH

Zack the Yak

Zack begins with the same sound as *Zechariah*. Like yaks, God's people are blessed, as Zechariah explained, with super-strong, zesty strength to accomplish whatever God asks them to do. When you see Zack the Yak in a picture, you'll know the daily devo is from Zechariah. Connected to Zack the Yak are number symbols. (See page 15.) They make the chapter location of the devo click and stick.

One yak is enough to yank out a tree stump by its roots or pull a plow through hard ground. Like yaks, God's people can be strong. But our strength is super-natural. We can do zilch on our own—we have to trust in the power of the Holy Spirit. Zechariah, along with his friend and fellow prophet Haggai, encouraged God's people to zero in on the task and trust God for the zeal to finish the Temple. The people did, and their leader Zerubbabel praised them for finishing what they'd started.

 MAKE IT STICK

Make a tab to mark the book of Zechariah in your Bible. (See Week 1, Monday, for directions.)

Do you know anything about yaks? See what you can find at a library or on the Internet. Can you find out how much they weigh? where they live? how they stay warm when it is icy cold in the mountains?

Whenever you see a yak or a picture of one, think about Zack the Yak and the book of Zechariah.

JUST FOR FUN

About 500 years before Jesus was born, Zechariah wrote about Jesus riding into Jerusalem on a donkey. Check out Zechariah, Chapter 9 (verses 9-10). You can also read in Matthew, Chapter 21 (verses 1-11) how that really happened on the first Palm Sunday.

PRAYER

Dear God, thank you for making me strong enough to do everything you want me to do. I'm trusting you to give me your strength whenever I need it. In Jesus' name, amen.

ZECHARIAH, CHAPTER 3 (VERSES 3-4)

Jeshua's clothing was filthy. . . . So the angel said to the others standing there, "Take off his filthy clothes." And turning to Jeshua he said, "See, I have taken away your sins, and now I am giving you these fine new clothes."

DAILY DEVO

God sees beyond the dirt on my shirt.

When the high priest stood before God, dirty from sin, Mr. Dirty himself showed up. Satan charged Jeshua with everything in his handbook of accusations. But God cut Satan off and told him to get lost. Satan got the message and left. But here's the really cool part. God then took Jeshua's dirty spiritual clothes and gave him new ones. Isn't that like God? He's so kind and forgiving. God still does that for us. All of us get our spiritual clothes dirty every day. But God sees beyond the dirt of sin—and, thanks to Jesus, gives us clean spiritual clothes to wear.

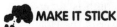 **MAKE IT STICK**

Politely ask your dad or mom for an old shirt that no one wears anymore. Get it really dirty, and ask yourself what your friends would think if you wore that dirty shirt to school. Then think about some of the sins that get your spiritual clothes dirty. As you say this daily devo, put on a fresh, clean shirt and thank God for also giving you clean spiritual clothes to wear every day.

PRAYER

Dear God, sometimes I feel like I'm wearing dirty clothes on the inside. Teach me to avoid doing things that make me feel that way. Please clean me up and make me like you. In Jesus' name, amen.

CLICK-ER: SHIRT

Whenever you see or clean off dirt on your *shirt*, let this daily devo wash your heart as it clicks and sticks. Zack the yak with his three-is-the-key reminds you that the devo is from Zechariah, Chapter 3.

WEEKEND ACTIVITY IDEAS

(1) Highlight the verses for Week 31 in your Bible. (2) Find the HoneyWord animal in each of the pictures for this week and identify the chapter-number symbols. (3) Add to your collection of Click-ers. (4) Say the daily devos for Week 31. (5) Check out Thursday of Week 21 for a related devo on dishing dirt on someone else's shirt.

FEELING THE HEAT

Yaks live in some of the highest mountains in the world, where the air is often icy cold. So how do yaks survive temperatures way below zero? As the yak digests its food, its stomach gets hot and provides heat—almost as if it were the animal's own furnace!

ZECHARIAH, CHAPTER 4 (VERSE 6)

This is what the LORD says to Zerubbabel: It is not by force nor by strength, but by my Spirit, says the LORD of Heaven's Armies.

DAILY DEVO

The Spirit is the source of my horsepower.

For thousands of years before anyone invented an engine, people traveled by horse. So when the train was invented, it was first called the *iron horse*. Later on, the automobile became known as the *horseless carriage*. In the Kingdom of God, however, true spiritual power is a horse of a different color. It doesn't come through horsepower or even from human strength. It comes only through the supernatural power of the Holy Spirit. As you seek to live for God, don't depend on your own strength. Go to the Source, and let him be your "horsepower."

 **MAKE IT STICK**

Draw this HoneyWord cartoon just as you see it, only put yourself in the driver's seat. Now show it to your dad or mom, and briefly explain how the Holy Spirit is the source of all your horsepower. Only he is strong enough to help you live for God.

PRAYER

Dear God, I'm not strong enough inside to do what's right and live for you every day. But I can be wise enough to depend on your Spirit. Thanks for giving me his supernatural power when I trust in you. In Jesus' name, amen.

CLICK-ER: CAR ENGINE

Whenever you experience or think about the horsepower of a *car engine*, let this daily devo rev up your heart as it clicks and sticks. Zack the Yak with his four-on-the-floorboard reminds you that the devo is from Zechariah, Chapter 4.

Week 32, Tuesday

BOOK OF MALACHI
Mala-gator

Mala-gator sounds like *Malachi*. The thick skin of an alligator is a picture of the leathery hearts of God's people in the days of Malachi. When you see Mala-gator in a picture, you'll know the daily devo is from Malachi. Connected to Mala-gator are number symbols. (See page 15.) They make the chapter location of the devo click and stick.

Many years had gone by since Zechariah and other prophets had painted a wonderful picture of the Messiah, who would soon be coming. So where was he? People were tired of waiting. Instead of trusting God, they turned away and became thick-skinned like alligators. And they kept their tough hearts underwater, hidden from God, while their eyes looked above for some sign of God's love. The book of Malachi ends with God kindly inviting his alligator-like people to come out of the muddy waters of bad attitudes. The invitation still stands today. How will you respond?

MAKE IT STICK

Make a tab to mark the book of Malachi in your Bible. (See Week 1, Monday, for directions.)

Learn what you can about an alligator's thick skin, and act out a wrestling match with a pretend alligator. Then look up the word *thick-skinned*. You'll discover that a thick-skinned person doesn't care what other people think. When might that be a good thing? How is it bad? Should we care about what God thinks?

Whenever you see an alligator or a picture of one, think about Mala-gator and the book of Malachi.

JUST FOR FUN
When God's people kept turning away from him, he kept promising that he'd save whoever turned back to him. You can read about it in Malachi, Chapter 4 (verse 2). Jesus, God's Son, is called a different kind of "sun" in this verse. He brings warmth and healing and freedom and joy!

PRAYER
Lord, I care about what you think and want to listen to what you say. Show me how to be a true follower as I walk with you in fun and freedom. In Jesus' name I pray. Amen.

MALACHI, CHAPTER 2 (VERSE 16)

*"I hate divorce!" says the L*ORD*, the God of Israel. "To divorce your wife is to overwhelm her with cruelty," says the L*ORD *of Heaven's Armies. "So guard your heart; do not be unfaithful to your wife."*

DAILY DEVO

God is hoarse from saying, "I hate divorce."

The pain from divorce can last for a lifetime. That's one reason why God hates it so much. Perhaps you have parents who are separated or divorced. Kids often blame themselves when that happens—don't do it. But do ask yourself this question: Is a child strong enough to break down the walls of a house? Of course not. When one parent moves out of the home, it may feel as if the walls have broken down. But remember, it's not the kids who broke the walls—or the parents—apart. If you or some of your friends have been hurt by divorce, pray for God's comfort and peace. Even though God is hoarse from speaking out against divorce, he loves you and will take care of you, no matter what happens.

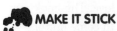 **MAKE IT STICK**

Draw a picture of Jesus holding his hand to his throat as if he were hoarse and could barely talk above a whisper. Write this daily devo below it. Now pray for yourself or someone you know who's been hurt by divorce.

PRAYER

Dear God, I know you feel sad when a family is hurt by divorce. Please give your comfort and strength to every hurting family right now. Thank you, God. In Jesus' name, amen.

CLICK-ER:
HOARSE THROAT

Whenever you hear, experience, or think about a raspy, *hoarse throat*, let this daily devo whisper comfort to your heart as it clicks and sticks. Mala-gator with his two-blue-shoes reminds you that the devo is from Malachi, Chapter 2.

Week 32, Thursday

BOOK OF MATTHEW

Matt the Mouse

Mouse begins with the same letter as *Matthew*.
The mouse pictures the chiseling, cheating ways of
Matthew the tax collector before Jesus, the Messiah, changed him from a thief to a servant of God. When you see Matt the Mouse in a picture, you'll know the daily devo is from Matthew. Connected to Matt the Mouse are number symbols. (See page 15.) They make the chapter location of the devo click and stick.

It's a little-known fact, but the word *mouse* comes from an old word from India that means "thief." In the days of Jesus, tax collectors were often thieves. Like mice, they made holes in the wallets and purses of God's people and stole their money. After becoming a follower of Jesus Christ, Matthew, a former tax collector, never forgot how God changed him from a money-grabber to a people-server for the Kingdom of God. That's why, in his Gospel, he kept calling himself "Matthew the tax collector." He wanted us to know that Jesus is the only true Messiah who can save us from our sins.

 MAKE IT STICK

Make a tab to mark the book of Matthew in your Bible. (See Week 1, Monday, for directions.)

Using one of your favorite Bible storybooks, find famous stories that come from the book of Matthew. Then tell one of these stories in your own words. You might want to consider the story of the wise men (Chapter 2), the Lord's Prayer (Chapter 6), or the story of the servant who wouldn't forgive (Chapter 18).

Whenever you see a mouse or a picture of one, think about Matt the Mouse and the book of Matthew.

JUST FOR FUN

You can read about Jesus and how he called Matthew to be his disciple in Chapter 9 (verses 9-13).

PRAYER

Dear God, I'm so glad you change people like Matthew and me, and make us clean from the inside out. Thank you for sending your Son, Jesus, to save us. Amen.

MATTHEW, CHAPTER 4 (VERSES 10-11)

*"Get out of here, Satan," Jesus told him. "For the Scriptures say, 'You must worship the L*ORD *your God and serve only him.'" Then the devil went away, and angels came and took care of Jesus.*

DAILY DEVO
I know how to zap Satan's trap.

Have you ever felt like doing something you knew you absolutely, positively shouldn't do? That's temptation. And the devil wants you to give in to the feeling to do what you know deep down isn't right. In fact, he even tried to make Jesus give in to temptation. But Jesus didn't fall for it. Instead, Jesus used God's Word to beat the devil and gave us a great example on how to beat temptation ourselves. Every time Satan set a "temptation trap," Jesus just zapped it with his zapper—the Word of God. Don't waste time letting the devil bother you. Instead, remember you've got a zapper that can't miss. Just keep repeating what the Bible says and zap Satan's trap every time.

MAKE IT STICK

Politely ask your dad or mom to show you how to work a small mousetrap. Then write this daily devo on a small piece of paper and fold it up into a little square. Now place it as the "bait" on your mousetrap. Each time you set and trigger your trap, say this daily devo.

PRAYER

Lord, please give me a heart that really wants to learn your Word. Then I'll know how to use it when Satan tempts me to do wrong. In Jesus' name I pray. Amen.

CLICK-ER: MOUSETRAP

Whenever you see, set, or think about a *mousetrap*, let this daily devo snap in your mind as it clicks and sticks. Matt the Mouse with his four-on-the-floorboard reminds you that the devo is from Matthew, Chapter 4.

MATTHEW, CHAPTER 5 (VERSE 13)

You are the salt of the earth. But what good is salt if it has lost its flavor? Can you make it salty again? It will be thrown out and trampled underfoot as worthless.

DAILY DEVO

I'm a saltshaker **flavor maker.**

Have you ever tasted french fries or popcorn without any salt? Adding at least a little salt makes them a lot tastier. Jesus calls us "the salt of the earth." It's like he's counting on us to shake out his flavor on the people around us, giving them a taste of what life could really be like. But you can't shake out what you haven't poured in. To make a difference in the lives of those around you, stock up on the salt of God's Word. Before you know it, you'll be a full-time saltshaker flavor maker for Jesus.

MAKE IT STICK

The next time you're in a restaurant, politely ask if your dad or mom knows how to balance a glass saltshaker on its edge. If not, try pouring a small pile of salt on a plate. Now carefully balance the saltshaker on one of its bottom glass edges in the salt. Once it's standing there by itself, slowly blow away the surrounding salt. Before someone knocks it down or shakes the table, say this daily devo.

PRAYER

Dear God, I want to do my part to help others know you better. Please show me how to give someone a taste of how great it is to love you and follow you. In Jesus' name, amen.

CLICK-ER: **SALTSHAKER**

Whenever you see, taste, or think about the salt in a *saltshaker*, let this daily devo season your mind as it clicks and sticks. Matt the Mouse with his five-on-a-hive-hat reminds you that the devo is from Matthew, Chapter 5.

WEEKEND ACTIVITY IDEAS
(1) Highlight the verses for Week 32 in your Bible. (2) Find the HoneyWord animal in each of the pictures for this week and identify the chapter-number symbols. (3) Add to your collection of Click-ers. (4) Say the daily devos for Week 32. (5) Check out Thursday of Week 36 for a related devo on why a lone leper wanted to pepper God with praise.

PEDAL TO THE METAL
Mice have such hard, sharp, chisel-like teeth,
they can even nibble into concrete and metal.

MATTHEW, CHAPTER 6 (VERSE 20)

Store your treasures in heaven, where moths and rust cannot destroy, and thieves do not break in and steal.

DAILY DEVO

I don't trust whatever gets rust or dust.

Rust and dust are as old as dirt. Dust is just little bits of dirt, sand, and other junk carried by the wind that lands on top of everything, from cars to coffee tables. Rust forms when iron or steel meets damp air. It's hard to think of anything that rust or dust can't reach and ruin. That's the point Jesus was making. Everything in this world will someday rust, rot, or collect dust. So please don't waste your life seeking and counting on stuff that won't last. Instead, go after what pleases God. Making God happy gives you treasure in heaven—the kind of treasure that nothing, absolutely nothing, can destroy. Don't trust whatever gets rust or dust. Trust God.

 ### MAKE IT STICK

Politely ask your dad or mom to help you hunt outside your home for a rusty nail or something else that's rusting. (Be sure, though, never to touch a rusty nail.) Repeat this daily devo as you carefully observe how rust eats away at the strength of the metal, turning it into a soft, dark brown, flaky crust.

PRAYER

Dear God, it's fun having a lot of stuff, but I know my things won't last forever. Teach me how to see your Son, Jesus, as my greatest treasure—in this life and the next. Thanks, God. Amen.

CLICK-ER: RUSTY NAIL

Whenever you see or think about a *rusty nail*, let your mind pound this daily devo into your heart as it clicks and sticks. Matt the Mouse with his six-pick-up-stix reminds you that the devo is from Matthew, Chapter 6.

MATTHEW, CHAPTER 7 (VERSE 4)

How can you think of saying to your friend, "Let me help you get rid of that speck in your eye," when you can't see past the log in your own eye?

DAILY DEVO

I can't jog with a log in my eye.

Jesus knows that some people are always looking for what others do wrong. It's as if they have a big log that fogs their eyes and keeps them from seeing their own sins. But they get upset about a little speck they see in someone else's eye—a mistake that person didn't make purposely to hurt anyone. If you tried to jog with a log in your eye, you couldn't see to run. But could a log really fit in your eye? No! Does Jesus know that? Yes! He also knows we need to let God remove the sins that keep us from seeing ourselves as we are. Then he'll give us wisdom to help others who've done wrong things too. Don't jog with a log in your eye. Let God take it out.

MAKE IT STICK

Draw a picture of a log and a speck. As you draw, ask God if you've been judging anyone for a little mistake that's like a speck, while hiding your own sin that's like a big log. Ask God to forgive you for judging and thank him for helping you remove the log from your own eye. Include this daily devo in your prayer.

PRAYER

Lord, forgive me for being so quick to see the wrong things others do. Please help me to focus instead on doing what *I* need to do to please you. In Jesus' name, amen.

CLICK-ER: LOG

Whenever you see, touch, or think about a *log*, let this daily devo jog your memory as it clicks and sticks. Matt the Mouse with his highway-seven-to-heaven sign reminds you that the devo is from Matthew, Chapter 7.

MATTHEW, CHAPTER 8 (VERSES 8-9)

The officer said, "Lord, I am not worthy to have you come into my home. Just say the word from where you are, and my servant will be healed. I know this because I am under the authority of my superior officers, and I have authority over my soldiers. I only need to say, 'Go,' and they go, or 'Come,' and they come."

DAILY DEVO

When God says, "Go!" I go.

Like Jesus, the Roman officer in Matthew 8 understood authority. When his boss said, "Come," he came. And when he told his soldiers to go, they went. He believed that all Jesus had to say was "be healed" and the bedridden servant at the officer's home would get well. That's exactly what happened. The officer's faith amazed Jesus. He wants to be amazed by your faith too. But first you must obey the people God has placed in authority over you. If you do, you'll understand Jesus' authority and develop the kind of faith that God loves to reward. Look at what Jesus did for a Roman officer and his young servant. Would you like to know God's power in this way? Then obey. And when God says, "Go," just go!

 MAKE IT STICK

For the next eight days, every time you pass through a green traffic light, say this daily devo out loud, or meditate on it quietly in your heart. While you're riding in your car, discuss with your dad or mom the kinds of actions and thoughts to which God says, "Go!"

PRAYER

Dear God, please help me to obey everyone who has authority over me. And give me faith in Jesus and his authority so I'll have his power in my life. Amen.

CLICK-ER:
"GO" TRAFFIC LIGHT

Whenever you see, go through, or think about a *"Go" traffic light*, let this daily devo turn green in your mind as it clicks and sticks. Matt the Mouse with his eight-under-skates reminds you that the devo is from Matthew, Chapter 8.

MATTHEW, CHAPTER 10 (VERSE 30)

The very hairs on your head are all numbered.

DAILY DEVO

God even cares about my hairs.

It's a little-known fact, but every day the average person loses about 100 hairs from his or her head. If you rolled that up over a year's time, that would make a pretty big hairball. Now if you multiply that by the other 6 billion or so people in the world, well . . . that's a pretty hairy thought, don't you think? But here's the really amazing thing: Somehow God numbers and keeps track of every single hair on every single person in the whole wide world. That's a lot of bookkeeping. Doesn't God have anything better to do? Nope. You see, God loves you so much that he cares about every detail of your life—even the number of hairs on your head.

 MAKE IT STICK

Go get your hairbrush. Pull out all the hair that's trapped in the bristles. See how many hairs you can untangle. For every single hair you separate, say this daily devo.

PRAYER

Thank you, Lord, for caring about me so much that you've even counted the number of hairs on my head. You know everything about me, but the most important thing is that you love me. I love you, too. In Jesus' name, amen.

CLICK-ER: HAIR

Whenever you see, brush, or think about your *hair*, let this daily devo comb through your mind as it clicks and sticks. Matt the Mouse with his one-on-a-bun and halo-is-a-hero-as-a-zero reminds you that the devo is from Matthew, Chapter 10.

MATTHEW, CHAPTER 11 (VERSES 28-29)

Then Jesus said, "Come to me, all of you who are weary and carry heavy burdens, and I will give you rest. Take my yoke upon you. Let me teach you, because I am humble and gentle at heart, and you will find rest for your souls."

DAILY DEVO

I find rest in his nest.

Every bird builds a special kind of nest. Some of these look neat, while others look messy. Wrens make tiny nests, while eagles form huge ones. But every nest is a safe, warm home for a family of birds. It's where they eat, sleep, and grow up. And when the baby birds are ready to fly the coop, it becomes a launching pad for their first flight. Think of the arms of Jesus as a warm, cozy nest where you can find rest from anything that seems hard or makes you feel bad. Do you get tired or worry a lot? Crawl into Jesus' nest. And let him teach you how to rest.

MAKE IT STICK

Politely ask your dad or mom to help you make bird's nest cookies. In the microwave, melt one cup of chocolate or butterscotch baking chips. Stir to make sure all the chips have melted. Mix them with one or two cups of chow mein noodles. Before the mixture cools, drop it by tablespoonfuls onto wax paper. Push down in the center of each with a spoon and add a few "eggs" (raisins or peanuts). When your "nests" are cool, say this daily devo each time you eat one.

PRAYER

Dear Jesus, sometimes things bother me, and I start feeling sad, worried, or tired. Teach me how to come to you and pour out my heart in prayer. Then I can find rest and peace in your arms. Thanks, Jesus. Amen.

CLICK-ER: BIRD'S NEST

Whenever you see, touch, or think about a *bird's nest*, let your heart find rest in this daily devo as it clicks and sticks. Matt the Mouse with his one-on-a-bun under each arm reminds you that the devo is from Matthew, Chapter 11.

MATTHEW, CHAPTER 17 (VERSE 20)

"You don't have enough faith," Jesus told them. "I tell you the truth, if you had faith even as small as a mustard seed, you could say to this mountain, 'Move from here to there,' and it would move. Nothing would be impossible."

DAILY DEVO

My faith can make a mountain quake.

Faith is a word that means "trust in God." Jesus taught his disciples that if they had even just a little trust, they could do big things for God. In fact, Jesus said that faith the size of a mustard seed—a seed so small you almost can't see it—would be enough for you to make an entire mountain move. How can you learn to trust God this much? Start by learning one thing about him from the Bible every day. And remember to pray and go to church. Over time these good habits will help you see God's power in action. As you learn to trust him, problems bigger than mountains will start moving away. And nothing will be impossible.

MAKE IT STICK

Politely ask your dad or mom to help you look up Pikes Peak in an encyclopedia. Then draw a picture of it. Underneath it, write down some mountain-size troubles you can trust God to take care of for you. Then say this daily devo.

PRAYER

Dear God, when I trust you, my problems get smaller and my love for you gets bigger. Thank you for your Son, Jesus, who helps me believe that nothing is impossible when I put my faith in you. Amen.

CLICK-ER: MOUNTAIN

Whenever you see, climb, or think about a *mountain*, let this daily devo move your mind to trust as it clicks and sticks. Matt the Mouse with his one-on-a-bun and highway-seven-to-heaven sign reminds you that the devo is from Matthew, Chapter 17.

WEEKEND ACTIVITY IDEAS

(1) Highlight the verses for Week 33 in your Bible. (2) Find Matt the Mouse in each picture for this week and identify the chapter-number symbols. (3) Add to your collection of Click-ers. (4) Say the daily devos for Week 33. (5) Check out Wednesday of Week 44 for a related devo on the kind of lava that grows and overflows.

CHEESE THIEF

The word mouse comes from a very old word
that means "thief." Any cheese missing?

MATTHEW, CHAPTER 18 (VERSE 10)

Beware that you don't look down on any of these little ones. For I tell you that in heaven their angels are always in the presence of my heavenly Father.

DAILY DEVO

Guardian angels see when anyone messes with me.

Jesus knows that some adults and older kids look down on younger kids and try to take advantage of them. It sort of makes sense if you think about it. When we're younger, we're shorter, smaller, weaker, and pretty much know less about everything . . . except how to please God by trusting him. And that trust—that faith—is what God loves seeing most in children. God loves you so much he's even given you personal angels to watch over you. Guardian angels, you see, are kind of like the best big brother or sister you could ever imagine, except a million times better. Your angels won't let any of Satan's bullies hurt you and get away with it.

MAKE IT STICK

Draw a picture of what you think a guardian angel looks like. Now think of a time when someone looked down on you or was unkind. What do you think that guardian angel whispered to God then? If you want to, ask God to forgive and help that person. Someone you feel comfortable with—your dad or mom, a teacher, a pastor, or another adult friend can help you know what to pray.

PRAYER

Dear God, I'm so happy that angels really do watch over me every day. Thank you for making my very own angels that help keep me safe. In Jesus' name, amen.

CLICK-ER: ANGEL

Whenever you see, wonder, read, or think about *angels*, let this daily devo stand by your heart as it clicks and sticks. Matt the Mouse with his one-on-a-bun and eight-under-skates reminds you that the devo is from Matthew, Chapter 18.

MATTHEW, CHAPTER 18 (VERSES 21-22)

Peter came to him and asked, "Lord, how often should I forgive someone who sins against me? Seven times?" "No, not seven times," Jesus replied, "but seventy times seven!"

DAILY DEVO

I give a new start when I forgive from the heart.

How many times should I forgive someone who hurts me? If you've ever asked yourself that question, you're not alone. Peter asked Jesus and was shocked at Jesus' answer of "seventy times seven." If you multiply 70 × 7, you get 490! That's a lot of forgiveness. But if you don't forgive someone who hurts you, your heart becomes like a car that won't start. When you forgive from the heart, you give yourself power—God's power—to get going again. And you give to the person you forgive that same power to start over again. Don't hold grudges! Give yourself and others a fresh start. Always forgive from the heart.

 MAKE IT STICK

For one week, every time you are in a car and the driver starts the engine, let it remind you to forgive someone who has hurt you. When the engine starts, say this daily devo. Then ask God to help you forgive from the heart. And thank him for giving you—and the person you forgave—a fresh, new start!

PRAYER

Thank you, Jesus, for teaching me about forgiveness. I'm glad you always forgive me when I come to you. Please help me to be just as forgiving as you are. Amen.

CLICK-ER: CAR STARTER

Whenever you see, hear, or think about a *car starter*, let your mind crank up this daily devo as it clicks and sticks. Matt the Mouse with his one-on-a-bun and eight-under-skates reminds you that the devo is from Matthew, Chapter 18.

MATTHEW, CHAPTER 22 (VERSE 37)

Jesus replied, "You must love the LORD your God with all your heart, all your soul, and all your mind."

DAILY DEVO

This I know: I love God from head to toe.

Can you imagine playing a game of basketball without using your arms or legs? How would you score if you couldn't move? You wouldn't be able to help your team win the game, and you wouldn't enjoy yourself either. Right? The same is true of your friendship with God. You can't love God with just one part of your body. Like playing good basketball, it takes everything you've got: your whole heart, soul, mind, and body. When it comes to loving God, don't be a one-part player. Give him your all. Love God from head to toe, and watch how he helps you win the game of life in this world and the next.

MAKE IT STICK

Trace around your big toe on a piece of paper. Using play dough or clay, make a big toe the size of your drawing. When your dough toe is done, show it to your dad or mom and tell them this daily devo.

PRAYER

Dear God, I love you so much. Do you know why? Because you love me! Thanks for everything you do for me. Please help me to show my love for you by the things I say and do. In Jesus' name I pray. Amen.

CLICK-ER: TOE

Whenever you see, touch, or think about a *toe*, let your whole body know this daily devo from head to toe as it clicks and sticks. Matt the Mouse with his two pairs of two-blue-shoes reminds you that the devo is from Matthew, Chapter 22.

MATTHEW, CHAPTER 28 (VERSES 19-20)

Therefore, go and make disciples of all the nations, baptizing them in the name of the Father and the Son and the Holy Spirit. Teach these new disciples to obey all the commands I have given you. And be sure of this: I am with you always, even to the end of the age.

DAILY DEVO

We are the invitations to all nations.

Everyone loves getting a personal invitation to a special event. God sends personal invitations, but he uses people instead of pen, paper, and stamps. Because of Jesus' death on the cross, God has personally invited everyone in the world to live in his big house in heaven. Many people, however, haven't received God's invitation because he is waiting for us to deliver it by hand. You see, God's people are his invitations to all nations. When we obey God and go into all the world, many people will respond to our offer to receive God's gift of eternal life. So don't hold back. Whether you go next door or to another country, talk to people about Jesus and invite them to heaven.

 **MAKE IT STICK**

Politely ask your dad or mom to help you create an invitation to heaven. When you're done, say this daily devo. Ask God to help you invite one person this week to believe in Jesus and spend forever in heaven.

PRAYER

Dear God, I pray that your Holy Spirit will show me who I can invite to become part of your family. And be with missionaries who have gone far away. Help them invite many people from other nations to believe in Jesus. Amen.

CLICK-ER: INVITATION

Whenever you see, open, or send a personal *invitation*, let your heart invite you to remember this daily devo as it clicks and sticks. Matt the Mouse with his two-blue-shoes and eight-under-skates reminds you that the devo is from Matthew, Chapter 28.

Week 34, Friday

BOOK OF MARK

Mark the Monkey

Monkey begins with the same letter as *Mark*. The monkey reminds us of the high-energy, action-packed movement of Mark's Gospel. When you see Mark the Monkey in a picture, you'll know the daily devo is from Mark. Connected to Mark the Monkey are number symbols. (See page 15.) They make the chapter location of the devo click and stick.

The stories in Mark's Gospel move quickly, like a monkey swinging through the trees of a giant forest. Mark used the word *immediately* more than any other New Testament writer, giving us a series of back-to-back stories. In his Gospel, he captured the highlights of Jesus' miracles, which were of great interest to his Roman readers. Mark wrote more about the things Jesus did than about the things he said. He described Jesus as the servant Son of God, always busily obeying his Father and meeting the needs of people.

MAKE IT STICK

Make a tab to mark the book of Mark in your Bible. (See Week 1, Monday, for directions.)

Mark was not one of the 12 disciples, but he knew who they were because he listed them in Chapter 3 (verses 16-19). Like a monkey darting from one scene to another, take a swing through Mark's gospel. Watch and listen for stories like these: Jesus teaching his disciples, feeding 5,000 people, healing a deaf man and a blind man, riding a donkey into Jerusalem, dying on a cross, and coming back to life.

Whenever you see a monkey or a picture of one, remember Mark the Monkey and the book of Mark.

JUST FOR FUN

You can learn about two of Mark's best friends in Acts, Chapter 13 (verses 4-5). What did Mark do with his friends?

PRAYER

Dear Jesus, thank you for all the things I learn about you when I read the books of Matthew, Mark, Luke, and John. In your name I pray. Amen.

MARK, CHAPTER 1 (VERSE 10)

As Jesus came up out of the water, he saw the heavens splitting apart and the Holy Spirit descending on him like a dove.

DAILY DEVO

I love the Dove from above.

The baptism of Jesus by John the Baptist was a special event. God's voice from heaven said, "You are my dearly loved Son, and you bring me great joy." As Jesus came up out of the water, the Spirit of God came down on him in the form of a dove. But why a gentle dove? Why not a fierce eagle instead? No one knows for sure, but we can guess. Like a dove, the Holy Spirit is very sweet and tenderhearted. In Ephesians, Chapter 4 (verse 30) we are told not to make the Holy Spirit sad. And 1 Thessalonians, Chapter 5 (verse 19) clearly says that we are not to choke out the Holy Spirit. You see, the Spirit is so kind and peace loving that he works at our invitation only. He's always with us, but we don't always follow him. So love the Dove from above, and let him have his way in your life.

MAKE IT STICK

Have fun making a frozen, dove-shaped juice bar. Use aluminum foil to form a hollow mold in the shape of a dove. Put it on a plate, fill it with juice and lay a Popsicle stick or spoon in the center so it tilts out and rests on an outside edge. Freeze your mold. Then take it out, remove the foil, and enjoy! As you eat your juice bar, repeat this daily devo.

PRAYER

Dear God, thank you for being so kind and gentle, and sending your Spirit down on your Son, Jesus. That shows how much you love him. Come, Holy Spirit. Fill me, too, with your love. Amen.

CLICK-ER: DOVE

Whenever you see, hear, or think about a *dove*, let this daily devo gently flutter through your mind as it clicks and sticks. Mark the Monkey with his one-on-a-bun reminds you that the devo is from Mark, Chapter 1.

WEEKEND ACTIVITY IDEAS

(1) Highlight the verses for Week 34 in your Bible. (2) Find the HoneyWord animal in each of the pictures for this week and identify the chapter-number symbols. (3) Add to your collection of Click-ers. (4) Say the daily devos for Week 34. (5) Check out Friday of Week 45 for a related devo on how to handle a candle with care.

SCRATCH ATTACH

Monkeys hug, kiss, and scratch one another's
backs to show they are friendly and caring.

MARK, CHAPTER 4 (VERSE 8)

Still other seeds fell on fertile soil, and they sprouted, grew, and produced a crop that was thirty, sixty, and even a hundred times as much as had been planted!

DAILY DEVO

I'm good seed on good soil.

Some seeds are round. Others are egg-shaped, triangular, or oval. Some seeds have horns, others have tails, and many have wings. Some are smooth, others have ridges. But the size or shape of the seed doesn't match the size of the plant that will grow from it. For example, the tallest tree in the world, the California redwood, grows from a seed six times smaller than the average watermelon seed. Every seed, though, needs rich, fertile ground. When you believe and receive all the different kinds of teaching in God's Word, you're like good seed on good soil. Over time, as you trust and obey God, your life in him will grow, and you'll become like a field filled with beautiful plants.

 MAKE IT STICK

Politely ask your dad or mom to buy some good, fresh soil and an envelope of seeds that you can grow in a planter inside your house. Carefully follow the instructions for planting the seeds, and watch them grow over the next several weeks. Write this daily devo on a small piece of paper, attach it to a toothpick, and stick it in your planter. Then, each time you pass by it, say this daily devo.

PRAYER

Lord, I want to be good seed on good soil for the rest of my life. Please make me the kind of person who really receives your Word and grows in your ways—more and more and more. In Jesus' name, amen.

CLICK-ER: SEEDS

Whenever you see, plant, or think about *seeds*, sow this daily devo deep into the good soil of your heart as it clicks and sticks. Mark the Monkey with his four-on-the-floorboard reminds you that the devo is from Mark, Chapter 4.

MARK, CHAPTER 7 (VERSES 19-21)

Food doesn't go into your heart, but only passes through the stomach. . . . It is what comes from inside that defiles you. For from within, out of a person's heart, come evil thoughts.

DAILY DEVO

I can eat-zza greasy, cheesy pizza.

The religious leaders back in Jesus' day had rules on top of rules. Don't do this. Don't do that. Don't eat this. Do eat that. Now, there's nothing wrong with rules. We all need them. But Jesus knew these people loved to keep rules more than they loved to know God. The key to a clean heart, then and now, is not what you put into your stomach. What's important is what you do with evil thoughts that come up out of your heart. You need to bring those thoughts to Jesus so he can wash them out and keep your friendship with God fresh and clean. You can choose to eat or not eat-zza greasy, cheesy pizza. But you can't make your heart pure for God. Only Jesus can do that.

MAKE IT STICK

The next time you're ready to eat pizza, stop and say this daily devo before you dig in. As you take your first bite, silently thank God for giving you a clean heart when you trusted in what Jesus did for you on the cross. Also tell him how glad you are that you're free to eat-zza greasy, cheesy pizza!

PRAYER

Thank you, Jesus, for dying on the cross for all my bad thoughts. Please teach me how to think good thoughts so my heart stays clean and pure. (Thanks for pizza, too!) Amen.

CLICK-ER: PIZZA

Whenever you see, eat, or think about a *pizza*, let your mind take a big bite of this daily devo as it clicks and sticks. Mark the Monkey with his highway-seven-to-heaven sign reminds you that the devo is from Mark, Chapter 7.

MARK, CHAPTER 9 (VERSE 41)

If anyone gives you even a cup of water because you belong to the Messiah, I tell you the truth, that person will surely be rewarded.

DAILY DEVO

I'm sold on giving cold cups of water.

Have you ever seen a sign offering a reward for a lost pet? You have to find that animal and return it to its owner before you get the money, right? That's the way rewards work. They only come when you do what's expected of you. The same is true with God. If we want to receive rewards from him, we must first learn what he expects of us. This passage gives us a clue. He wants us to notice what people need and give it to them. He wants us to welcome visitors and serve them. Even if we just offer a guest a cup of cold water, God will see that and reward us—maybe in this life, but for sure in heaven. Get sold on giving cold cups of water. And get ready to receive some really cool rewards.

 ### MAKE IT STICK

Before bedtime tonight, offer to get a cup of cold water for your dad, mom, brother, or sister. If he or she asks why, explain how this daily devo is the reason for your doing this. But don't ask for a reward. God will give you that—probably when you're not even expecting it!

PRAYER

Dear God, I like having people do nice things for me, but I need help to see what you want me to do for others. Make me willing to do simple things like giving someone a cup of water. And it's okay even if you don't reward me. Amen.

CLICK-ER: CUP OF WATER

Whenever you see, drink, or think about a cold *cup of water*, let this daily devo refresh your heart as it clicks and sticks. Mark the Monkey with his nine-foot-pine reminds you that the devo is from Mark, Chapter 9.

MARK, CHAPTER 11 (VERSES 8-9)

Many in the crowd spread their garments on the road ahead of him, and others spread leafy branches they had cut in the fields. Jesus was in the center of the procession, and the people all around him were shouting, "Praise God! Blessings on the one who comes in the name of the LORD!"

DAILY DEVO

Go bananas! Shout hosannas!

Most parades take tons of preparation and practice. But the big parade in this story came together in a few seconds. Grown-ups and kids joined in, doing whatever they could to celebrate this one-float parade—Jesus riding into Jerusalem. He rode on a young donkey, a colt that had never been ridden before. People were going bananas and shouting hosannas all over the place. *Hosanna* is a Hebrew word of praise that means "save us now." Some people spread their coats on the road. Others cut leafy branches off trees to wave in the air or spread on the road. We'd probably have done the same thing. After all, this was the Son of God they were excited about. It's the same Jesus who came to save you from your sins so he can take you to heaven someday. So go ahead. Go bananas and shout a few hosannas!

 MAKE IT STICK

Hold a banana up to your mouth and pretend that it's a microphone. Shout this daily devo three times. After your third hosanna, peel your banana and enjoy eating it.

PRAYER

Wow, Lord, that must have been a fun parade, with people waving and shouting as you rode by. But I know you hear me, too. Hosanna! Thank you, Jesus, for coming to earth to be my Savior. Amen.

CLICK-ER: BANANA

Whenever you see, peel, or think about a *banana*, let this daily devo slip through your mind as it clicks and sticks. Mark the Monkey walking with his pair of one-on-a-bun stilts reminds you that the devo is from Mark, Chapter 11.

MARK, CHAPTER 12 (VERSE 10)

Didn't you ever read this in the Scriptures? "The stone that the builders rejected has now become the cornerstone."

DAILY DEVO

Jesus is my very own cornerstone.

Cornerstones give connecting walls the strength and direction to stand at just the right angle to one another. Without a cornerstone, a building could fall down. Jesus is like a cornerstone. As we build our lives on the foundation of God's Word, Jesus is the One who helps us stand straight and strong. When the storms and pressures of life come against us and we are tempted to fall, he holds us up. Let Jesus be your very own cornerstone. He'll never let you down.

MAKE IT STICK

Politely ask your dad or mom to help you look up the word *cornerstone* in a dictionary and in Isaiah, Chapter 28 (verse 16). Learn how these stones make buildings strong and safe. Then repeat this daily devo out loud.

PRAYER

Dear God, thank you for letting Jesus be my very own cornerstone. I know he will always keep me going, no matter how many problems I have to face. Thank you, Jesus. Amen.

CLICK-ER: CORNERSTONE

Whenever you see, touch, or think about a building with a *cornerstone*, let this daily devo corner your mind as it clicks and sticks. Mark the Monkey with his one-on-a-bun and two-blue-shoes reminds you that the devo is from Mark, Chapter 12.

Week 35, Saturday/Sunday

BOOK OF LUKE
Luke the Lion

Lion begins with the same letter as *Luke*. The lion reminds us of Dr. Luke's powerful report on Jesus, who was the bold Lion of the tribe of Judah.

When you see Luke the Lion in a picture, you'll know the daily devo is from Luke. Connected to Luke the Lion are number symbols. (See page 15.) They make the chapter location of the devo click and stick.

Good doctors know how important it is to pay attention to small details. So Dr. Luke, a medical doctor, gives us a complete examination of the life and words of Jesus, the most amazing person in history. His words roar off the pages of this Gospel like a powerful lion. Luke shows how Jesus, the royal Son of God, boldly came to seek and save those who are lost. But Jesus was also gentle like a lion cub. In fact, Dr. Luke points out how Jesus went out of his way to care about people who were poor, hurt, sick, sinful, and not well-liked.

 MAKE IT STICK

Make a tab to mark the book of Luke in your Bible. (See Week 1, Monday, for directions.)

Luke cared about people and wanted them to understand God's love. In Chapter 15, Luke writes stories about a lost sheep, a lost coin, and a lost son. Ask a friend to help you act out one of these stories. What do you learn about God's love from the story you chose to act out?

Whenever you see a lion or a picture of one, think about Luke the Lion and the book of Luke.

JUST FOR FUN
Luke is the only Gospel writer who tells the story of a short man you might have learned about a long time ago. Jesus found the man in a tree and went home with him. Read about Jesus and that man in Chapter 19 (verses 1-10).

PRAYER
Lord Jesus, I learn many things from Scripture about you and your heavenly Father. I'm glad you are powerful enough to save those who are lost from God. I'm also glad you are loving enough to care about me. Amen.

WEEKEND ACTIVITY IDEAS

(1) Highlight the verses for Week 35 in your Bible. (2) Find the HoneyWord animal in each of the pictures for this week and identify the chapter-number symbols. (3) Add to your collection of Click-ers. (4) Say the daily devos for Week 35. (5) Check out Tuesday of Week 17 for a related devo on God being the guide by your side.

NOW, THAT'S LOUD!

A male lion's roar can be heard up to five miles away.

LUKE, CHAPTER 4 (VERSES 17-18)

The scroll of Isaiah the prophet was handed to him. He unrolled the scroll and found the place where this was written: "The Spirit of the LORD is upon me. . . ."

DAILY DEVO

With HoneyWord I can race to the right place.

In the days of Jesus, the New Testament hadn't been written yet. The Old Testament had been written on scrolls that were rolled up. It took stacks and stacks of them to hold the entire Old Testament. So when the scroll of Isaiah the prophet was handed to Jesus, how did he know where to find the words he wanted to read? He had learned God's Word so well that he had no trouble finding just the right verse at just the right time. These daily devos will help you do the very same thing. As you learn the book and chapter location of more and more daily devos, you'll be able to find the words you need for any situation you face. The more you let these daily devos click and stick, the more quickly you'll be able to race to the right place every time.

MAKE IT STICK

List the Click-ers for some of your favorite daily devos. Now hand the list to one of your parents. Let him or her check to see how fast you can say and race to the right book and chapter place of each one. You'll amaze your mom or dad with how many you know!

PRAYER

Dear God, I want to remember how to find stuff in your Word. Then I'll always know how to obey you. Thank you for my daily devos. They remind me where to find all the things I need to know. Amen.

CLICK-ER: RACE CAR

Whenever you see, play with, or think about a *race car*, let this daily devo zoom through your mind as it clicks and sticks. Luke the Lion with his four-on-the-floorboard reminds you that the devo is from Luke, Chapter 4.

LUKE, CHAPTER 9 (VERSE 62)

Jesus told him, "Anyone who puts a hand to the plow and then looks back is not fit for the Kingdom of God."

DAILY DEVO

I vow to plow with God.

Just talking about your commitment to follow God is easy. But putting God first and actually doing what he wants is probably the hardest thing you'll ever do. This verse is from a story about some men who walked with Jesus to Jerusalem, where he would die on the cross for the sins of the world. All of the guys talked a good game about their decision to follow Jesus. But when he challenged them to prove it with their actions, they all came up with excuses that sounded good but really weren't. What are your excuses? Whatever they are, get rid of them. Vow to plow with God today. And never turn back.

 MAKE IT STICK

When a person "puts a hand to the plow," he's starting a job that needs to be finished. Farmers plow big fields to get the dirt ready for planting crops. What job do you need to finish? How about cleaning your room from top to bottom! Keep "plowing" until you're totally finished. Then say this daily devo as you make a commitment to keep following God until he takes you to heaven someday.

PRAYER

Dear God, I'm still young, but I already know that following you is a big commitment. It's easy to make excuses, but I want to do what you want. Help me to live for you now so that someday I can live with you forever. In Jesus' name, amen.

CLICK-ER: PLOW

Whenever you see, use, or think about a *plow*, let this daily devo cut through your heart as it clicks and sticks. Luke the Lion with his nine-foot-pine reminds you that the devo is from Luke, Chapter 9.

LUKE, CHAPTER 10 (VERSE 21)

Jesus was filled with the joy of the Holy Spirit, and he said, "O Father, Lord of heaven and earth, thank you for hiding these things from those who think themselves wise and clever, and for revealing them to the childlike. Yes, Father, it pleased you to do it this way."

DAILY DEVO

God himself puts his cookies on the lower shelf.

Kids like you have hearts of faith—the number one thing that pleases God. That's why Jesus broke out in praise to God for kids who keep the Christian life simple, as it's supposed to be. The hidden things Jesus referred to here are the yummy spiritual cookies of God's Word. He stores them on the lower shelf so trusting hearts like yours can easily grab a fistful. Are you eating God's cookies? If you'll commit to "eating" (learning) a verse a day, you'll be amazed at how delicious each "cookie" (message from God) actually is. So open your Bible, reach in, and grab one.

 MAKE IT STICK

Write out 10 daily devos and their locations. Beside each daily devo, write its Click-er. Then politely ask your dad or mom if you can have a "spiritual cookies" contest. Put a bag of cookies on the table. When your parent names a Click-er, place one cookie in front of you if you can say its daily devo and the book and chapter location. You get to keep as many cookies as you win, but you can't eat them until you get permission!

PRAYER

Dear God, I'm glad you give kids like me the gift of faith. Help me to learn the meaning of lots of verses from your Word so my faith in you will keep growing and growing. In the name of Jesus I pray. Amen.

CLICK-ER: COOKIES

Whenever you see, eat, or think about your favorite *cookies*, let your mind snack on this yummy daily devo as it clicks and sticks. Luke the Lion with his one-on-a-bun and halo-is-a-hero-as-a-zero reminds you that the devo is from Luke, Chapter 10.

LUKE, CHAPTER 17 (VERSES 15-17)

One [leper], when he saw that he was healed, came back to Jesus, shouting, "Praise God!" He fell to the ground at Jesus' feet, thanking him for what he had done. This man was a Samaritan. Jesus asked, "Didn't I heal ten men? Where are the other nine?"

DAILY DEVO

Like the lone leper, I pepper God with praise.

You'd think that after being instantly cured of leprosy, a terrible disease many people had in Jesus' day, all ten lepers would have shouted their thanks to God. But only one did. And to him Jesus said, "Didn't I heal ten men? Where are the other nine?" We're often a lot like those nine men. We pray and pray and pray when we need God's help. Then after he answers, we forget to thank him. Let's be like the lone leper and pepper God with praise for everything he does for us. If you start being thankful now, not only will you develop a great attitude, but you'll positively stand out for the rest of your life.

 MAKE IT STICK

Shake some pepper from a pepper shaker into your hand. All the grains that sprinkle out are a picture of how often we should pepper God with praise. Just for fun, go outside and say this daily devo as you sprinkle some pepper on the ground. Then thank God for one special thing he's done for you today.

PRAYER

Dear God, I praise you for making the world, the sun, the moon, and the stars. I praise you for all the ways you show that you love me. Most of all, I praise you for your Son, Jesus. Amen.

CLICK-ER:
PEPPER SHAKER

Whenever you see, use, or think about a *pepper shaker*, let this daily devo season your heart with praise as it clicks and sticks. Luke the Lion with his one-on-a-bun and highway-seven-to-heaven sign reminds you that the devo is from Luke, Chapter 17.

LUKE, CHAPTER 18 (VERSE 16)

Then Jesus called for the children and said to the disciples, "Let the children come to me. Don't stop them! For the Kingdom of God belongs to those who are like these children."

DAILY DEVO

Jesus never puts the lid on any kid.

Some of the 12 disciples must have believed the line "Children should be seen and not heard." Why else would they have told parents to keep their kids away from Jesus and not bother him? Thankfully, Jesus heard them trying to put lids on all those kids and warmly welcomed the kids into his arms. You see, Jesus knows how wiggly, giggly kids can sometimes irritate the stew out of adults. But he also knows how much these grown-ups need the same kind of faith as squirmy, softhearted kids. As we're growing up, we need the loving boundaries that parents and other adults place around us. But when it comes to trusting God, remember this: Jesus never puts the lid on any kid. Ever.

MAKE IT STICK

Write this daily devo on a slip of paper and put it in a container with a lid. Put the lid on and then take it off as you say this daily devo.

PRAYER

Thank you, Jesus, for letting me talk to you anytime I want. I know you're never too busy for me. And you'll never send me away. Thanks for listening to me right now. I love you, Jesus, with all my heart. Amen.

CLICK-ER: LID

Whenever you see, take off, or think about a *lid*, let this daily devo open your heart and mind as it clicks and sticks. Luke the Lion with his one-on-a-bun and eight-under-skates reminds you that the devo is from Luke, Chapter 18.

LUKE, CHAPTER 24 (VERSES 1, 3-6)

The women went to the tomb . . . but they didn't find the body of the Lord Jesus. As they stood there puzzled, two men suddenly appeared to them, clothed in dazzling robes. The women were terrified and bowed with their faces to the ground. Then the men asked, "Why are you looking among the dead for someone who is alive? He isn't here! He is risen from the dead!"

DAILY DEVO

Give me five—he's alive!

"He isn't here! He is risen from the dead!" Those are exciting words. God won! He defeated death! Jesus took on Satan and his entire army and came back a triumphant champion. Because of Jesus' resurrection—his coming back to life from the dead—we too will one day have life after death. And right now, this resurrection power can make us clean from our sin. Because Jesus lives, his resurrection power gives us, as his followers, a supernatural desire to learn about God from his Word and to live the way he wants us to. And we have the power to experience God's love, joy, and peace in our hearts. So give me five—he's alive!

 MAKE IT STICK

Politely ask your dad or mom to read you Luke, Chapter 24 (verses 1-34). Ask what the resurrection of Jesus means to him or her. After your brief discussion, give each other a high five and say this daily devo in unison.

PRAYER

Jesus, you're alive! And because you came back to life, I know that someday I'll do that too. Thank you for being with me even now, and filling me with love and joy and peace. Amen.

CLICK-ER: HIGH FIVE

Whenever you feel alive and give someone a *high five*, point to heaven as this daily devo clicks and sticks. Luke the Lion with his two-blue-shoes and four-on-the-floorboard reminds you that the devo is from Luke, Chapter 24.

WEEKEND ACTIVITY IDEAS

(1) Highlight the verses for Week 36 in your Bible. (2) Find Luke the Lion in each of the pictures for this week and identify the chapter-number symbols. (3) Add to your collection of Click-ers. (4) Say the daily devos for Week 36. (5) Check out Wednesday of Week 40 for a related devo on Jesus being your divine Valentine.

PREY AWAY

Lions live in family groups called prides. All groups of lions fiercely defend themselves against any outside lions attempting to break in and join their families.

Week 37, Monday

BOOK OF JOHN
John the Giraffe

Giraffe begins with the same sound as *John*. The giraffe, with its long neck, pictures the long reach of John's Gospel. When you see John the Giraffe in a picture, you'll know the daily devo is from John. Connected to John the Giraffe are number symbols. (See page 15.) They make the chapter location of the devo click and stick.

John was Jesus' best friend. He wrote the book of John to prove that Jesus really is the Son of God and that all who believe in him will have eternal life. Like a giraffe, John reached up to grab high thoughts about God and brought them down to our level on earth. He put the spiritual cookies on the lower shelf. That's why the Gospel of John is a great place to start reading the Bible.

 MAKE IT STICK

Make a tab to mark the book of John in your Bible. (See Week 1, Monday, for directions.)

John is the only Gospel writer who tells about Jesus' first miracle—turning water into wine. The story is in John, Chapter 2 (verses 1-12). Ask a grown-up to please read it to you, or find it in a Bible storybook and read it by yourself. You may want to draw a picture of the wedding and put yourself in the picture. Do you think you would have believed Jesus is God's Son if you had been there?

Whenever you see a giraffe or a picture of one, think about John the Giraffe and the book of John.

JUST FOR FUN

In the book of John, there is a prayer that Jesus prayed for *you*! Look it up and read it in John, Chapter 17 (verses 20-26). What did Jesus pray about when he talked to God about you?

PRAYER

Lord God, thank you for all the stories in the Bible that help me believe Jesus really is your Son. And thank you so much, Jesus, for praying to God, your heavenly Father, for me. Amen.

JOHN, CHAPTER 1 (VERSE 14)

So the Word became human and made his home among us. He was full of unfailing love and faithfulness. And we have seen his glory, the glory of the Father's one and only Son.

DAILY DEVO
Jesus is the picture-book story of God's amazing glory.

The Bible is one huge picture-book story about the glory of God. It paints picture after picture of the great things God did that bring glory to his name. To give someone glory simply means to bring honor to that person. When we follow God's ways, we honor him and give him glory. But the greatest picture-book story about the glory of God is Jesus. Everything he said and did while he lived on earth is a perfect picture of the one true God—because Jesus *is* God! Would you like to get to know God better? If so, just keep reading his book and following the pictures.

MAKE IT STICK

Make your own picture book by stapling at least three sheets of paper together. Write this daily devo on the front. On the rest of the pages, draw pictures of your favorite stories about Jesus. On the last page draw yourself giving glory to God. Then thank God for letting you honor him by telling others about his glory.

PRAYER

Thank you, God, for the way Jesus helps me understand what you are like. When I learn about him, I learn about you. Help me to honor you the way Jesus did, by telling others about your greatness and glory. Amen.

CLICK-ER: PICTURE BOOK

Whenever you see, read, or flip through a *picture book*, paint this daily devo in your mind as it clicks and sticks. John the Giraffe with his one-on-a-bun reminds you that the devo is from John, Chapter 1.

JOHN, CHAPTER 3 (VERSE 16)

For God loved the world so much that he gave his one and only Son, so that everyone who believes in him will not perish but have eternal life.

DAILY DEVO

God's gift is my only lift to heaven.

Hey, did you know God has a gift for you? John, Chapter 3 (verse 16) is probably the best and most famous one-verse summary of God's gift in the Bible. In fewer than 30 words we see and feel his deep desire for all people everywhere to live with him forever after we die. God loves us too much to let us miss out on heaven, so he sent us a gift. That gift is a person—God's own Son, Jesus, who died on the cross for our sins. All we have to do is believe in Jesus and reach out to accept him like a gift. He's better than any other gift we could ever get. Will you receive God's gift right now? Please do. Jesus, God's gift, is your only lift to heaven.

 MAKE IT STICK

Find a picture of Jesus in a Sunday school paper or draw a picture of him and write his name under it. Then fold it, place it in a small box, and gift wrap it. After your gift is ready, sit down with your dad, mom, or a friend and use John, Chapter 3 (verse 16) to tell the story of Jesus. Hand over the gift, and give that person the joy of receiving it and opening it up.

PRAYER

Dear God, thank you for sending me Jesus, the best gift I've ever gotten! And Jesus, I'm so glad I can believe in you and receive you as my Savior. Thank you for promising eternal life to everyone who believes in you. Amen.

CLICK-ER: GIFT

Whenever you give, receive, or think about a *gift*, let your heart unwrap this daily devo as it clicks and sticks. John the Giraffe with his three-is-the-key reminds you that the devo is from John, Chapter 3.

JOHN, CHAPTER 4 (VERSES 17-18)

"I don't have a husband," the woman replied. Jesus said, "You're right! You don't have a husband—for you have had five husbands, and you aren't even married to the man you're living with now. You certainly spoke the truth!"

DAILY DEVO

Be true 'cause Jesus can see right through.

Sometimes we tell lies to make ourselves look good. We might say we hit two home runs when we only hit a single. Other times it just seems easier to lie or not be totally honest. But the best choice is to tell the whole truth. The woman at the well found that out when she told Jesus, "I don't have a husband." Jesus said, "You're right! . . . You have had five husbands, and you aren't even married to the man you're living with now." Then the woman understood just how special Jesus was—he knew the whole truth and still cared about her. Jesus could see into her heart, and he can see into yours and mine, too. So let's speak the whole truth—always.

MAKE IT STICK

Write this daily devo on a three-by-five card. Now tape it facedown to the outside of a see-through water pitcher (or large glass). Fill the pitcher with water and read the daily devo through the water from the opposite side. Jesus can see through your heart in the same way! For the next day or two, each time you pour water from that pitcher, say this daily devo.

PRAYER

Lord Jesus, please help me remember to always tell the truth, especially when I speak with you. I know you can see right through me, so teach me how to talk to you about everything in my heart. Amen.

CLICK-ER: SEE-THROUGH WATER PITCHER

Whenever you see, use, or think about a *see-through water pitcher*, let this daily devo pour into your heart as it clicks and sticks. John the Giraffe with his four-on-the-floorboard reminds you that the devo is from John, Chapter 4.

JOHN, CHAPTER 5 (VERSE 18)

The Jewish leaders tried all the harder to find a way to kill [Jesus]. For he not only broke the Sabbath, he called God his Father, thereby making himself equal with God.

DAILY DEVO

I'm good at godly math: Jesus = God.

Almost everyone knows that $1 + 1 = 2$. The basic laws of math never change, and neither does God. But heavenly math is different from earthly math. The Bible teaches that the one true God exists in three different persons: God the Father, Son, and Holy Spirit. If we showed this as a spiritual math equation, it would look like this: $1 + 1 + 1 = 1$. From God's point of view, this makes perfect sense. Jesus equals God, just as the Father equals God and the Holy Spirit equals God—one God in three persons who all exist at the same time. This mystery is hard to understand, but it's clearly what God wants us to believe.

MAKE IT STICK

Here's a way to "see" how the one true God exists in three different persons. Put three ice cubes in a bowl. Microwave them until they melt into a pool of water. Then politely ask your dad or mom to boil the water until it turns into steam. God the Father, Son, and Holy Spirit are one God just as the steam, liquid, and ice are the same water seen in three different ways. As you think this through, thank God for helping you believe that Jesus equals God.

PRAYER

Thank you, Lord, for helping me believe that you are one God in three persons—God the Father, God the Son, and God the Holy Spirit. It's a mystery I don't understand, but I still believe it. Amen.

CLICK-ER: EQUAL SIGN (=)

Whenever you see, write, or think about an *equal sign (=)*, let this daily devo add up in your mind as it clicks and sticks. John the Giraffe with his five-on-a-hive-hat reminds you that the devo is from John, Chapter 5.

JOHN, CHAPTER 6 (VERSES 8-9)

Andrew, Simon Peter's brother, spoke up. "There's a young boy here with five barley loaves and two fish. But what good is that with this huge crowd?"

DAILY DEVO

I have a hunch Jesus wants my lunch.

Jesus was such an amazing healer that people would follow him around for hours, sometimes even forgetting to eat. In this story, almost everyone had forgotten to bring a lunch. What would they eat? Andrew found a boy with a heart full of love who was willing to share his lunch. Kids like him—like you—almost always have hearts full of love for God. So Jesus took the boy's little lunch and made it feed a lot of people—just the men numbered 5,000! Everybody got an all-you-can-eat meal, with more left over than what the little boy first gave Jesus. The point is this: It's not the *little* that we can give, but the *big* that Jesus can do when we put it in his hands.

 MAKE IT STICK

Think of one thing you do well or would like to do well. Write it on a slip of paper and put it in a brown lunch bag at bedtime. For the next six nights, hold your "little lunch" up to God in prayer, asking him to take your *little* and make it *a lot*. Then get ready. Over time, you'll be amazed at how God takes your little and turns it into a lot.

PRAYER

Dear God, I want to be like the little boy who shared his lunch. Please take my little, and give me the patience to wait and see what amazing things you do with it. In Jesus' name, amen.

CLICK-ER:

BROWN-BAG LUNCH

Whenever you see, eat, or think about a *brown-bag lunch*, let your heart hunger for this daily devo as it clicks and sticks. John the Giraffe with his six-pick-up-stix reminds you that the devo is from John, Chapter 6.

WEEKEND ACTIVITY IDEAS

(1) Highlight the verses for Week 37 in your Bible. (2) Find John the Giraffe in each picture for this week and identify the chapter-number symbols. (3) Add to your collection of Click-ers. (4) Say the daily devos for Week 37. (5) Check out Friday of Week 44 for a related devo on how you can be a can-do kid for God.

A TALL ORDER

As the world's tallest animal, a giraffe stands
20 feet tall and can run 35 miles an hour.

JOHN, CHAPTER 6 (VERSE 48)
Yes, I am the bread of life!

DAILY DEVO

Jesus is the bread that keeps me fed.

After Jesus fed over 5000 people, everybody was excited about the free lunch program they thought he'd started. So they found him again the next day. Jesus knew they were just looking for another meal deal. But instead of giving out yummy sub sandwiches, Jesus gave the people a message on how he wanted to be their spiritual bread. Just as food fills your stomach and keeps your body going, Jesus, the Bread of Life, gives your spirit and soul the spiritual get-up-and-go to follow God. Believe in Jesus today and receive him into your life. Then, as you "feed" on him in God's Word, he'll lead the way, day by day.

 MAKE IT STICK

Make your favorite sandwich. Carefully write the name *Jesus* on each piece of bread, using a squirt bottle of mustard, ketchup, or mayonnaise. Before eating your meal, say this daily devo. Then think about how Jesus feeds your soul like this sandwich fills your stomach.

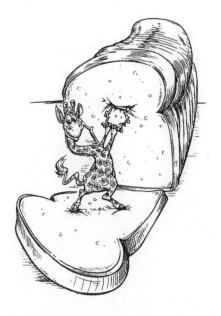

PRAYER

Thank you, Lord, for feeding my body, soul, and spirit with your life-giving Word. Thank you for being the spiritual bread that keeps me going day after day as I follow you. In the name of Jesus I pray. Amen.

CLICK-ER: **BREAD**

Whenever you see, eat, or think about any kind of *bread*, let your mind take a big bite of this daily devo as it clicks and sticks. John the Giraffe with his six-pick-up-stix reminds you that the devo is from John, Chapter 6.

JOHN, CHAPTER 8 (VERSE 12)

Jesus spoke to the people once more and said, "I am the light of the world. If you follow me, you won't have to walk in darkness, because you will have the light that leads to life."

DAILY DEVO

Jesus is my flashlight, day and night.

Have you ever gone camping? If you're not used to it, night in the country can be quite a shock—it's very dark without city lights. That's when a flashlight really makes a big difference. It can keep you from stumbling over a fallen tree branch on the way to the bathroom. And when you get the munchies, your flashlight can help you find the snack bag. Jesus tells us that he is light. When we follow him, he lights the way in front of us just like a flashlight. Step by step, he shows us the right path to take. He also shows us there are wrong things we should stay away from. And one more thing: The light of Jesus never goes out, never needs new batteries. He's always there, lighting the way day and night, so stick tight to him.

 MAKE IT STICK

Write this daily devo on a slip of paper and tape it to a flashlight. If your family doesn't have a flashlight, draw a picture of the one you'd like to have. Then imagine yourself using it in the dark as you say this daily devo.

PRAYER

Dear God, sometimes I feel like I'm in the dark and don't know what to do. But I'm so glad your Son, Jesus, is the light who shows me the right way to go and the right things to do. Amen.

CLICK-ER: FLASHLIGHT

Whenever you see, use, or think about a *flashlight*, let this daily devo flash through your mind as it clicks and sticks. John the Giraffe with his eight-under-skates reminds you that the devo is from John, Chapter 8.

JOHN, CHAPTER 10 (VERSE 27)

My sheep listen to my voice; I know them, and they follow me.

DAILY DEVO

Jesus steers through listening ears.

Back in the days of Jesus, shepherds brought their flocks together at night for sheep sleepovers. They all stayed in a special pen with high walls that kept the sheep safe from wild animals. So how did the shepherds know which sheep were theirs each morning? Simple. Sheep aren't the smartest animals in the world, but they do recognize and follow the voices of their own shepherds. Every day each shepherd called his sheep by name and led them out to green pastures. Jesus said that we're like sheep and he is our Shepherd. He shows us how to follow him by speaking quietly to our souls as we read God's Word and pray. Then he steers through listening ears. Are you listening?

MAKE IT STICK

Look in a mirror and use your fingers to wiggle your ears back and forth while repeating this daily devo. Then ask God to give you ears that listen for his voice.

PRAYER

Dear Lord, I'm really glad you want to be my good Shepherd, because I really want to be one of your good sheep. As I read your Word and listen to your voice, please give me a heart that wants to follow only you. Thanks! Amen.

CLICK-ER: EAR

Whenever you see, touch, or think about an *ear*, let this daily devo steer your heart as it clicks and sticks. John the Giraffe with his one-on-a-bun and halo-is-a-hero-as-a-zero reminds you that the devo is from John, Chapter 10.

JOHN, CHAPTER 14 (VERSE 6)

Jesus told [Thomas], "I am the way, the truth, and the life. No one can come to the Father except through me.

DAILY DEVO

Jesus is my complete one-way street to heaven.

What if your parents got lost while taking you to a friend's house? Would they want directions from someone who had no idea where your friend lived, or from somebody who really knew how to get there? Unfortunately, many people think they know the way to heaven and believe there are many ways to get there. As you grow older, you'll hear more and more about this. But Jesus, who came to earth from heaven and really knows the way, made it super clear that the only way to heaven is through him. Don't believe anyone who says differently. Jesus, the Son of God, is *the* only complete, one-way street to heaven. And if you truly believe in him as your only way to God the Father, then you're on the road to heaven.

 ### MAKE IT STICK

Make a one-way street sign on a piece of paper or cardboard. Then tape it to the door of a room in your house that only has one door. Just as there is only one door into this room, there is only one way to God. That Way is a person, and his name is Jesus!

PRAYER

Lord Jesus, thank you for making it so clear that believing in you is the only true way to get to heaven. No matter what others may say, please help me to believe that it's only what you say that really counts. Amen.

CLICK-ER: ONE-WAY STREET SIGN

Whenever you see, follow, or think about a *one-way street sign*, let this daily devo direct your mind as it clicks and sticks. John the Giraffe with his one-on-a-bun and four-on-the-floorboard reminds you that the devo is from John, Chapter 14.

JOHN, CHAPTER 15 (VERSE 5)

Yes, I am the vine; you are the branches. Those who remain in me, and I in them, will produce much fruit. For apart from me you can do nothing.

DAILY DEVO

I only shine when I stick to the Vine.

Bananas don't grow on grocery-store shelves. And strawberries don't sprout from green plastic bins. All fruit comes from branches attached to living plants. Apples grow on apple tree branches. Peaches grow on peach tree branches. And grapes come through grapevine branches. But no fruit grows on branches that have broken off the vine. That's why it's so important that we as branches stay connected to Jesus, our Vine. When we do, we become more and more like him as his spiritual fruit grows in us—fruit like love, joy, peace, patience, kindness, goodness, faithfulness, gentleness, and self-control. (See the book of Galatians, Chapter 5, verses 22-23.) So stick to the Vine. It's the only way to shine.

MAKE IT STICK

The next time your dad or mom buys grapes, politely ask if you can have a small bunch. If you are given one, use a string to tie it to a plant in your house or garden for a day. Let the vine stem remind you to stick to Jesus so you can shine on his vine.

PRAYER

Dear God, thank you for all the things I can be and all the things I can do for you when I let Jesus' love shine through me. Please teach me how to stick close to you every day, Lord Jesus. In your name I pray. Amen.

CLICK-ER: VINE

Whenever you see, touch, or think about a *vine*, let this daily devo wind around your mind as it clicks and sticks. John the Giraffe with his one-on-a-bun and five-on-a-hive-hat reminds you that the devo is from John, Chapter 15.

JOHN, CHAPTER 19 (VERSES 17-18)

Carrying the cross by himself, [Jesus] went to the place called Place of the Skull (in Hebrew, Golgotha). There they nailed him to the cross. Two others were crucified with him, one on either side, with Jesus between them.

DAILY DEVO

My Boss suffered on the cross.

Jesus suffered terrible pain for the sins of the world. He was beaten, mocked, and forced to wear a crown of thorns. When he was completely worn out, he had to carry his own cross to the place where he was nailed to it. But greater than the physical pain was the spiritual pain he went through as he took the blame for our sins. By taking our sins onto himself, he was separated from God the Father for the first time. It was more painful than anything he'd ever experienced. But he did it so we could become part of God's family. It was a strange but wonderful moment in history. Here the one true Boss of the universe was willing to suffer on a cross made by people he had created. Now that's love. True love.

 MAKE IT STICK

Make a cross out of two small sticks, wires, or Popsicle sticks. Then stop for a moment and think about the price Jesus paid for your sins. Thank him for dying for you and coming back to life to be your Savior.

PRAYER

Dear Jesus, it's hard to understand why you had to go through so much pain. But it makes me know how much you love me. Thank you for dying on the cross and coming back to life so I can be forgiven. Amen.

CLICK-ER: CROSS

Whenever you see, touch, or think about a *cross*, let this daily devo crisscross your heart as it clicks and sticks. John the Giraffe with his one-on-a-bun and nine-foot-pine reminds you that the devo is from John, Chapter 19.

284

WEEKEND ACTIVITY IDEAS

(1) Highlight the verses for Week 38 in your Bible. (2) Find John the Giraffe in each picture for this week and identify the chapter-number symbols. (3) Add to your collection of Click-ers. (4) Say the daily devos for Week 38. (5) Check out Wednesday of Week 52 for a related devo on being hot sauce for the one true Boss.

HEART OF HEARTS

A giraffe has a big heart—it's 2 feet long and weighs 24 pounds.

Week 39, Monday

BOOK OF ACTS
Emmett the Ant

Ant begins with the same letter as *Acts*. Like an ant, the early church carried loads many times heavier than itself. When you see Emmett the Ant in a picture (Emmett means "ant"), you'll know the daily devo is from Acts. Connected to Emmett the Ant are number symbols. (See page 15.) They make the chapter location of the devo click and stick.

After Jesus left the earth and went back to heaven, the Holy Spirit came. And *kaboom!* It was as if he lit a firecracker in the opening of a small anthill. Before the sand had settled, these supercharged "human ants" were scurrying around, taking the gospel to everyone in the world. But these followers of Jesus didn't do this in their own power. Just as God gives an ant strength to carry loads many times heavier than itself, the Holy Spirit energized God's antlike people to tirelessly do mighty "acts" beyond their natural strength and know-how. And he wants to do the same thing through you today.

MAKE IT STICK

Make a tab to mark the book of Acts in your Bible. (See Week 1, Monday, for directions.)

Find a picture book that shows ants working together in an ant colony. Notice how each one works hard doing its own job. After Jesus returned to heaven, all of his followers worked together like busy ants, each with a special job to do. See Acts, Chapter 6 (verses 2-4).

Whenever you watch an ant or look at a picture of one, remember Emmett the Ant and the book of Acts.

JUST FOR FUN

The amazing story about how Jesus appeared to Paul is found in the book of Acts, Chapter 9 (verses 1-19). You can read about it with your family. Then look for maps that show the busy life Paul lived traveling for the Lord on missionary trips.

PRAYER

Dear God, like the first followers of your Son, Jesus, I want to do my part in making your Kingdom grow. Please give me the power to do the acts of love and kindness that you want me to do. In Jesus' name, amen.

ACTS, CHAPTER 1 (VERSE 8)

You will receive power when the Holy Spirit comes upon you. And you will be my witnesses, telling people about me everywhere—in Jerusalem, throughout Judea, in Samaria, and to the ends of the earth.

DAILY DEVO

I delight in Holy Spirit dynamite.

Dynamite was invented in 1866 by Alfred Nobel, who figured out how to mix a little of this with a little of that to make big explosions. The primary purpose of dynamite is to move a huge pile of rocks or dirt quickly, as when digging a canal or blasting out a foundation. In the same way, the Holy Spirit is at work all over the world today, moving great kids like you to speak up about Jesus. Whether he blasts you next door or across the world someday, you need his power to be his witness. So ask God to fill you with his Spirit. Then delight in the dynamite things he does through you.

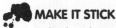

MAKE IT STICK

Politely ask your dad or mom to help you locate the city of Jerusalem on a world map. Think about how the message of Jesus moved from there to your town. The Holy Spirit moved someone to tell somebody else, who told the next person, until someone told you. Ask God to help you think of one person he'd like for you to introduce to Jesus. Now say this daily devo as you pray for God's power to be his witness.

PRAYER

Thank you, God, for the Holy Spirit, who gives me all the power I need to be a faithful witness for you. Please show me what to do and say to help my friends learn about Jesus. In his name I pray. Amen.

CLICK-ER: DYNAMITE

Whenever you see or hear a blast of *dynamite* on TV or at a movie, let this daily devo blow your mind as it clicks and sticks. Emmett the Ant with his one-on-a-bun reminds you that the devo is from Acts, Chapter 1.

ACTS, CHAPTER 4 (VERSE 37)

[Barnabas] sold a field he owned and brought the money to the apostles.

DAILY DEVO

I'm willing to yield my field.

Yield signs remind drivers to slow down and give way to the flow of traffic *before* entering it. As Christians, we have similar signs along the road of life that teach us how to go with the flow of God's Kingdom. When he begins leading us in a new direction, God wants us to slow down and yield to whatever he's doing at that time. God gave Barnabas a new direction, asking him to sell a field he owned and give it to Jesus' disciples, who could use the money to help those in need. So Barnabas, who was willing to yield, sold his field and went where God wanted him to be at that time. In what direction is God leading you? Whatever it is, yield. It's the only way to go.

 MAKE IT STICK

Draw a picture of yourself holding a yield sign in your hand. Write this daily devo below your drawing. Then ask God in prayer if there's anything he wants you to yield to him today so you can help someone else. End your prayer by saying this daily devo.

PRAYER

Dear God, please make me willing to yield some of my things to you. Help me to give something away today that someone needs. Show me what to give and who to give it to. In Jesus' name I pray. Amen.

CLICK-ER: YIELD SIGN

Whenever you see, pass by, or think about a *yield sign*, let your heart give way to this daily devo as it clicks and sticks. Emmett the Ant with his four-on-the-floorboard reminds you that the devo is from Acts, Chapter 4.

ACTS, CHAPTER 12 (VERSES 6–7)

[Peter] was asleep, fastened with two chains between two soldiers. Others stood guard at the prison gate. Suddenly, there was a bright light in the cell, and an angel of the Lord stood before Peter. The angel struck him on the side to awaken him and said, "Quick! Get up!" And the chains fell off his wrists.

DAILY DEVO

I can't explain, but prayer can break a chain.

Because of his great love for God, Peter was unfairly thrown in jail and chained between two soldiers. So the church prayed for his release. Then, right in the middle of their prayer meeting, Peter himself knocked on the front door. The servant girl was so happy to hear his voice that she left him outside behind the closed door. When she told everybody that God had answered their prayers, they all told her she was crazy. You see, nobody can explain the power of prayer. Sometimes God answers quickly. Sometimes he seems to take forever. Other times he says no, so we think he didn't answer at all. But God wants us to know that our prayers always make a difference. Don't try to explain. Just pray and watch God break chains.

MAKE IT STICK

Write each word of this daily devo on a narrow strip of paper. Then have fun making a paper chain by stapling or gluing the strips together in order. When you're done, say this daily devo out loud as you break your chain in two. Now pray about some "chain" (problem) that you want God to help you break.

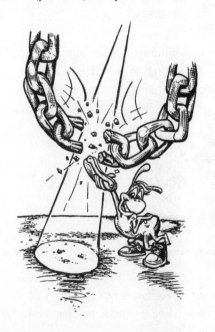

PRAYER

Dear God, I'm glad you always know the best way to answer my prayers. Thank you for taking care of me in just the right way at just the right time. In Jesus' name, amen.

CLICK-ER: CHAIN

Whenever you see, use, or think about a heavy *chain*, let this daily devo unshackle your heart as it clicks and sticks. Emmett the Ant with his one-on-a-bun and two-blue-shoes reminds you that the devo is from Acts, Chapter 12.

ACTS, CHAPTER 12 (VERSE 23)

Instantly, an angel of the Lord struck Herod with a sickness, because he accepted the people's worship instead of giving the glory to God. So he was consumed with worms and died.

DAILY DEVO

I squirm just thinking about Herod's worms.

God made tons of different kinds of worms. He made flatworms, roundworms, pinworms, and hookworms. He also made helpful earthworms and cute little inchworms. We don't know what kind of worms God gave Herod, but it's a safe bet they weren't the nice kind, because they killed him. This story isn't disgusting because of slimy worms. It's gross because a man was so full of himself that he could think of no one else—not even God. This sad, evil king was so taken with himself that he actually allowed his people to worship him like a god. When you squirm just thinking about Herod's worms, remember this: We are to worship no one but God—not ourselves or anyone else.

MAKE IT STICK

Politely ask your dad or mom to buy you a pack of gummy worms the next time he or she is at the grocery store. Before you pop one of these tasty worms in your mouth, say this daily devo about some not-so-good worms. Then thank God for teaching you to worship no one but him.

PRAYER

Dear God, since you alone are the one true King of the universe, I promise to give you all my praise and worship. Thank you for reminding me to never glorify anyone but you. In Jesus' name I pray. Amen.

CLICK-ER: WORMS

Whenever you see, touch, or think about *worms*, let this daily devo wiggle through your mind as it clicks and sticks. Emmett the Ant with his one-on-a-bun and two-blue-shoes reminds you that the devo is from Acts, Chapter 12.

ACTS, CHAPTER 14 (VERSES 21-22)

Paul and Barnabas . . . strengthened the believers. They encouraged them to continue in the faith, reminding them that we must suffer many hardships to enter the Kingdom of God.

DAILY DEVO

I need grace to reach home base.

Life is like the game of baseball. The goal is to get around all the bases and score a run. But every batter is up against nine players on the opposite team who will try hard to get him or her out. When Paul and Barnabas talked to believers, they reminded everyone that life also is full of opposition. If you're going through a difficult time, God hasn't left you. In fact, it's a sure sign that he loves you. Huh? You see, God allows all the players on his team to go through hard times. This is so we will learn to depend on his grace—his kindness and help—to get us from base to base. Receive God's grace. It's the only way to get to home base.

 MAKE IT STICK

Draw a picture of yourself up at bat. Then draw Jesus standing behind you with his hands on the bat with yours. That's a picture of God's grace. He stays with us throughout our lives, helping us step by step, base by base, until we safely reach heaven, our home base.

PRAYER

Dear God, even when I go through hard times, I know you're with me. Thank you for everyone who encourages me to keep going and keep trusting you all the way home to heaven. Amen.

CLICK-ER: HOME BASE

Whenever you see, touch, or think about *home base*, let this daily devo slide into your heart as it clicks and sticks. Emmett the Ant with his one-on-a-bun and four-on-the-floorboard reminds you that the devo is from Acts, Chapter 14.

WEEKEND ACTIVITY IDEAS

(1) Highlight the verses for Week 39 in your Bible. (2) Find the HoneyWord animal in each of the pictures for this week and identify the chapter-number symbols. (3) Add to your collection of Click-ers. (4) Say the daily devos for Week 39. (5) Check out Wednesday of Week 37 for a related devo on the gift that's your only lift to heaven.

ANTS ON YOUR PLANTS

Standing on its own six legs, an ant can lift stuff 20 to 50 times its own weight.

Week 40, Monday

BOOK OF ROMANS
Roman the Rhino

Rhinoceros begins with the same letter as *Romans*. Just as a rhino makes a point with its horn, Paul makes one big point in the book of Romans: God loves you and wants to be your best friend. When you see Roman the Rhino in a picture, you'll know the daily devo is from Romans. Connected to Roman the Rhino are number symbols. (See page 15.) They make the chapter location of the devo click and stick.

The new Christians in Rome had all sorts of questions about the Christian faith, and Paul answered them in this remarkable book. But reading the book of Romans is like standing in the way of a charging rhinoceros. If you stay still long enough, sooner or later you'll get the "Big Point": God loves you and has already taken the first step in becoming your best friend. He sent his Son, Jesus, to die on the cross for your sins. In this letter to the Romans, Paul tells us point by point why Jesus came, why he died, and why faith is important. So read the book and get the point.

 **MAKE IT STICK**

Make a tab to mark the book of Romans in your Bible. (See Week 1, Monday, for directions.)

For a cone-shaped rhino horn, roll up a piece of heavy paper so it comes to a point at one end. Make a hole on each side of the wide end, and at each hole attach a string that's long enough to go around your head. Wear this horn over your nose, and gently nudge family and friends with the "Big Point" of Romans: God loves you and wants to be your best friend.

Whenever you see a rhinoceros or a picture of one, remember Roman the Rhino and the book of Romans.

JUST FOR FUN

Read about God's love in Romans, Chapter 8 (verses 38-39). Is there anything that can separate you from God and his love?

PRAYER

Lord, I'm so glad you want to be my best friend, because I want to be yours, too. Thank you for the promise in your Word that nothing will ever be able to separate me from your love. That's really cool, God. Amen.

ROMANS, CHAPTER 1 (VERSE 18-19)

God shows his anger from heaven against all sinful, wicked people who suppress the truth by their wickedness. They know the truth about God because he has made it obvious to them.

DAILY DEVO

I don't dismiss God's inner compass.

Have you ever wondered how airplanes fly at night through dense fog or how ships make it through big storms? They do it by using compasses that show them the direction in which they're headed. Compasses work magnetically by pointing to the North Pole. Pilots and sea captains aren't the only ones who use compasses. Campers, hunters, and even car drivers use them to get from one place to another. All of us are born with special compasses in our hearts that know how to get a bearing on God's true north. They steer us in the right direction and let us know when we get off track. Whenever you're tempted to dismiss God's inner compass, don't push the truth away. Follow it carefully and stay on course.

 MAKE IT STICK

Politely ask your school librarian to help you look up the word *compass* in a set of encyclopedias. (Or look up the word on the Internet.) Then draw a picture of a compass as you whisper this daily devo to your heart.

PRAYER

Dear God, thank you for putting your truth in my heart to guide me like a compass. I'm trusting you for strength to obey your Word. And I'm counting on you to steer me in the right direction all the days of my life. Thank you! In Jesus' name, amen.

CLICK-ER: COMPASS

Whenever you see, use, or think about a *compass*, let this daily devo navigate your heart to God as it clicks and sticks. Roman the Rhino with his one-on-a-bun reminds you that the devo is from Romans, Chapter 1.

ROMANS, CHAPTER 5 (VERSE 8)

God showed his great love for us by sending Christ to die for us while we were still sinners.

DAILY DEVO

Jesus is my divine Valentine.

One of several different legends says that many years ago the Romans put a man named Valentine in prison for his Christian faith. He was such a loving man that many children in his town missed him and tossed him love notes. Sadly, he was put to death on February 14. But his heart of love lives on as we exchange Valentine's Day cards with one another. Jesus, our divine Valentine, died too. He loved us so much that he died in our place. But he came back to life so we can live for God. And someday we can live *with* him. Your heart must open up and receive Jesus' gift of salvation, just like your hand opens up and receives a valentine. Won't you please be his valentine?

MAKE IT STICK

Make your own valentines—even if it isn't Valentine's Day! Write "Jesus is my divine Valentine" on the front of each card. On the inside write: "And he wants to be yours too!" On the back, write out Romans, Chapter 5 (verse 8). Pray about how many of these you should make and to whom you should give them. Then get ready to experience love and joy as you see how God uses you.

PRAYER

Dear Jesus, thanks for being the best Valentine I've ever received. You loved me and died in my place to forgive my sins. No one has ever loved me that much. But you do. And I love you, too! Amen.

CLICK-ER: VALENTINE

Whenever you send, receive, or think about a *valentine*, let this daily devo fill your heart with love from above as it clicks and sticks. Roman the Rhino with his five-on-a-hive-hat reminds you that the devo is from Romans, Chapter 5.

ROMANS, CHAPTER 8 (VERSE 28)

We know that God causes everything to work together for the good of those who love God and are called according to his purpose for them.

DAILY DEVO

I believe in God's perfect weave.

Weaving is the process of making cloth by crossing two sets of threads over and under each other. One set, the *warp*, is stretched up and down on a loom or frame. The other set, the *weft*, gets woven from left to right. (Get it? Weft—left!) To make cloth, a weaver threads the weft over and under the warp again and again. God is the Master Weaver. He promises to make every up-and-down and over-and-under weave of your life work together for your good. But his promise is only for those who love him. Do you love God? Believe in his perfect weave. It will increase your love for him.

 MAKE IT STICK

Politely ask your dad or mom to help you make a wooden hand loom. Use an old wooden picture frame, or just nail four small strips of wood together in a square or rectangle shape. Then hammer small nails into the wood all around the outer edges. Be careful to space them equally and leave them sticking up halfway. Now use rubber bands, yarn, or string to weave a fun pattern.

As you weave, say this daily devo.

PRAYER

Dear God, I believe you make everything in my life work together for my good. Sometimes it's hard to see that. But I love you and trust you to pull everything together at the right time. In Jesus' name I pray. Amen.

CLICK-ER: **WOVEN CLOTH**

Whenever you see, feel, or closely observe a piece of *woven cloth*, let this daily devo weave its way into your heart as it clicks and sticks. Roman the Rhino with his eight-under-skates reminds you that the devo is from Romans, Chapter 8.

ROMANS, CHAPTER 9 (VERSE 21)

When a potter makes jars out of clay, doesn't he have a right to use the same lump of clay to make one jar for decoration and another to throw garbage into?

DAILY DEVO

I'm go-with-the-flow play dough.

Squishing and squashing play dough into whatever shape we want is fun. It even smells sort of good and comes in different colors. Kids playing with play dough is a good picture of a great truth in God's Word. You see, we are like play dough in the hands of God. And he lovingly shapes us and makes us into exactly what he wants us to be. His job, as the Play-Dough Master, is to decide all about whether we're tall or short, blue eyed or brown eyed, good at sports or music, science or language. Our job, as play dough, is to stretch and bend and go with the flow of whatever God is molding us to be. Don't fight his strong, loving hands. Go with the flow. And marvel at what he's making of you.

MAKE IT STICK

If you don't have any store-bought Play-Doh, politely ask your dad or mom to help you make some out of biscuit dough and food coloring. (Or use a recipe you find by searching for "homemade play dough" on the Web.) Have fun squishing and squashing it into whatever shape you want as you say this daily devo.

PRAYER

Thank you, God, for the way you're shaping me. Help me do the best I can with my schoolwork and other activities. Then please teach me to be happy with myself, as I become what you want me to be. Amen.

CLICK-ER: PLAY DOUGH

Whenever you see, play with, or think about *play dough*, let this daily devo take shape in your heart as it clicks and sticks. Roman the Rhino with his nine-foot-pine reminds you that the devo is from Romans, Chapter 9.

ROMANS, CHAPTER 10 (VERSE 15)

How will anyone go and tell them without being sent? That is why the Scriptures say, "How beautiful are the feet of messengers who bring good news!"

DAILY DEVO

I use my shoes to share the Good News.

Have you ever stopped to think about all the different kinds of shoes in the world? We've got baseball shoes, basketball shoes, soccer shoes, tennis shoes, even jogging shoes. And then there are sandals, clogs, sneakers, loafers, moccasins, boots, and bedroom slippers. The list could probably go on forever, but all shoes have one main purpose: to protect our feet while we're getting to where we're going. As Christians, we, too, have a primary purpose: to share the Good News about Jesus wherever our shoes take us. You see, people wearing shoes that go and share the gospel are beautiful in the eyes of God. Some beautiful person brought it to you. And you can take it to others.

 MAKE IT STICK

Write this daily devo on two slips of paper and place one in each of your shoes for a day or two. Every time you remember they're there, ask God for boldness to use your shoes to go and share the Good News with one person who needs it. Then get ready. That's the kind of prayer God loves to answer.

PRAYER

Lord God, thank you for each person who has shared the Good News about Jesus with me. Now please make me willing to go wherever you send me with that same news. In Jesus' name I pray. Amen.

CLICK-ER: SHOES

Whenever you see or put on *shoes*, let this daily devo take a walk through your mind as it clicks and sticks. Roman the Rhino with his one-on-a-bun and halo-is-a-hero-as-a-zero reminds you that the devo is from Romans, Chapter 10.

WEEKEND ACTIVITY IDEAS
(1) Highlight the verses for Week 40 in your Bible. (2) Find the HoneyWord
animal in each picture for this week and identify the chapter-number symbols.
(3) Add to your collection of Click-ers. (4) Say the daily devos for Week 40.
(5) Check out Monday of Week 8 for a related devo on who steps in when you
step out.

TIPTOE LIKE A RHINO
Though built like an armored tank, the rhino
walks on its tiptoes like a ballet dancer.

ROMANS, CHAPTER 12 (VERSE 2)

Don't copy the behavior and customs of this world, but let God transform you into a new person by changing the way you think. Then you will know God's will for you, which is good and pleasing and perfect.

DAILY DEVO

I don't put tar in my mental DVD or VCR.

The TV, the computer, the VCR, the CD player, and the DVD player had not been invented when the Bible was written. So it says nothing about them—just as it doesn't mention skateboards, ski jumps, or Skittles. But it has much to say about what we put into our minds. Our brains are like VCRs or DVD players. If we put good thoughts and pictures into our minds, good attitudes and actions come out in our behavior. And the opposite is also true: garbage in means garbage out. Please be extremely careful about what you cram into your mind. Don't clog up your mental DVD player or VCR with trashy tar. Instead, pop a copy of God's Word into your mind. And enjoy the benefits of his care and protection.

 MAKE IT STICK

Show your dad or mom that you know this daily devo. Politely ask one of them to come with you to the family TV. As you pop in your favorite good, clean movie, point to your forehead and say this daily devo and its location: Romans, Chapter 12. Then read the verse above or find it in your Bible.

PRAYER

Dear God, I want my mind filled with thoughts about you and your love. Please help me to turn away from the thoughts of the world. Thanks for changing me into the new person you want me to be. Amen.

CLICK-ER:
DVD PLAYER/VCR

Whenever you see, use, or think about a *DVD player* or a *VCR*, let this daily devo pop into your mind as it clicks and sticks. Roman the Rhino with his one-on-a-bun and two-blue-shoes reminds you that the devo is from Romans, Chapter 12.

ROMANS, CHAPTER 13 (VERSE 8)

Owe nothing to anyone—except for your obligation to love one another. If you love your neighbor, you will fulfill the requirements of God's law.

DAILY DEVO

I'm on guard with credit cards.

When your parents want to buy you something—say, a shirt—they can give the store a credit card and the credit-card company pays the store for the shirt. Then you start wearing the shirt that your parents haven't yet paid for. This isn't a problem if your parents pay the credit-card company back. But some people let down their guard when it comes to credit cards. They let their debts pile up, and soon they're in "Big Trouble." If you owe something to someone—whether it's money, a promise, or a kind word—God wants you to pay it right away. Be on guard. Don't pay later what you can pay back today.

MAKE IT STICK

Politely ask your dad or mom to help you make a pretend credit card from an index card or a piece of cardboard. Then look through newspaper flyers and make two lists: things you need and things you want. Say this daily devo as you talk through whether anything on either list should be bought with a credit card. Maybe your parents will let you "charge" one item from each list, as long as you agree to pay them back in a month or pay extra.

PRAYER

Dear God, please teach me to be wise in the way I use my money. I know you don't want me to spend what I don't have. So help me make it my goal to owe no one a thing but a hug or a kind word. In Jesus' name, amen.

CLICK-ER: CREDIT CARD

Whenever you think about or see someone use a *credit card*, let your heart charge this daily devo to your mind as it clicks and sticks. Roman the Rhino with his one-on-a-bun and three-is-the-key reminds you that the devo is from Romans, Chapter 13.

Week 41, Wednesday

BOOK OF 1 CORINTHIANS
Cori Chameleon the 1st

Chameleon starts with the same letter as *Corinthians*. Like a chameleon, the new believers in Corinth blended in with their environment. When you see Cori Chameleon the 1st in a picture, you'll know the daily devo is from 1 Corinthians. Connected to Cori Chameleon the 1st are number symbols. (See page 15.) They make the chapter location of the devo click and stick.

The chameleon is a lizard that can change its color to match whatever's around it. Its body is flat, and its bulging eyes can see in separate directions. While one eye looks at a leaf on the left, the other can follow a roach on the right. In this letter, Paul let the new believers in Corinth know they were like chameleons. By keeping one eye on God and the other on the world, they got mixed up and therefore nixed out the power of God. The result was all kinds of sin. Paul promised that if they focused both eyes on God, they would reflect the color of love, the most important characteristic of a Christian.

 MAKE IT STICK

Make a tab to mark the book of 1 Corinthians in your Bible. (See Week 1, Monday, for directions.)

In the middle of a large piece of drawing paper, draw a picture of yourself with one eye looking to the left, and the other to the right, just like a chameleon. Near the eye on the left, show something you're looking at that pleases God, like someone giving an offering or reading a Bible. Near the eye on the right, show something that doesn't please God, like kids fighting or someone stealing something. That's a picture of the divided hearts of the Corinthian believers.

Whenever you picture a chameleon with the number *one* on it, remember Cori Chameleon the 1st and the book of 1 Corinthians.

JUST FOR FUN

1 Corinthians, Chapter 13, is called the love chapter. Read verses 4-7 with your family to see how God expects you to act if you really love someone.

PRAYER

Dear God, please teach me how to keep my eyes on you so I'll keep my eyes off the things that drag me down. In Jesus' name I pray. Amen.

1 CORINTHIANS, CHAPTER 9 (VERSES 24–25)

Don't you realize that in a race everyone runs, but only one person gets the prize? So run to win! All athletes are disciplined in their training. They do it to win a prize that will fade away, but we do it for an eternal prize.

DAILY DEVO

I win first prize through spiritual exercise.

The Bible is big on using sports (like cross-country racing, wrestling, and boxing) to describe spiritual ideas. As Paul watched athletes train for and compete in their games, he saw their struggles and victories as a picture of the Christian life. He observed that many try, but few actually win. God, however, wants each one of us to win. And he knows that's possible only when we keep our eyes on him. We win, not by comparing ourselves to what others do or don't do, but by doing *exactly* what our heavenly Coach wants us to do. That takes a lot of practice. So go for it. Win first prize through spiritual exercise. It's a decision that you—and God—will always be proud of.

MAKE IT STICK

Draw, color, and cut out a first-prize blue ribbon. As you pin it to your shirt, pretend that God is the one awarding it to you. Now do nine jumping jacks, and count out loud as you jump. When you finish, say this daily devo. Just for fun, do it again and again, as many times as you like.

PRAYER

Lord, please be my heavenly Coach. I promise to do my spiritual exercises this week by praying, reading my Bible, and tithing. I'm following you all the way to the finish line. Amen.

CLICK-ER: FIRST-PRIZE BLUE RIBBON

Whenever you see, win, or think about a *first-prize blue ribbon*, let this daily devo take first place in your heart as it clicks and sticks. Cori Chameleon the 1st with his nine-foot-pine reminds you that the devo is from 1 Corinthians, Chapter 9.

1 CORINTHIANS, CHAPTER 10 (VERSE 13)

The temptations in your life are no different from what others experience. And God is faithful. He will not allow the temptation to be more than you can stand. When you are tempted, he will show you a way out so that you can endure.

DAILY DEVO

When I'm in a jam, I look to the Lamb.

To make jam, fruit like strawberries is crushed, mixed with sugar, and boiled to a pulp. After it cools and jells, you have a delicious strawberry jam. The process of making jam is a picture of the way temptation works in our life. When we wind up in a pot of boiling-hot events, all of us are tempted to give in and do things we know are wrong. But God wants us to look to Jesus, the Lamb of God, who always knows what to do "in a jam." As we trust him for the strength to keep going and the wisdom to do what's right, he promises to show us a way out. Are you in a jam? Then look to the Lamb. God will use the heat of this temptation to bring sweet-tasting results in your life.

 MAKE IT STICK

Politely ask your dad or mom if you may eat a spoonful of jam. (If you only have clear jelly, without any pieces of fruit, pretend that it's jam.) As you enjoy its flavor, let it be a taste of how good things happen when you trust God during times of temptation. Now say this daily devo.

PRAYER

Dear Jesus, when I'm tempted this week to do something wrong, please show me the way out. I'm trusting you to help me get through every temptation I face. Amen.

CLICK-ER: JAM

Whenever you see, taste, or think about *jam*, let this daily devo spread over your heart as it clicks and sticks. Cori Chameleon the 1st with his one-on-a-bun and halo-is-a-hero-as-a-zero reminds you that the devo is from 1 Corinthians, Chapter 10.

1 CORINTHIANS, CHAPTER 12 (VERSE 12)

The human body has many parts, but the many parts make up one whole body. So it is with the body of Christ.

DAILY DEVO

Everybody is somebody in the body of Christ.

God created the human body with about 650 muscles, 206 bones, 2 eyes, a brain, and around 5 quarts of blood. Just one drop of blood contains about 5 million red blood cells. And here's the most amazing thing of all: Each part of the body has its own job and knows how to serve all the other parts! That's why the apostle Paul used the human body as a picture of how Christians are to work together. Each of us is an important part of the worldwide family of God—"the body of Christ." Nobody is a nobody. Everybody is somebody, with a job to do. And that includes you!

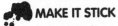

MAKE IT STICK

Politely ask your mom or dad to help you look up the subject "human body" in an encyclopedia. Find out how the different parts work together. On one half of a sheet of paper, list the jobs some of these parts do, such as the brain, the stomach, the lungs, the blood vessels, the muscles, and the bones. On the other half of your paper, list jobs in the body of Christ. Then say this daily devo.

PRAYER

Lord, it feels good knowing I was born to do a very special job in your family. Help me understand exactly what it is, so I can do it with all my heart. In Jesus' name I pray. Amen.

CLICK-ER: BODY

Whenever you look at, touch, or think about your *body*, let this daily devo make you feel like somebody as it clicks and sticks. Cori Chameleon the 1st with his one-on-a-bun and two-blue-shoes reminds you that the devo is from 1 Corinthians, Chapter 12.

WEEKEND ACTIVITY IDEAS

(1) Highlight the verses for Week 41 in your Bible. (2) Find the HoneyWord
animal in each picture for this week and identify the chapter-number symbols.
(3) Add to your collection of Click-ers. (4) Say the daily devos for Week 41.
(5) Check out Wednesday of Week 34 for a related devo on how to know if you
love God from head to toe.

EYES ON THE PRIZE

Chameleons have two goofy, googly eyes that
move in different directions at the same time.

1 CORINTHIANS, CHAPTER 15 (VERSE 52)

It will happen in a moment, in the blink of an eye, when the last trumpet is blown. For when the trumpet sounds, those who have died will be raised to live forever. And we who are living will also be transformed.

DAILY DEVO

When his trumpet sounds, I'll be heaven bound.

One day, when people least expect it, there'll be in the distance a sudden mighty blast: *Tooh-tooh-tooh-t'-too!* The trumpet of heaven will sound and one of the most spectacular events in the history of the world will take place. In the twinkling of an eye, believers—both dead and alive—will be given brand-new, perfect bodies that will last forever in heaven. This breathtaking event could happen in your lifetime! All Christians everywhere are looking forward to the return of Christ, especially those of us affected by sickness or physical disabilities. In a flash, all our pain and heartache will be over. Do you ever hurt or feel sad? Put your hope in Christ's return. Someday you might hear his trumpet sound, and you'll be heaven bound.

MAKE IT STICK

Politely ask your school music teacher or band director to play a few notes on a trumpet for you. Or ask if you can listen to a CD with trumpet music. Be sure to say thanks for the help. As you listen to the sound of a trumpet, imagine what Jesus' second coming will be like, and say this daily devo.

PRAYER

Wow, God! It'll be so exciting to hear the sound of that last trumpet! Then everyone in your family will live forever with Jesus, and no one will ever be sick or sad again. Thanks, God! In Jesus' name, amen.

CLICK-ER: TRUMPET

Whenever you hear or think about a *trumpet*, let this daily devo sound off in your mind as it clicks and sticks. Cori Chameleon the 1st with his one-on-a-bun and five-on-a-hive-hat reminds you that the devo is from 1 Corinthians, Chapter 15.

Week 42, Tuesday

BOOK OF 2 CORINTHIANS
Cori Chameleon the 2nd

Chameleon starts with the same letter as *Corinthians*. Like a chameleon, some of the new believers in Corinth kept trying to blend in with their environment. When you see Cori Chameleon the 2nd in a picture, you'll know the daily devo is from 2 Corinthians. Connected to Cori Chameleon the 2nd are number symbols. (See page 15.) They make the chapter location of the devo click and stick.

Back in his first letter to the church at Corinth, Paul had said the people were like chameleons, changing their colors to match the sinful lifestyles of those around them. Many listened and stopped living that way, but some were upset with Paul's message and said unkind things about him. So in this second letter, Paul wrote from his heart, sharing his deepest joys and greatest sorrows. While 1 Corinthians is practical, 2 Corinthians is personal and focuses on Paul's love for the people. It hurt him to see some of his friends follow false teaching, and he wanted to do everything he could to stop it.

MAKE IT STICK

Make a tab to mark the book of 2 Corinthians in your Bible. (See Week 1, Monday, for directions.)

With a sticky tongue as long as its body, a chameleon can lash out and catch insects, lizards, and even birds. Log on to a search engine and look for pictures and videos of chameleons catching stuff. Notice the eyes. While you're at it, you should be able to find almost all of the HoneyWord animals online. Which three are missing?

Whenever you picture a chameleon with the number *two* on it, think about Cori Chameleon the 2nd and the book of 2 Corinthians.

JUST FOR FUN

Read what Paul compares us to in 2 Corinthians, Chapter 4 (verses 6-7). Why do you think Paul uses this picture? See what God says in Jeremiah, Chapter 18 (verses 5-6) and Romans, Chapter 9 (verse 21).

PRAYER

Lord, I don't want to live like a chameleon—with one eye on you and one eye on something else. Please help me keep both eyes firmly fixed on you in everything I do. In Jesus' name I pray. Amen.

2 CORINTHIANS, CHAPTER 3 (VERSE 3)

Clearly, you are a letter from Christ showing the result of our ministry among you. This "letter" is written not with pen and ink, but with the Spirit of the living God. It is carved not on tablets of stone, but on human hearts.

DAILY DEVO

I'm a living, giving letter.

Even though we live in a world of instant e-mail, don't you love getting a handwritten letter from a friend or a relative? There's something so personal about what this person writes and says that we can almost see him or her as we read. That's a picture of how people see us as Christians. Whether we realize it or not, we are living, breathing letters from God to the world. How we live and the way we treat others tells people what God is like. The responsibility of being a walking, talking, living, giving letter from God can feel scary. But it's not, really. Day by day, trust God for the strength to live up to this tall assignment.

MAKE IT STICK

Address an envelope to a friend, a parent, or another family member. Write a brief note thanking that person for something he or she has done for you. At the end of your letter, write this daily devo and draw your picture beside it. Now deliver it by hand or through the mail.

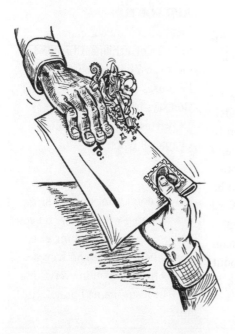

PRAYER

Dear God, if I say I'm a Christian but don't act like one, the people around me don't get a good picture of what you're like. Please help me do a better job of treating others the way you want me to. In Jesus' name, amen.

CLICK-ER:
LETTER ENVELOPE

Whenever you send, receive, or see a *letter* in an *envelope*, let this daily devo address your heart as it clicks and sticks. Cori Chameleon the 2nd with his three-is-the-key reminds you that the devo is from 2 Corinthians, Chapter 3.

2 CORINTHIANS, CHAPTER 4 (VERSE 18)

We don't look at the troubles we can see now; rather, we fix our gaze on things that cannot be seen. For the things we see now will soon be gone, but the things we cannot see will last forever.

DAILY DEVO

All my troubles are like bubbles.

Adults and kids all feel the stress and strain of life. When we're sick from worry, the only thing that helps is trusting God. He shows us that all our troubles are like bubbles ready to burst. The very worst things in life down here will burst and give way to the joys of heaven up there. "But how do I deal with troubles that just won't go away?" you might ask. Every difficulty is small compared with the eternal happiness we'll someday have in heaven. Are you going through troubled times? Don't worry. Instead, trust God for the strength to see through all your bubbles of troubles. When it's time, they'll pop and disappear into thin air.

MAKE IT STICK

Politely ask your dad or mom to help you make a batch of homemade bubbles to blow. Squeeze a small amount of concentrated liquid dish soap into a small glass of water. Now bend one end of a large paper clip into a circle or oval, and use it as a bubble blower. Each time you dip your blower into the suds and blow bubbles, say this daily devo.

PRAYER

Dear God, I wish all of my troubles would just go away. But help me think about you and your plans for me. I know that trusting you will keep me from worrying about my troubles. In Jesus' name, amen.

CLICK-ER: BUBBLES

Whenever you see, make, or think about *bubbles*, let this daily devo burst your heart with joy as it clicks and sticks. Cori Chameleon the 2nd with his four-on-the-floorboard reminds you that the devo is from 2 Corinthians, Chapter 4.

Week 42, Friday

BOOK OF GALATIANS

Sea-gull-atians

Lunch?!

Gull begins with the same sound as *Galatians*. Like a seagull, the Galatian believers had careless eating habits. For their spiritual diet, they had eaten a "new gospel" that was making them spiritually sick. When you see Sea-gull-atians in a picture, you'll know the daily devo is from Galatians. Connected to Sea-gull-atians are number symbols. (See page 15.) They make the chapter location of the devo click and stick.

Seagulls eat almost anything: fish, eggs, dead birds, garbage, and even rats. Yuck! Like seagulls, the Galatian believers were careless in their diet—their spiritual diet. Some Jewish leaders had fed them the lie that becoming a Christian meant believing in Jesus *plus* perfectly keeping certain rules. So Paul said over and over: Faith alone sets us free. No person can do anything perfectly. When we do our best to obey the rules that please God, we do it because we love him. But salvation comes simply by believing Jesus is God's Son. Don't be a spiritual seagull and gobble up lies. Read and gulp down the truth. It's the only way to stay fit for life.

 MAKE IT STICK

Make a tab to mark the book of Galatians in your Bible. (See Week 1, Monday, for directions.)

On a sheet of paper, draw some foods that make you feel sick. What happens when you eat them? Do you break out in hives? Maybe you cough or start sneezing. Whatever happens, that's a picture of what your spirit looks like when you eat the wrong spiritual food the way a seagull gobbles up garbage.

Whenever you see a seagull or a picture of one, think about Sea-gull-atians and the book of Galatians.

JUST FOR FUN

Turn to Galatians, Chapter 5 (verses 22-23) and see what the Holy Spirit wants to produce in you. How many things are listed? And which one do you want the most? Now ask God to give it to you.

PRAYER

Father, I want to receive all the good things the Holy Spirit wants to give me. Please produce in me the kind of fruit that honors you and helps others. In Jesus' name I pray. Amen.

GALATIANS, CHAPTER 1 (VERSES 6-7)

I am shocked that you are turning away so soon from God, who called you to himself through the loving mercy of Christ. You are following a different way that pretends to be the Good News but is not the Good News at all. You are being fooled by those who deliberately twist the truth concerning Christ.

DAILY DEVO

I resist whoever twists the truth.

Have you ever tried hanging up clothes on bent coat hangers? It's impossible, isn't it? The teachings of the Bible are like spiritual clothes we are to carefully hang in the closets of our hearts. But the only hanger strong enough to hold them up is the truth of the Good News. Anybody who twists and changes the truth about Christ is offering you a twisted, useless hanger. And twisted truth doesn't hold anything up. The Bible is filled with the truth about God. It tells us that believing in Jesus is the only way to be rescued from sin. So resist believing anyone with a different twist on the truth. Instead, hang on to this truth: Salvation is by faith in Christ. Period.

 MAKE IT STICK

Politely ask your dad or mom for permission to bend a wire clothes hanger out of shape. Then try to hang a piece of clothing on it. You can't, can you? Don't believe people who twist God's truth. As you throw away your bent hanger, thank God for the truthfulness of his Word and say this daily devo.

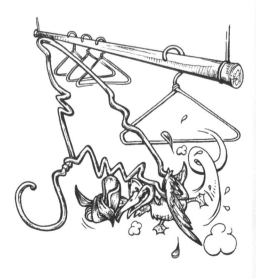

PRAYER

Dear God, thank you for teaching me that everything in the Bible is true—and that believing in Jesus is the main thing I need to do to stay strong in you. I love you, Lord. Amen.

CLICK-ER: TWISTED COAT HANGER

Whenever you see, bend, or think about a *twisted coat hanger*, let your mind hang this daily devo in your heart as it clicks and sticks. Sea-gull-atians with his one-on-a-bun reminds you that the devo is from Galatians, Chapter 1.

WEEKEND ACTIVITY IDEAS

(1) Highlight the verses for Week 42 in your Bible. (2) Find the HoneyWord animal in each picture for this week and identify the chapter-number symbols. (3) Add to your collection of Click-ers. (4) Say the daily devos for Week 42. (5) Check out Friday of Week 37 for a related devo on getting good at godly math.

JUNK-FOOD JUNKIE

Gulls look for and eat almost anything: fish, insects, rotten meat, eggs, and food or garbage that floats. Seagulls have even been known to snatch snacks from kids on the playground.

GALATIANS, CHAPTER 2 (VERSE 10)

Their only suggestion was that we keep on helping the poor, which I [Paul] have always been eager to do.

DAILY DEVO

Let's agree to stamp out poverty.

For most of us, "being poor" means having just enough money to buy one hamburger instead of two, or having only three pairs of shoes when we'd like ten. Usually we don't think about how much we *do* have, or how much the rest of the world does *not* have. And too often we see "the world" as somewhere "over there." But no matter where you live, there are people near you who don't have enough money for food, shelter, clothes, and medical bills. You can't help everyone, but you can help a few. Take a meal, give a shirt, hold a hand. Let's be like Paul and help stamp out poverty.

MAKE IT STICK

Politely ask one of your parents to help you write and mail a letter like this to your pastor: "Dear Pastor, I learned today from Galatians, Chapter 2 (verse 10) that we are to help the poor. Would you please let me know how I can help someone in our church? Maybe I can buy some food, give some clothes, or help pay a medical bill. Thanks for showing me how to help." As you put the postage stamp on your envelope, say this daily devo.

PRAYER

Dear God, I know that a lot of people don't have as much stuff as I do. Thank you for your goodness to me. Please help me to be less selfish and more willing to share what I have. In Jesus' name, amen.

CLICK-ER:
POSTAGE STAMP

Whenever you see, use, or think about a *postage stamp*, let your mind seal this daily devo to your heart as it clicks and sticks. Sea-gull-atians with his two-blue-shoes reminds you that the devo is from Galatians, Chapter 2.

GALATIANS, CHAPTER 3 (VERSE 28)

There is no longer Jew or Gentile, slave or free, male and female. For you are all one in Christ Jesus.

DAILY DEVO

Red and yellow, black and white, **all are equal in his sight.**

We humans tend to make a big fuss over color. Some people eat only red apples—they won't touch green or yellow ones. Some folks dye their hair black, and others dye it blonde. When it comes to differences in clothing, we look like a field of multicolored flowers. If God had a middle name, it could be "Variety." We see it everywhere throughout his creation. But unfortunately, some of us can't see how this applies to the color of people's skin. In fact, many people don't like anyone who doesn't look just like they do. But God doesn't think like that. Red and yellow, black and white, men and women, boys and girls, old and young, all are beautiful . . . and totally equal . . . in his sight. God created all the colors of the rainbow and loves all of them. You can too.

 MAKE IT STICK

Use crayons to draw the outlines of four people. Now color each person a different color. As you color, repeat this daily devo. If you know children of different races, politely ask your dad or mom if you may invite one of them over to play sometime.

PRAYER

Thank you, God, for all the colors you've created. I love seeing them in rainbows, in flowers, and in people. I'm so glad you don't have any favorites, God. Every color and every person is beautiful to you—and to me, too! Amen.

CLICK-ER: CRAYONS

Whenever you see, use, or think about different *crayons*, let this daily devo color your heart as it clicks and sticks. Sea-gull-atians with his three-is-the-key reminds you that the devo is from Galatians, Chapter 3.

GALATIANS, CHAPTER 6 (VERSE 2)

Share each other's burdens, and in this way obey the law of Christ.

DAILY DEVO

I'm there to help you up that stair.

Have you ever had one of those days when everything goes wrong? You wake up late for school, spill milk on yourself, and discover that your kid brother or sister scribbled all over your homework. Later that day, you accidentally fall down the stairs and find out your best friend doesn't like you anymore. Sometimes bad things can beat us down so low, we don't think we can ever get up again. God understands. When your troubles seem too much for you to handle, go to God and pour out your heart in prayer. Over time, he'll show you how he's there to help you up that next stair. And then, in turn, you'll be glad to do what God asks: Be there to help others up their stairs.

 MAKE IT STICK

Walk up and down some stairs several times at your house, in your apartment building, or at school. As you do, repeat this daily devo and ask God to help you think of a friend who is hurting because of some kind of problem. Then find your friend and kindly offer to help him or her get back up and get going again. Just talk, listen, or pray with your friend so the problem won't feel so hard to deal with.

PRAYER

Lord, I really want to help my friends with their problems. But sometimes I don't know what to do. Please help me to remember how others helped me so I can do the same thing for a friend. In Jesus' name I pray. Amen.

CLICK-ER: STAIRWAY

Whenever you see, go up and down, or think about a *stairway*, let this daily devo step into your heart as it clicks and sticks. Sea-gull-atians with his six-pick-up-stix reminds you that the devo is from Galatians, Chapter 6.

Week 43, Thursday

BOOK OF EPHESIANS
Ele-phesians

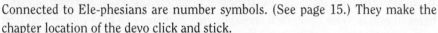

Elephant begins with the same letter as *Ephesians*. Like an enormous elephant, God's love is as high as it is long. When you see Ele-phesians in a picture, you'll know the daily devo is from Ephesians. Connected to Ele-phesians are number symbols. (See page 15.) They make the chapter location of the devo click and stick.

The book of Ephesians shows us the huge size of God's love, which is much more enormous than an elephant! Did you know that an elephant can use its trunk to pick up a peanut just as easily as a 600-pound log? In the same way, God's strong love lifts and removes our biggest burdens while it delicately wipes our smallest tears. And just as an elephant has large ears, so God's big heart of love is attached to a gigantic ear. He's crazy about you and longs to listen to everything you say and to talk with you every day. If you'd like to get closer to God's love for you, snuggle up with the book of Ephesians. As you hear and feel its message, you'll never be the same.

 MAKE IT STICK

Make a tab to mark the book of Ephesians in your Bible. (See Week 1, Monday, for directions.)

You might also like to make an elephant from play dough. Give it big, thick legs and a long trunk. Stand your elephant in your room where you can see it every day and be reminded of just how big God's love for you really is.

Whenever you see an elephant or a picture of one, think about Ele-phesians and the book of Ephesians.

JUST FOR FUN
Read what Paul wants you to learn about loving others the way God loves you. Check out Ephesians Chapter 4 (verses 31-32) and Chapter 5 (verses 1-2).

PRAYER
Dear God, I've got a lot to learn about loving others. But I'm so glad you love me just the way I am. Please teach me how to live like Jesus, who is kind, forgiving, and loving. Amen.

EPHESIANS, CHAPTER 1 (VERSE 5)

God decided in advance to adopt us into his own family by bringing us to himself through Jesus Christ. This is what he wanted to do, and it gave him great pleasure.

DAILY DEVO

I'm plugged in to God's plan.

Just before Moses was born, Pharaoh had ordered all Hebrew baby boys to be killed. So Moses, born into a poor family of slaves, had a death sentence over his head. His parents, however, put him in a basket-boat along the Nile River. And according to God's plan, Moses was discovered and adopted by an Egyptian princess, the daughter of Pharaoh himself. This adoption took Moses from death to life, from slavery to freedom, and from poverty to riches. It's a wonderful picture of how Jesus died on the cross so that God could adopt us. And here's the most amazing thing: God's plan to adopt us into his family was in place even before he made the world. If you believe in Jesus, you're plugged in to God's plan. And he won't ever unplug you.

 MAKE IT STICK

Sometime when your dad or mom is with you, hold the electrical plug of a radio, lamp, or DVD player. As you plug it in and take it out of an electrical socket, repeat this daily devo. Think about the parallel between electricity and God's power, and determine to stay plugged in to God's plan.

PRAYER

Dear Lord, it's amazing how you planned to adopt me into your family even before you made the world! I don't really understand this, but I thank you for plugging me in to your plan. Amen.

CLICK-ER: **ELECTRIC PLUG**

Whenever you see or think about an *electric plug*, let this daily devo connect your heart and mind as it clicks and sticks. Ele-phesians with his one-on-a-bun reminds you that the devo is from Ephesians, Chapter 1.

EPHESIANS, CHAPTER 3 (VERSE 20)

Now all glory to God, who is able, through his mighty power at work within us, to accomplish infinitely more than we might ask or think.

DAILY DEVO
Like a yo-yo, I get my go-go from the hand of God.

The yo-yo may have been invented as a hunting weapon thousands of years ago in the Philippines. There's also evidence that the ancient Greeks played with this toy. Over the years, many fun tricks have been developed for the yo-yo, from "Loop the Loop" to "Walk the Dog" to "Rock the Baby." But a yo-yo has go-go only when it's attached to a hand. By itself it's totally useless. In the same way, we're spiritually powerless without God. But when we place ourselves in his hands, his mighty power accomplishes more through us than we could ever dare ask or hope. Be like a yo-yo. Get your go-go from the hand of God. Then get ready to watch God use you to "loop-the-loop" and "walk-the-dog" all over your world.

MAKE IT STICK

If you don't have a yo-yo, politely ask your dad or mom to help you find a way to earn money for one. Once you have one, notice how it doesn't come to life until you pick it up. The same is true of our walk with God. As you experiment with different tricks, say today's daily devo.

PRAYER
Jesus, please put your hand on my life and keep it there so that your power can flow through me. I agree right now to do whatever you want me to do and say whatever you want me to say. Amen.

CLICK-ER: YO-YO
Whenever you see, play with, or think about a *yo-yo*, let this daily devo go up and down in your mind as it clicks and sticks. Elephesians with his three-is-the-key reminds you that the devo is from Ephesians, Chapter 3.

WEEKEND ACTIVITY IDEAS

(1) Highlight the verses for Week 43 in your Bible. (2) Find the HoneyWord animal in each picture for this week and identify the chapter-number symbols. (3) Add to your collection of Click-ers. (4) Say the daily devos for Week 43. (5) Check out Tuesday of Week 39 for a related devo on how to delight in Holy Spirit dynamite.

MELLO HELLO

An elephant gently says hello by putting its trunk in another elephant's mouth or ear.

EPHESIANS, CHAPTER 4 (VERSES 26-27)

"Don't sin by letting anger control you." Don't let the sun go down while you are still angry, for anger gives a foothold to the devil.

DAILY DEVO

I won't let the Evil Spider be a divider.

Did you know there are more than 34,000 known kinds of spiders in the world? Most spiders are creepy—except for Charlotte, of course! They're best known for the silk webs they spin to catch bugs for food. Some spiders build webs so strong, they snag insects several times larger and stronger than themselves. That's why a good name for the devil is "Evil Spider." He's always spinning a web of lies that he hopes will entangle and disconnect God's people, who are much more powerful than he is. Anger is one of his biggest traps. Anger, you see, is usually expressed in words. And words delivered in a single moment of anger can divide and sometimes cripple relationships for life. Don't let the slimy Evil Spider be a divider. Instead, sweep away his lies every time he tries to trap you.

 **MAKE IT STICK**

Do some research on spiders on the Internet, also known as the World Wide *Web*. Make a list comparing how the ways of spiders are similar to the traps and tricks of Satan. Then, the next time you see or sweep away a spider web, say this daily devo.

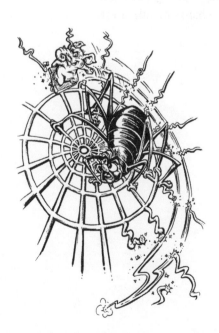

PRAYER

Dear God, sometimes I'm afraid that my anger might get my friends so upset that they won't be my friends anymore. Please don't let me get trapped by the devil that way. Show me how to give my anger to you whenever it comes up. Amen.

CLICK-ER: SPIDER

Whenever you see or get grossed out by a *spider*, let this daily devo weave a web around your heart as it clicks and sticks. Ele-phesians with his four-on-the-floorboard reminds you that the devo is from Ephesians, Chapter 4.

Week 44, Tuesday

BOOK OF PHILIPPIANS

Philip the Firefly

Firefly begins with the same sound as *Philip-pians*. Like a firefly flashing in the sky at night, Paul was lit up with joy even while he was a prisoner in Rome. When you see Philip the Firefly in a picture, you'll know the daily devo is from Philippians. Connected to Philip the Firefly are number symbols. (See page 15.) They make the chapter location of the devo click and stick.

Philippians is Paul's happiest letter. He wrote it while he was chained to a Roman guard, facing possible death for the "crime" of sharing the gospel with others. Yet he was filled to overflowing with joy. How was that possible? The secret of joy is learning that it's never based on happenings. Real joy comes only when life is seen from the Bible's point of view. This focus kept God's light shining so brightly in Paul's heart that he was like a firefly flashing in the sky at night. If you need some cheering up, check out Philippians and receive its light into your soul.

 MAKE IT STICK

Make a tab to mark the book of Philippians in your Bible. (See Week 1, Monday, for directions.)

If you're able to find a book or a Web site about fireflies, you'll learn that they're really beetles, not flies. And they're often called lightning bugs because they flash like lightning. Here's one more fun fact: In some parts of South America, people have used net bags full of fireflies as flashlights to light their way at night.

Whenever you see a firefly or a picture of one, remember Philip the Firefly and the book of Philippians.

JUST FOR FUN

Look up the book of Philippians, Chapter 4 (verse 4). What does Paul say about joy in that verse?

PRAYER

Thank you, God, for the joy you give when I live for you and follow your ways. And during those times when I don't feel any joy, please help me to trust you anyway. In Jesus' name, amen.

PHILIPPIANS, CHAPTER 1 (VERSE 9)

I pray that your love will overflow more and more, and that you will keep on growing in knowledge and understanding.

DAILY DEVO

Like a volcano, my love grows and overflows.

We love to love ourselves. But God wants us to grow and overflow in our love for others. He understands, however, our need to receive love before we can give it. That's why the book of 1 John, Chapter 4 (verse 19) says, "We love each other because he loved us first." True love is like a volcano. Deep inside a volcanic mountain, lava gets hotter and hotter over time, until it overflows everywhere. In the same way, our love overflows into the lives of others because of the love that Christ has first poured into our hearts.

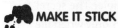 **MAKE IT STICK**

Politely ask your mom or dad to help you make a volcano. You'll need a plastic cup, washable red paint powder (or red food coloring—stains are hard to get out, though), vinegar, baking soda, and a paper plate. Put on some old clothes and go outside. Place the cup on the plate and put about two tablespoons of baking soda in it. Add red paint powder or two drops of food coloring to a half cup of vinegar, and pour it into the cup. As you watch your "volcano" erupt, say this daily devo.

PRAYER

Thank you, Lord Jesus, for filling my heart with your love. Make it burn so deeply within me that it flows out freely to others. I love you, Lord. Amen.

CLICK-ER: VOLCANO

Whenever you see, study, or think about a *volcano*, let this daily devo overflow your heart as it clicks and sticks. Philip the Firefly with his one-on-a-bun reminds you that the devo is from Philippians, Chapter 1.

PHILIPPIANS, CHAPTER 2 (VERSES 14-15)

Do everything without complaining and arguing, so that no one can criticize you. Live clean, innocent lives as children of God, shining like bright lights in a world full of crooked and perverse people.

DAILY DEVO

I'm a spark in the dark.

You've seen sparklers sparking at night, haven't you? Maybe you've even held one. Isn't it amazing how itty-bitty sparks can light up so much darkness? Sparklers are a picture of the way God wants us to brightly shine in a dark world filled with people who don't trust God. A good way to shine, Paul explains, is to stop griping and grumbling. Our hearts are built for faith, and the person who is always moaning and groaning has zero trust in God's ability to run the universe. But the fact is, everything about God's plan for the world is humming along just fine, and right on time. To believe that, you need a heart of faith. So don't be grouchy. Light up your world. Trust God and be a spark in the dark.

MAKE IT STICK

Draw a picture of yourself with your mom or dad, safely holding a lit sparkler in the dark. Be sure to draw a big smile on your face to show how happy you are to be a spark in the dark for God. Along the bottom of your picture, write this daily devo.

PRAYER

Dear God, you know I've done my share of moaning and groaning, but it's not any fun living that way. Please help me live with real joy in my heart and a sincere smile on my face. In Jesus' name, amen.

CLICK-ER: SPARKLER

Whenever you see, hold, or think about a *sparkler*, let this daily devo dazzle your heart as it clicks and sticks. Philip the Firefly with his two-blue-shoes reminds you that the devo is from Philippians, Chapter 2.

PHILIPPIANS, CHAPTER 4 (VERSE 13)

I can do everything through Christ, who gives me strength.

DAILY DEVO
I'm a can-do kid for God.

What's Paul's point in the Bible verse above? Does he mean you can jump up and touch a 12-foot-high ceiling? And what about people who are paralyzed from the neck down? Their "can't do" list is longer than their "can-do" one. Will God really help everyone do *everything*? The answer is no. This verse isn't a guarantee that any of us can do everything we want. But it *is* a promise that we can do everything God *asks* us to do. And he will ask of us only what he knows we can handle with his help. Think of it this way: The only difference between *can* and *can't* is the letter *t*, which looks like the cross of Jesus. Anytime you think or say *can't*, that little cross is there reminding you that you *can*. So be a can-do kid for God. You can do it!

MAKE IT STICK

Get an empty soda-pop can and stand in front of a mirror. As you think of one thing God is asking you to do that feels impossible, balance the can on top of your head and say this daily devo. Then thank God by faith for the way he's going to super-naturally strengthen you.

PRAYER

Dear God, what do you want me to do for you today? Show me what it is, and help me believe you'll give me the strength to do it. Then I'll do it! Amen.

CLICK-ER: CAN

Whenever you see, use, or think about any kind of *can*, let this daily devo fill your heart with a can-do attitude as it clicks and sticks. Philip the Firefly with his four-on-the-floorboard reminds you that the devo is from Philippians, Chapter 4.

Week 44, Saturday/Sunday

BOOK OF COLOSSIANS

Colossians the Collie

Collie starts with the same sound as *Colossians*. Like a good collie, Paul tried to round up God's sheep in Colosse and protect them from false teachers. When you see Colossians the Collie in a picture, you'll know the daily devo is from Colossians. Connected to Colossians the Collie are number symbols. (See page 15.) They make the chapter location of the devo click and stick.

The Christians in the city of Colosse had gotten off to a good start as they followed Christ, their Good Shepherd. But then false teachers slithered into the church and taught wrong things about Jesus and the Christian life. So, like a good collie, Paul set a goal to round up God's sheep and protect them. He did it by humbly trying to help them see that Jesus is the Son of God and the only Savior. Even today, Jesus must be the main focus of all that we do—the still center of our turning world. Christ alone is the head of the church everywhere. So he deserves first place in everything, including our hearts.

 MAKE IT STICK

Make a tab to mark the book of Colossians in your Bible. (See Week 1, Monday, for directions.)

Play "round up the sheep" with your family or several friends. The sheep hide, and the "collie" must find them one by one, bringing them together in a safe place. In much the same way, Paul gently rounded up God's people so he could keep them safe by correctly teaching them about Jesus.

Whenever you see a collie or a picture of one, think about Colossians the Collie and the book of Colossians.

JUST FOR FUN

Read about the astounding things Jesus did in Colossians, Chapter 1 (verses 15-17). What's the most amazing thing about his part in the creation of the universe?

PRAYER

Thank you, God, for each person you've used to round me up and teach me the truth about Jesus. Please bless them for their faithfulness to you. I pray in the name of Jesus. Amen.

WEEKEND ACTIVITY IDEAS

(1) Highlight the verses for Week 44 in your Bible. (2) Find the HoneyWord animal in each picture for this week and identify the chapter-number symbols. (3) Add to your collection of Click-ers. (4) Say the daily devos for Week 44. (5) Check out Wednesday of Week 38 for a related devo on how the Good Shepherd steers through listening ears.

COAL-LIKE COLLIE

Bred in Scotland in the 1600s, early Collie dogs had a dark, coal-like color. Some say this is what led to the nickname *Coaly*, which over time became known as *Collie*.

COLOSSIANS, CHAPTER 2 (VERSE 7)

Let your roots grow down into [Christ Jesus], and let your lives be built on him. Then your faith will grow strong in the truth you were taught, and you will overflow with thankfulness.

DAILY DEVO

As my roots grow down, my faith grows up.

Did you know that roots have four very important jobs? Healthy roots drink water, find food, anchor their plant in the soil, and hold it upright above the ground. Paul wrote about our need to let our "roots grow down" into Jesus so we can draw up nourishment from him. Why? Because Christians need spiritual water, food, and strength to grow and mature. You see, when our spiritual roots grow down into the rich soil of God's Word, our hearts are fed and our faith grows up. Faith is the only thing that keeps us growing and prevents us from getting blown away by the harmful winds of false teaching. Dig deep in God's Word. It's the only way to grow.

MAKE IT STICK

Ask your mom or dad to please give you a small cutting from a houseplant. Put the cutting in a glass of water. Over the next few days, watch how it begins to grow roots. After your cutting has developed strong roots, plant it in a pot of good soil. Then say this daily devo each time you water its soil.

PRAYER

Lord Jesus, I'm so thankful that the tender roots of my faith are growing deep in the rich soil of your Word. Please protect me and cause me to grow up tall and strong in you. I love you. Amen.

CLICK-ER: ROOTS

Whenever you see, pull up, or think about *roots*, let this daily devo deeply take root in your heart as it clicks and sticks. Colossians the Collie with his two-blue-shoes reminds you that the devo is from Colossians, Chapter 2.

COLOSSIANS, CHAPTER 4 (VERSES 5-6)

Live wisely among those who are not believers, and make the most of every opportunity. Let your conversation be gracious and attractive so that you will have the right response for everyone.

DAILY DEVO

I weigh **what I say.**

When you hang out with a friend or chitchat over the phone, you like to hear positive words, right? Words are amazing. They don't weigh a thing, yet they have the power to strenghten the soul or crush the heart. That's why God wants us to weigh what we say *before* we say it. He wants us to be especially careful about the way we talk to someone who doesn't believe in Jesus. When you feel yourself cutting someone down, ask God for the strength to say kind words instead. When that person feels built up, not torn down, he or she just might decide to believe in Jesus.

MAKE IT STICK

Write an unkind word on one slip of paper and this daily devo on another. Then stand on a scale holding the unkind word, and think how easily you could knock someone down if you put your weight behind that bad word. That's a picture of the destructive power of unkind words. Now pick up the paper with this daily devo and see yourself using all your strength to help a friend get up off the ground and start following Jesus. Positive words have uplifting power like that. From now on, every time you weigh yourself, say this daily devo.

PRAYER

Heavenly Father, please help me to watch what I say, especially when I'm with people who don't believe in you. Use my words to show how much you love and care for them. Amen.

CLICK-ER: **SCALE**

Whenever you see, step on, or think about a *scale*, let this daily devo weigh on your heart as it clicks and sticks. Colossians the Collie with his four-on-the-floorboard reminds you that the devo is from Colossians, Chapter 4.

Week 45, Wednesday

BOOK OF 1 THESSALONIANS
Sloth-a-lo-nians the 1st

Sloth ends with the same sound as *Thessalonians* begins with. Like a sloth, the Thessalonians were sometimes slow moving and lazy as they waited for Jesus to return. When you see Sloth-a-lo-nians the 1st in a picture, you'll know the daily devo is from 1 Thessalonians.

Connected to Sloth-a-lo-nians the 1st are number symbols. (See page 15.) They make the chapter location of the devo click and stick.

As the Thessalonian believers read Paul's first letter, they felt the love of a pastor who had jumping-up-and-down excitement about their first steps in the faith. He was so proud of them for trusting the Lord in the midst of suffering. But he also wrote to teach them about the return of Christ. Paul carefully explained that the Lord, upon his return, will first raise all Christians who have died. Then the believers who are still alive will join them in the clouds to meet the Lord and remain with him forever. Paul warned the people not to be lazy and slow like a sloth, but to be joyful, prayerful, and thankful, always ready for Christ's return.

MAKE IT STICK

Make a tab to mark the book of 1 Thessalonians in your Bible. (See Week 1, Monday, for directions.)

Did you know that sloths spend most of their time sleeping as they hang from trees in South America? If you have a tree with low-hanging branches in your backyard, ask an adult to watch you hang by your arms from one. Or hang like a sloth on the monkey bars at school or a nearby park. How would it feel to spend most of your day that way?

Whenever you see a sloth and picture it wearing the number *one*, remember Sloth-a-lo-nians the 1st and the book of 1 Thessalonians.

JUST FOR FUN

Read the "to do" list Paul put together for Christians in 1 Thessalonians, Chapter 5 (verses 12-22). Which item on the list feels like the hardest thing to do? Which one is the easiest? Why? (You'll learn more about verse 19 on Friday.)

PRAYER

Lord, sometimes I'm not sure how I can do all the things you want me to do. Please show me one special thing you want me to do every day. As I listen to your voice, help me to obey whatever you say. In Jesus' name I pray. Amen.

1 THESSALONIANS, CHAPTER 4 (VERSES 16-17)

The Lord himself will come down from heaven with a commanding shout, with the voice of the archangel, and with the trumpet call of God. First, the Christians who have died will rise from their graves. Then, together with them, we who are still alive and remain on the earth will be caught up in the clouds to meet the Lord in the air. Then we will be with the Lord forever.

DAILY DEVO

When the Lord comes down, I'll rocket off the ground.

There are some key facts about the future return of Christ. The Lord will first raise from the dead all Christians who have died. Then, together with them, all believers who are still alive will be beamed up to the clouds to meet the Lord in the air, and he will keep us with him forever. When Christ returns, no true Christian, including you, will be left behind. If you have any doubts about your salvation, please talk with your dad, mom, a Sunday school teacher, or your pastor. Ask that person to help you know for sure that when the Lord comes down, you'll rocket off the ground.

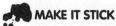

MAKE IT STICK

Draw a picture of a rocket with your name clearly written on its side. Beneath it write this daily devo. Now take a second to imagine how amazing this moment will be. Put your picture on the refrigerator, and be ready to explain this daily devo to family and friends who ask about it.

PRAYER

Lord Jesus, I want to be there when you come back to earth from heaven. It's exciting to think about meeting you in the sky! Thank you for telling me your plan ahead of time. Amen.

CLICK-ER: ROCKET

Whenever you see, play with, or think about a toy *rocket*, let this daily devo take off in your mind as it clicks and sticks. Sloth-a-lo-nians the 1st with his four-on-the-floorboard reminds you that the devo is from 1 Thessalonians, Chapter 4.

1 THESSALONIANS, CHAPTER 5 (VERSE 19)

Do not stifle the Holy Spirit.

DAILY DEVO

I handle his candle with care.

Have you ever heard the word *stifle*? It means to choke or murder by strangling. How can we kill God the Holy Spirit? We can't. But we can choke out the work he wants to do through us. The Holy Spirit is all-powerful, yet he operates in our hearts so gently that he's like a flickering candle. Because the Spirit of God is holy just like God the Father, he won't have anything to do with sin. The Holy Spirit never leaves you, but sin can certainly dampen his plans for you. So handle his candle with care. Whenever you sin, admit it to God. Each time he'll forgive you and ignite his flame within you once again.

 MAKE IT STICK

Ask your dad or mom to please help you light a candle. Now take 10 steps back and try to blow it out. Could you do it? Probably not. Take one step toward the candle and try again. Keep trying, step-by-step, until you blow it out. Sometimes sin creeps up on us until it blows out the light of God's Spirit within us. We need to confess our sins so we don't "stifle the Holy Spirit." With help, relight the candle and say this daily devo.

PRAYER

Holy Spirit, I don't ever want to snuff you out of my heart, but I know I sometimes do. Please forgive my sins and make me more aware of your holy presence in my life. Thank you so much for living in me. Amen.

CLICK-ER: CANDLE

Whenever you see, light, or snuff out a *candle*, let this daily devo flicker in your heart as it clicks and sticks. Sloth-a-lo-nians the 1st with his five-on-a-hive-hat reminds you that the devo is from 1 Thessalonians, Chapter 5.

Week 45, Saturday/Sunday

BOOK OF 2 THESSALONIANS
Sloth-a-lo-nians the 2nd

Sloth ends with the same sound as *Thessalonians* begins with. Like a sloth, the Thessalonians were sometimes slow-moving and lazy because of their sloppy beliefs about the return of Christ. When you see Sloth-a-lo-nians the 2nd in a picture, you'll know the daily devo is from 2 Thessalonians. Connected to Sloth-a-lo-nians the 2nd are number symbols. (See page 15.) They make the chapter location of the devo click and stick.

The good Christians in Thessalonica totally misunderstood Paul's first letter to them. Their phony beliefs about the return of Christ had infected their thoughts and poisoned their behavior. Because they mistakenly thought Jesus would return any minute, many of them quit their jobs and stopped helping around the church. They just sat around waiting for the end of the world. When that didn't come, a lot of people, having run out of money, started mooching off others for food. Paul's response to such foolishness was simple and direct: No work-ey, no turkey. It's great to wait for Christ's return. But work while you wait.

MAKE IT STICK

Make a tab to mark the book of 2 Thessalonians in your Bible. (See Week 1, Monday, for directions.)

Discover how you spend your time each day by drawing a pie chart. First draw a circle. Then draw a straight line through the center from top to bottom. Draw another line through the center from left to right. Ask your dad or mom to help you label each "piece of your day." The total should be 24 hours. How many hours a day do you spend sleeping? eating? going to school?

Whenever you see a sloth and picture it wearing the number *two*, remember Sloth-a-lo-nians the 2nd and the book of 2 Thessalonians.

JUST FOR FUN
What's the one thing Paul says you should never get tired of doing? Read 2 Thessalonians, Chapter 3 (verse 13) to find out.

PRAYER
Dear God, being lazy is easy, but I know it's not the way to live. Certain stuff just has to get done. I'm not that excited about asking you this, but please help me learn how to work. In Jesus' name I pray. Amen.

WEEKEND ACTIVITY IDEAS

(1) Highlight the verses for Week 45 in your Bible. (2) Find the HoneyWord animal in each picture for this week and identify the chapter-number symbols. (3) Add to your collection of Click-ers. (4) Say the daily devos for Week 45. (5) Check out Wednesday of Week 22 for a related devo on what leads to a garden of weeds.

RAINDROPS KEEP FALLING ON THEIR HEADS

Sloths spend most of their time sleeping as they hang from trees in South American rain forests. A sloth's neck muscles hold its head almost totally right-side up while the rest of its body hangs upside down.

2 THESSALONIANS, CHAPTER 3 (VERSE 10)

Even while we were with you, we gave you this command: "Those unwilling to work will not get to eat."

DAILY DEVO

No work-ey, no turkey.

Many of the Thessalonians kept thinking, *If Christ is coming back any second, why work or do anything at all?* And many of them began sitting on the sidelines of life. They quit their jobs. They even quit their chores. So Paul had to remind them that daily duties are just a fact of life. Every day somebody's got to walk the dog, feed the cat, set the table, take out the trash, and clean the bathroom. Are you helping out around the house? If not, learn from Paul's letter to the Thessalonians: No work-ey, no turkey. In other words, if you don't pull your own weight, others shouldn't be put upon to wait on you hand and foot.

MAKE IT STICK

The next time you eat a turkey sandwich or dinner, think through how that turkey got to you—from a turkey farm to a turkey factory to your grocery store. Then your parents had to work and earn enough money to buy it. There's a lot of work-ey that went into that big turkey you're eating. As you savor its flavor, say this daily devo.

PRAYER

Dear God, when I eat with my family, please remind me that food doesn't just show up on the table. Someone worked to get it there. Teach me to do my part at home to show my thanks for all the things you give me. Amen.

CLICK-ER: TURKEY

Whenever you see, eat, or think about sliced *turkey*, let your heart gobble up this daily devo as it clicks and sticks. Sloth-a-lo-nians the 2nd with his three-is-the-key reminds you that the devo is from 2 Thessalonians, Chapter 3.

Week 46, Tuesday

BOOK OF 1 TIMOTHY
Timmy Tiger the 1st

Tiger begins with the same letter as *Timothy*. Like a tiger, Timothy earned his stripes by fiercely defending his spiritual turf as he guarded God's people and pounced on false teachers. When you see Timmy Tiger the 1st in a picture, you'll know the daily devo is from 1 Timothy. Connected to Timmy Tiger the 1st are number symbols. (See page 15.) They make the chapter location of the devo click and stick.

Sad but true: Many false teachers have gotten into the church from its earliest days to the present. Somehow they sneak in among us and teach things that upset the faith of many. Good pastors, like good parents and good kids, are always on the alert about what their families are hearing, seeing, thinking, and believing. That's why Paul urged Timothy, his young pastor-friend, to fight the good fight of faith. Like a tiger, Timothy earned his stripes by fiercely defending his spiritual turf, guarding God's people, and pouncing on false teachers.

 MAKE IT STICK

Make a tab to mark the book of 1 Timothy in your Bible. (See Week 1, Monday, for directions.)

Play a whispering game with your family by whispering a short sentence in the ear of the person next to you. You'll probably find that the last person doesn't repeat back exactly what you said. False teachings about God get started just that easily. Always test everything you hear against the Word of God.

Whenever you see a tiger and picture it wearing the number *one*, remember Timmy Tiger the 1st and the book of 1 Timothy.

JUST FOR FUN

Read 1 Timothy, Chapter 6 (verse 10). What is the root of all kinds of evil? Name three things that prove this is true.

PRAYER

Dear Lord, I don't understand why anyone would want to teach something that isn't true. It's scares me to think that people like that might even be in my church. Please protect my family and me. Teach us what is true so we'll know if someone does not speak the truth. In Jesus' name I pray. Amen.

1 TIMOTHY, CHAPTER 2 (VERSES 1-2)

Pray for all people. Ask God to help them . . . and give thanks for them. Pray this way for kings and all who are in authority so that we can live peaceful and quiet lives marked by godliness and dignity.

DAILY DEVO
My prayers never cease for teachers and police.

Honest-to-goodness prayer, according to Paul, is more than mumbling a few bless 'ems before drifting off to sleep. It's coming to God with requests about the real needs of real people. God wants us to pray for kings and everyone else "in authority." That means parents, teachers, city mayors, state governors, and the president. And it means police officers who keep the peace by enforcing the law, preventing crime, and protecting us and our properties. Increase your prayers for teachers, police, and others who are in authority over you. They'll appreciate it more than you'll know.

MAKE IT STICK
Politely ask your dad or mom to call the police department and get the name of an officer who is regularly assigned to your area. Then begin praying for him or her every night. After one week, call this person's voice mail and say you're praying for him or her. Respectfully ask for a return phone call about specific things you could pray about this week. Conclude your message with this daily devo.

PRAYER
Dear God, please help my parents, my teachers, and leaders everywhere to hear your voice and carefully follow your ways. Thanks for all of them. In Jesus' name, amen.

CLICK-ER: POLICE BADGE
Whenever you see, give respect to, or think about a *police badge* and the police officer who wears it, let your heart salute this daily devo as it clicks and sticks. Timmy Tiger the 1st with his two-blue-shoes reminds you that the devo is from 1 Timothy, Chapter 2.

1 TIMOTHY, CHAPTER 4 (VERSE 12)

Don't let anyone think less of you because you are young. Be an example to all believers in what you say, in the way you live, in your love, your faith, and your purity.

DAILY DEVO

I stand out like a steeple among God's people.

Being young has never been easy. Just ask Timothy. Even though he was a pastor, people in his church said he was too young and too boyish. So Paul stepped in and gave him the secret for handling the bullies trying to push him around. His advice was not to be scared, but instead to stand out like a steeple among God's people. Steeples stand tall and strong. They tower above the buildings that hold them up. And they always point to heaven. As the leader over God's people, Timothy's job was to be like a steeple in the way he lived and showed his love, faith, and purity. He was to stand tall, stay strong, and always point people to God. You may not have been called to be a pastor—at least not yet—but your assignment is still the same: Stand out like a steeple among God's people. It's the only kind of life worth living.

 MAKE IT STICK

Ask an adult to please drive you through your town to see how many different church steeples you can find. Each time you spot one, say this daily devo. If the person you're with is interested, tell the story of Paul and his young friend, Timothy.

PRAYER

Heavenly Father, it's a big deal for you to ask me to be an example to people who are older than I am. I'm going to need your help—a lot. But please help me to live for you whether anyone is looking or not. Amen.

CLICK-ER: STEEPLE

Whenever you see or think about a church *steeple*, let this daily devo stand tall in your heart as it clicks and sticks. Timmy Tiger the 1st with his four-on-the-floorboard reminds you that the devo is from 1 Timothy, Chapter 4.

Week 46, Friday

BOOK OF 2 TIMOTHY
Timmy Tiger the 2nd

Tiger begins with the same letter as *Timothy*. Like a tiger, Timothy earned his stripes by fiercely defending his spiritual turf as he guarded God's Word and pounced on anyone seeking to fleece God's flock. When you see Timmy Tiger the 2nd in a picture, you'll know the daily devo is from 2 Timothy. Connected to Timmy Tiger the 2nd are number symbols. (See page 15.) They make the chapter location of the devo click and stick.

Sometimes life feels like you're being stalked in a jungle at night. The slightest snap of a twig can shake you to the bone. Timothy knew firsthand about this kind of fear. Surrounded by false teachers who were tearing his church apart, Timothy was looking for answers. Paul, writing his last letter, once again stepped in and urged him to fight like a tiger. Instead of being timid, Paul wanted Timothy to earn his stripes by fiercely defending his spiritual turf. He challenged him to guard God's Word and pounce on anyone seeking to fleece God's flock.

MAKE IT STICK

Make a tab to mark the book of 2 Timothy in your Bible. (See Week 1, Monday, for directions.)

Check out a book about tigers, or look them up on the Internet. One of the things you might learn is this: Armed with dagger-sharp teeth over three inches long, the tiger can usually kill its prey with just one bite. What other fun facts about tigers can you find?

Whenever you see a tiger and picture it wearing the number *two*, remember Timmy Tiger the 2nd and the book of 2 Timothy.

JUST FOR FUN

You can pray that your pastors and spiritual leaders will do what Paul told Timothy to do. Read 2 Timothy, Chapter 4 (verses 2-3) and ask God to help your pastors obey these verses.

PRAYER

Lord, being a pastor is a big responsibility. Please protect all the pastors in my church. Keep them strong as they patiently teach us your Word week after week. In Jesus' name I pray. Amen.

2 TIMOTHY, CHAPTER 2 (VERSE 15)

Work hard so you can present yourself to God and receive his approval. Be a good worker, one who does not need to be ashamed and who correctly explains the word of truth.

DAILY DEVO

I know eggs-actly how to slice and dice the Word.

The best restaurants have master chefs. You've probably seen them on TV in their tall white hats, slicing and dicing food so fast you think you're watching on fast-forward mode. But they didn't get that good overnight. They experimented with different recipes over a period of time. The Bible is like one giant 66-book set of recipes for every kind of spiritual food you'd ever want to eat. As a young chef, don't try out every Bible recipe at once. But do start sampling a few. And God will be pleased as over time, you discover his truth—his food—in each book. Then you'll know how to slice and dice every spiritual food there is.

 MAKE IT STICK

Ask your dad or mom to please help you hard-boil an egg. After it's cool, peel off the shell under cold running water, slice it on an egg slicer, and say this daily devo. The slices are like the 66 books of God's Word. Together, the books form the Bible, which contains all of the spiritual food you'll ever need.

PRAYER

Lord, your Word is such a big book, I hardly know where to start. Make me willing to read page after page, as I slowly get to know it. And help me to remember it too. In Jesus' name, amen.

CLICK-ER: **EGG SLICER**

Whenever you eat *eggs* or see, use, or think about an *egg slicer*, let your mind slice and dice this daily devo as it clicks and sticks. Timmy Tiger the 2nd with his two-blue-shoes reminds you that the devo is from 2 Timothy, Chapter 2.

WEEKEND ACTIVITY IDEAS

(1) Highlight the verses for Week 46 in your Bible. (2) Find the HoneyWord animal in each picture for this week and identify the chapter-number symbols. (3) Add to your collection of Click-ers. (4) Say the daily devos for Week 46. (5) Check out Monday of Week 36 for a related devo on how to race to the right place every time.

CREEPING, LEAPING

After carefully creeping up on it prey, a tiger can leap more than 30 feet when it pounces—that's about the length of three minivans parked in a row.

2 TIMOTHY, CHAPTER 3 (VERSES 16-17)

All Scripture is inspired by God and is useful to teach us what is true and to make us realize what is wrong in our lives. It corrects us when we are wrong and teaches us to do what is right. God uses it to prepare and equip his people to do every good work.

DAILY DEVO

God's ruler keeps me straight and strong.

A one-foot ruler equals 12 inches. Not some of the time. All of the time. Rulers help us draw straight lines and measure things accurately. In the same way, God's Word is a ruler that helps us mark out straight paths for our lives. And the Bible is *the* standard that never changes. It's what we use to measure all things spiritual. How are you measuring up? If you don't know, it's probably because you're just starting to learn the Scriptures. For now, just remember this: God's ruler for our lives is a supernatural Book. He chose just the right writers and gave them the ability to create one living Book, which perfectly speaks his exact Word straight to your heart. Line up with God's ruler. It will keep you straight and strong the rest of your life.

 MAKE IT STICK

Write each letter of the word *ruler* on a sheet of paper, using the straight edge of your Bible's cover as a ruler. When you finish, stand up straight and say this daily devo as you hold your "ruler" sheet in one hand and your Bible in the other.

PRAYER

Heavenly Father, thank you that every Bible writer wrote exactly what you wanted to say. Thank you that the Bible corrects me when I'm wrong and gets me ready for all the good things you want me to do. Amen.

CLICK-ER: RULER

Whenever you see, use, or think about a *ruler*, let this daily devo draw a straight line through your mind as it clicks and sticks. Timmy Tiger the 2nd with his three-is-the-key reminds you that the devo is from 2 Timothy, Chapter 3.

Week 47, Tuesday

BOOK OF TITUS
Titus the Tortoise

Tortoise begins and ends with the same sounds as *Titus*. Like a tortoise, Titus steadily plodded along, step by step, and proved himself to be the perfect person to help solve the church crisis on Crete. When you see Titus the Tortoise in a picture, you'll know the daily devo is from Titus. Connected to Titus the Tortoise are number symbols. (See page 15.) They make the chapter location of the devo click and stick.

The church on the island of Crete was in a crisis. False teachers were everywhere, and Christians living a pure life for the Lord were few and far between. So Paul sent Titus to take care of the turmoil. Like a tortoise, he was thick-skinned yet softhearted, mild mannered yet tough as nails. Titus steadily plodded along and proved himself to be the perfect person for the job. He carefully practiced the truth he calmly preached, and he faithfully chose good leaders with strong character in every town. Come out of your shell and enjoy a slow read through this short letter. If you do, you'll see how Titus fit the situation like a turtleneck sweater.

MAKE IT STICK

Make a tab to mark the book of Titus in your Bible. (See Week 1, Monday, for directions.)

Have you ever wondered about the difference between a tortoise and a turtle? Log on to the Internet and have fun finding out. Among other things, you'll learn that a turtle is found in or around water, while a tortoise is only found on dry land. Also, the back legs of a tortoise are stumpy like an elephant's. But the legs of a turtle are webbed for swimming. Kinda cool, huh?

Whenever you see a tortoise or a picture of one, think about Titus the Tortoise and the book of Titus.

JUST FOR FUN
Read what Paul said to Titus in Chapter 3 (verses 13-14). What do you think these guys needed for their trip? Who do you know that might have an urgent need today?

PRAYER
Lord, your Word has a lot to say about people who get off track. I don't ever want to be one of them. What I want is to follow you with all my heart—for the rest of my life. In Jesus' name I pray. Amen.

TITUS, CHAPTER 3 (VERSES 4-5)

When God our Savior revealed his kindness and love, he saved us, not because of the righteous things we had done, but because of his mercy. He washed away our sins, giving us a new birth and new life through the Holy Spirit.

DAILY DEVO

I'm super clean from God's washing machine.

After we do something we shouldn't have done, we often feel dirty inside. That's because sin makes our hearts gross and grimy. But God sent his Son, Jesus Christ, to save us from our sin. And he sent the Holy Spirit to clean us up when we sin. His Spirit is like a heavy-duty washing machine that gets out even the toughest of sinful stains. When we sin, we can't create our own washing machines or spit-and-shine our way to cleanliness. But we can let the Holy Spirit clean up and scrub out all our muck and yuck. Do you need a spiritual bath? Ask Jesus to forgive you, and then ask the Holy Spirit to clean you up. He will make you sudsy-soapy-squeaky clean. And that's a promise.

MAKE IT STICK

How about shocking your dad or mom by offering to help do the laundry? Collect and sort dirty clothes from all over the house. At some point, one parent will probably ask, "What's gotten into you?" Then smile and say this daily devo. If no one faints on the spot, tell about God's heavy-duty washing machine in Titus, Chapter 3 (verses 4-5).

PRAYER

Lord, please forgive me for my sins. And Holy Spirit, please give me the spiritual bath I need. Wash away all my sins and make me clean inside. Thank you. In the name of Jesus I pray. Amen.

CLICK-ER:
WASHING MACHINE

Whenever you see, use, or think about a *washing machine*, let this daily devo wash your heart as it clicks and sticks. Titus the Tortoise with his three-is-the-key reminds you that the devo is from Titus, Chapter 3.

Week 47, Thursday

BOOK OF PHILEMON
Philemon the Flamingo

Flamingo begins with the same sound as *Philemon*.
Like a flamingo, Onesimus seemed to have long,
stiltlike legs, which he used to run away from Philemon. When you see Philemon
the Flamingo in a picture, you'll know the daily devo is from Philemon. Connected
to Philemon the Flamingo are number symbols. (See page 15.) They make the
chapter location of the devo click and stick.

Onesimus was tickled pink like a flamingo as he used his long legs to run
away from his master, Philemon. Thinking he was finally footloose and fancy-free,
he sought refuge in the city of Rome. But as God would have it, he ran smack into
the apostle Paul and became a Christian. Now what? Paul sent him back to Philemon
with a letter asking for total forgiveness. We don't know if Paul's plan succeeded, but
it probably did because of how forgiveness works. God forgives us and expects us to
forgive others so they can forgive others, and on and on, and on and on, forever and
ever. Forgiveness is contagious. Once it starts, it spreads and keeps on going.

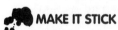 **MAKE IT STICK**

Make a tab to mark the book of Philemon
in your Bible. (See Week 1, Monday, for
directions.)

Find some photos of flamingos by
clicking on the "Images" section of a search
engine. Notice how long and skinny their legs
are. Then do a regular search on "flamingo
fun facts." Did you know a flamingo's eye is
larger than its brain?

Whenever you see a flamingo or a
picture of one, think about Philemon the
Flamingo and the book of Philemon.

JUST FOR FUN
Read about the nice things Paul
said about Philemon when he
wrote to him. Check out Chapter
1 (verses 4-7). Since Philemon
was a kind, loving person, how do
you think he treated Onesimus
when he came back?

PRAYER
Dear God, it's hard sometimes
to forgive others for the wrong
things they do. I know you've
forgiven me for a lot of stuff. So
please help me to remember your
forgiveness when it's my turn to
forgive. In Jesus' name I pray.
Amen.

PHILEMON, CHAPTER 1 (VERSE 15)

It seems you lost Onesimus for a little while so that you could have him back forever.

DAILY DEVO

God always uses the right wrench to reach me.

God is a master at everything he does. He's a Master Teacher. He's a Master Farmer. He's even a Master Mechanic, always using the right wrench to reach us. If you're having any doubts, just ask Onesimus. As a slave belonging to Philemon, he ran away from his master, ran to Rome, ran into Paul, and became a Christian by giving his runaway life to Christ. You see, no matter how far or how fast we run, God is always out in front of us with his special box of search-and-rescue tools. And he's got plenty of wrenches with long handles and adjustable jaws for gripping and turning nuts and bolts—like you and me—in the right direction. Don't run from God. It's no use. He'll always find the right wrench to reach you.

 MAKE IT STICK

Trace around a wrench on a piece of cardboard, or just draw one by looking at a picture in a catalog or the picture on this page. Cut it out and cover it with aluminum foil. Then have fun going around the inside or outside of your house, finding nuts and bolts you can pretend to tighten. Each time you turn and "tighten" a nut, say this daily devo. Remember that you're like that nut, and God is gently gripping you to bring you back to him.

PRAYER

Dear God, I'm glad you come after me whenever I try to run from you. It makes me feel good that you love me that much. Thank you for the safety I have in you. In Jesus' name I pray. Amen.

CLICK-ER: WRENCH

Whenever you see, use, or think about a *wrench*, let your mind tighten this daily devo around your heart as it clicks and sticks. Philemon the Flamingo with his one-on-a-bun reminds you that the devo is from Philemon, Chapter 1.

Week 47, Saturday/Sunday

BOOK OF HEBREWS

Hebrews the Hippo

Hippo begins with the same letter as *Hebrews*.

Many Jewish Christians (Hebrews) felt so blue and underwater, they looked liked a hippo with just their eyes, ears, and noses above the surface. When you see Hebrews the Hippo in a picture, you'll know the daily devo is from Hebrews. Connected to Hebrews the Hippo are number symbols. (See page 15.) They make the chapter location of the devo click and stick.

The Jewish Christians in this book, who were also known as Hebrews, had a bad case of the blues. They'd lost homes, loved ones, and almost their very lives. Feeling low from harsh criticism, they looked like a hippo barely above the surface. To keep them from bailing out of the Christian faith, they needed to know for sure that Christianity was true. And they needed to know that Jesus was the Messiah, who had come to save them from sin. So the author of Hebrews filled their hungry hippo hearts with proof that Jesus is superior to everyone: Joshua, Moses, the prophets, and even angels. Jesus is God's full and final revelation.

 MAKE IT STICK

Make a tab to mark the book of Hebrews in your Bible. (See Week 1, Monday, for directions.)

Play musical chairs with your family and make a paper crown to honor the winner. Play several rounds until everyone gets to wear the crown. Then think about Jesus, who has the place of honor at the right hand of God the Father in heaven. He never has to fight to get that seat, because it can never belong to anyone else.

Whenever you see a hippo or a picture of one, think about Hebrews the Hippo and the book of Hebrews.

JUST FOR FUN

To read about God the Son (Jesus) being even greater than angels, check out Hebrews, Chapter 1 (verses 3-4).

PRAYER

Dear God, I'm glad you've given the best seat in heaven to your Son, Jesus. He is the only one who belongs there, because he was brave enough to come to earth and die on the cross for everyone's sins. Thank you, God, for Jesus, my Savior. Amen.

WEEKEND ACTIVITY IDEAS

(1) Highlight the verses for Week 47 in your Bible. (2) Find the HoneyWord animal in each picture for this week and identify the chapter-number symbols. (3) Add to your collection of Click-ers. (4) Say the daily devos for Week 47. (5) Check out Thursday of Week 38 for a related devo on your only complete one-way street to heaven.

HORSE OF A DIFFERENT COLOR

Hippopotamus comes from a Greek word that means "water horse" or "river horse." But hippos are not related to horses. Their closest living relative is the pig!

HEBREWS, CHAPTER 4 (VERSE 12)

The word of God is alive and powerful. It is sharper than the sharpest two-edged sword, cutting between soul and spirit, between joint and marrow. It exposes our innermost thoughts and desires.

DAILY DEVO

The Word of the Lord is my sword.

A sword is an ancient weapon of war used for defending good guys and defeating bad guys. The word of God is sharper than the sharpest sword. It lets the air out of every inflated thought that rises up against what's true about God. The Jewish Christians in this book were holding on to, and believing in, a big bag of hot air. They were puffed up with the wrong notion that Jesus might not really be God. So the writer to these Hebrews warned them that God's Word would cut through their false beliefs and expose their true hearts. Come under the sword of the Lord, and let it deflate whatever is defeating you.

MAKE IT STICK

Politely ask your dad or mom for help in doing this activity. Pry open and bend a paper clip into the shape of a little sword. Now blow up a balloon and tie it around your forehead so it sticks up above your head. As you use your sword to pop the hot air around your mind, say this daily devo. Then look up some of your favorite daily devos and think about how each one cuts out wrong thoughts.

PRAYER

Dear God, I like how you compare your Word to a sword that is sharp enough to cut away all of my wrong thoughts. I'm glad that the Bible helps me see if I'm following what is true. In the name of Jesus, amen.

CLICK-ER: SWORD

Whenever you see, play with, or think about a plastic *sword*, let this daily devo pop the wrong thoughts in your mind as it clicks and sticks. Hebrews the Hippo with his four-on-the-floorboard reminds you that the devo is from Hebrews, Chapter 4.

HEBREWS, CHAPTER 6 (VERSES 18-20)

We who have fled to him for refuge can have great confidence as we hold to the hope that lies before us. This hope is a strong and trustworthy anchor for our souls. It leads us through the curtain into God's inner sanctuary. Jesus has already gone in there for us.

DAILY DEVO

Jesus is my ready, steady anchor.

You know what an anchor is, don't you? It's that heavy, metal gizmo that's attached to a rope and thrown overboard to keep a boat from moving. Anchors only work when they hit bottom and hold on from below. But there's another kind of anchor that holds on from above. This downside-up anchor is Jesus himself, who's already gone through the curtain of heaven and into the very presence of God the Father. It's as if Jesus has a super-long, unbreakable, invisible rope tied to his waist that hangs down to earth all the way from heaven. And here's the really cool part. This rope is permanently tied around your waist, so you're connected to Jesus no matter where you go. You can be sure that he'll hear and answer your prayers. So hang tough.

 MAKE IT STICK

Draw yourself with a rope tied around your waist. Now show that rope stretching up to Jesus in heaven, tied to an anchor around his waist. That shows your eternal connection to Jesus. Now say this daily devo as you thank God for how securely you're anchored to him.

PRAYER

Thank you, Jesus, for keeping me safe as I hang on to you. And thanks for letting me pray to God the Father in your name. I know you're right beside him, listening to my prayers, and answering every one of them. Amen.

CLICK-ER: ANCHOR

Whenever you see, use, or think about an *anchor*, let this daily devo hold your heart in place as it clicks and sticks. Hebrews the Hippo with his six-pick-up-stix reminds you that the devo is from Hebrews, Chapter 6.

HEBREWS, CHAPTER 9 (VERSE 14)

Just think how much more the blood of Christ will purify our consciences from sinful deeds so that we can worship the living God. For by the power of the eternal Spirit, Christ offered himself to God as a perfect sacrifice for our sins.

DAILY DEVO

His blood cleans the mud off my heart.

Did you know that each of us is born with a thick layer of sinful mud on our hearts? This sin-mud resists everything that tries to clean it off, except for one thing: the blood of Christ. Don't be grossed out by the word *blood*. Often in the Bible *blood* simply means "death." In the Old Testament, the death of animals covered muddy sin from God's eyes. In the New Testament it was Jesus' perfect life, death, and resurrection that not only covered our muddy sins, but also removed the mud forever. Now no one needs to give animals as an offering to God (like in the Old Testament). Jesus is your offering. His blood has cleaned the mud off your heart.

MAKE IT STICK

Politely ask your dad or mom to help you understand what a "blood bank" is. Talk about how our blood can give life on this earth to other people and how Jesus' blood gives eternal life to everyone who believes in him. Repeat this daily devo and ask your parents about any part of the devo you don't understand.

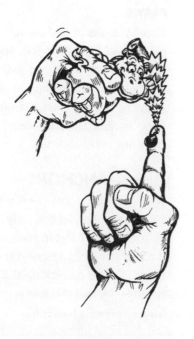

PRAYER

Thank you, Jesus, for sacrificing your life on the cross and for cleaning away my sin. You gave your blood so I can live with you forever. I love you, Lord, and I praise you for everything you've done for me. Amen.

CLICK-ER: BLOOD

Whenever you see, touch, or think about your own *blood*, let this daily devo circulate through your mind as it clicks and sticks. Hebrews the Hippo with his nine-foot-pine reminds you that the devo is from Hebrews, Chapter 9.

HEBREWS, CHAPTER 11 (VERSE 1)

Faith is the confidence that what we hope for will actually happen; it gives us assurance about things we cannot see.

DAILY DEVO

Can't see what's ahead—gotta trust instead.

One of the hardest things about being friends with God is getting used to the fact that he's invisible—at least in this life. And furthermore, this God, whom we can't see, requires that we follow him by faith, not by sight. So what's that mean? It means that most of us aren't told in advance exactly where he's leading us or how he's going to get us there. It's a bit like blindfolding a close friend and taking that person on a "trust walk." No true friend would ever purposely bump you into a stump or lead you off a cliff. And God is the same way. First Peter, Chapter 1 (verses 8-9) puts it this way: "You love him even though you have never seen him. Though you do not see him now, you trust him. . . . The reward for trusting him will be the salvation of your souls." You see, God seldom lets us see what's ahead. He simply wants us to trust instead. And when we do, he always gets us there safe and sound.

MAKE IT STICK

Have fun taking turns blindfolding a friend or someone in your family and taking that person on a walk around your house. At the end of each turn, have the blindfolded person say this daily devo.

PRAYER

Heavenly Father, even though I can't see what's ahead, I have faith that you'll go with me. I know you're with me now, and I trust you to stay with me forever. In Jesus' name I pray. Amen.

CLICK-ER: BLINDFOLD

Whenever you see, wear, or think about a *blindfold*, let your heart open your eyes to this daily devo as it clicks and sticks. Hebrews the Hippo with a one-on-a-bun on each side reminds you that the devo is from Hebrews, Chapter 11.

HEBREWS, CHAPTER 13 (VERSE 3)

Remember those in prison, as if you were there yourself. Remember also those being mistreated, as if you felt their pain in your own bodies.

DAILY DEVO

I deeply feel for those living in cages of steel.

Imagine this, if you can. Soldiers with machine guns force their way into your house and ask, "Do you believe that Jesus is God?" Everyone in your family says yes, so you are all taken to jail. This happens to families every day of the week in different parts of the world. And we know it happened to the Jewish Christians at the time the book of Hebrews was written, because in Chapter 10 (verse 34), the writer said, "You suffered along with those who were thrown into jail." Not everybody in prison deserves to be there. Can you deeply feel for those living in cages of steel? If not, pray that you can.

MAKE IT STICK

Draw a picture of you and your entire family behind the bars of a jail. Now close your eyes and try to imagine what it would feel like for you to be cooped up in a small, one-room prison cell, day after day, week after week. Pray that God will strengthen those Christians throughout the world who are in jail right now because of their faith. End your prayer by saying this daily devo.

PRAYER

Dear God, I'm so sorry that some people are put in jail just for believing in Jesus. Please stay close to those people. Keep their faith strong, and help them know that you really love them. In Jesus' name I pray. Amen.

CLICK-ER:
CAGES OF STEEL

Whenever you see, visit, or think about *cages of steel*, let this daily devo lower the bars in your heart as it clicks and sticks. Hebrews the Hippo with his one-on-a-bun and three-is-the-key reminds you that the devo is from Hebrews, Chapter 13.

Week 48, Saturday/Sunday

BOOK OF JAMES

James the German Shepherd

German shepherd begins with the same sound as *James*. Like a German shepherd, James doggedly loved God's sheep and showed them how to live a faith-filled, action-packed life. When you see James the German Shepherd in a picture, you'll know the daily devo is from James. Connected to James the German Shepherd are number symbols. (See page 15.) They make the chapter location of the devo click and stick.

Centuries ago in Europe, some shepherds decided to raise a dog that would meet the special needs of their sheep. It had to be an intelligent, alert, brave, loyal, obedient, good-natured, and protective outdoor guard dog. It worked. The new breed they developed became known as the German shepherd. James, the writer of this letter, was a half brother of Jesus. And as the leader of God's sheep—the church—in Jerusalem, his heart for God's people is best compared to that of a German shepherd. He doggedly loved God's sheep and wrote this letter to teach them how to show their faith through kind words and good deeds.

 MAKE IT STICK

Make a tab to mark the book of James in your Bible. (See Week 1, Monday, for directions.)

Take turns with family members or friends pretending to be a German Shepherd rounding up sheep. When the "shepherd" catches a "sheep," he or she says something kind. (For example: "I'm really glad you're my little sister.") Or the "shepherd" might do a good deed, like sharing a treat.

Whenever you see a German shepherd or a picture of one, think about James the German Shepherd and the book of James.

JUST FOR FUN

Read what James wrote in James, Chapter 1 (verses 22-25) about looking at your face in a mirror. What he says makes sense, doesn't it?

PRAYER

Dear God, your Word makes it clear that it's not what I know that counts. It's what I do. So please help me to actually do what I know you've taught me to do. And I thank you for your promise to bless me for doing it. In Jesus' name, amen.

WEEKEND ACTIVITY IDEAS

(1) Highlight the verses for Week 48 in your Bible. (2) Find the HoneyWord animal in each picture for this week and identify the chapter-number symbols. (3) Add to your collection of Click-ers. (4) Say the daily devos for Week 48. (5) Check out Wednesday of Week 43 for a related devo on being there to help someone up that stair.

TOP DOG

German shepherds are called police dogs when they are trained to catch criminals. And they're called Seeing Eye dogs when they are trained to guide people who are blind, becoming like eyes to help them see.

JAMES, CHAPTER 3 (VERSE 5)

The tongue is a small thing that makes grand speeches. But a tiny spark can set a great forest on fire.

DAILY DEVO

Like a match, my tongue can strike and burn.

Did you know the first friction match was sold way back in 1827? The man who discovered this bright idea was a British chemist named John Walker. He glued a dab of chemicals on the tip of a long stick. Holding the stick between his fingers, he found he could strike it anywhere, and in a flash he had a burning match. What Mr. Walker did with the match, we can do with our tongues. Our burning words can strike people's hearts and sometimes almost burn them up. Please be very, very careful about what you say. Without God's help, your tongue might strike and burn someone to a crisp.

 MAKE IT STICK

Politely ask your dad or mom to help you look up *match* or *safety match* online or in an encyclopedia. Have fun learning together about the history of the match and how it works. When you're done, say this daily devo as you draw a picture of yourself with flames shooting out from the tip of your tongue. Ask God to bring to mind someone you may have struck and burned. Then go to that person and humbly ask for forgiveness.

PRAYER

Dear God, I don't want my words to burn like fire, so please help me be careful about what I say. If I have hurt someone, make me willing to go to that person and ask for forgiveness. In Jesus' name I pray. Amen.

CLICK-ER: MATCH

Whenever you see or think about a *match*, let this daily devo kindle kindness in your heart as it clicks and sticks. James the German Shepherd with his three-is-the-key reminds you that the devo is from James, Chapter 3.

JAMES, CHAPTER 5 (VERSES 14-15)

Are any of you sick? You should call for the elders of the church to come and pray over you, anointing you with oil in the name of the Lord. Such a prayer offered in faith will heal the sick, and the Lord will make you well. And if you have committed any sins, you will be forgiven.

DAILY DEVO

Oil and faith can heal the sick mighty quick.

Can God heal? He can, and he does. How? Through rest, exercise, healthy food, vitamins, medicine, surgery, physical therapy, faith, and, of course, the prayers of Bible-believing friends, family, and church buddies. When you are sick, James says to call for the elders—the spiritual leaders—of your church to pray and put oil on your head in Jesus' name. In the Bible, oil was used as a medicine and to show that God's Spirit was present. So oil, along with faith, is a reminder that God will heal you physically and spiritually. But only God, who made you, knows the best way and the best time for both. None of us will be completely whole until we're in heaven.

MAKE IT STICK

Make a get-well card for someone who is sick or hurt. Include a prayer offered in faith. Perhaps you and someone from your family or church can deliver the card. If not, ask one of your parents if you could please have the address, an envelope, and a stamp so you can mail it. When you're finished, say this daily devo.

PRAYER

I'm thankful, God, for all the times you've made me well, and for people who have prayed for me. Help me believe that you heal in many ways: through doctors, pills, prayers, rest, and miracles. In Jesus' name, amen.

CLICK-ER: OLIVE OIL

Whenever you see, think about, or eat something cooked in *olive oil*, let this daily devo lube your heart as it clicks and sticks. James the German Shepherd with his five-on-a-hive-hat reminds you that the devo is from James, Chapter 5.

Week 49, Wednesday

BOOK OF 1 PETER

Peter Panda the 1st

Panda begins with the same letter as *Peter*. Like a giant panda, Peter stepped in and gave hurting believers a big bear hug of encouragement. When you see Peter Panda the 1st in a picture, you'll know the daily devo is from 1 Peter. Connected to Peter Panda the 1st are number symbols. (See page 15.) They make the chapter location of the devo click and stick.

Times were tough when this letter was written. Throughout the Roman Empire, Christians were being hurt and even killed for their faith. Church people were leaving Jerusalem and scattering throughout the Mediterranean world. So Peter, like a giant panda, stepped in and gave God's people a big bear hug of encouragement. Peter understood that the believers needed to bear in mind that since Christ suffered, many of his followers would also suffer. God doesn't promise to keep you from the pain and trials of life, but he does promise to hold you like a giant panda, hugging you and helping you through.

 MAKE IT STICK

Make a tab to mark the book of 1 Peter in your Bible. (See Week 1, Monday, for directions.)

Look up pandas on the Internet. See if you can learn the name of the only country where pandas can be found, other than in zoos.

Whenever you see a panda and picture it wearing the number *one*, remember Peter Panda the 1st and the book of 1 Peter.

JUST FOR FUN

Read 1 Peter, Chapter 1 (verses 6-7) to see what Peter said to people going through hard times. What did he say was ahead for them?

PRAYER

Lord Jesus, I wish suffering would never be a part of life. But I know it is. Help me to see your purpose in it and to trust you through the good times and bad times. Amen.

1 PETER, CHAPTER 2 (VERSES 2-3)

Like newborn babies, you must crave pure spiritual milk so that you will grow into a full experience of salvation. Cry out for this nourishment, now that you have had a taste of the Lord's kindness.

DAILY DEVO

I know the milky way to grow.

Many experts believe that milk is the most nourishing of all foods. It has almost everything we need for growth and good health. And there are lots of ways to take it in: butter, buttermilk, cheese, evaporated milk, whole milk, low-fat milk, skim milk, yogurt, chocolate milk, cream, sour cream, and even ice cream. Peter compares the Word of God to pure spiritual milk. When we read it, remember what it says, and do what it teaches, it helps us, as God's children, to grow up. We become strong Christians, very sure about what we believe. We understand the salvation that's ours if we believe Jesus is God's Son. He will forgive our sins as we put our trust in him. But this milky way to grow isn't automatic. You've got to pick it up and drink in big glassfuls of it. Do you really want to grow up big and strong in your faith? Then read God's Word and wear his milk mustache *every* day.

 MAKE IT STICK

Write this daily devo on a slip of paper and tape it to the outside of a clear glass. Now fill it with milk. Before drinking it, say the daily devo.

PRAYER

Dear God, I know that babies cry when they need milk. And kids like me grow strong by drinking milk. Please help me remember to drink my spiritual milk too by reading my Bible every day. In Jesus' name, amen.

CLICK-ER: MILK

Whenever you see, drink, or think about *milk*, let this daily devo nourish your soul as it clicks and sticks. Peter Panda the 1st with his two-blue-shoes reminds you that the devo is from 1 Peter, Chapter 2.

1 PETER, CHAPTER 3 (VERSES 8-9)
Finally, all of you should be of one mind. Sympathize with each other. Love each other as brothers and sisters. Be tenderhearted, and keep a humble attitude. Don't repay evil for evil. Don't retaliate with insults when people insult you. Instead, pay them back with a blessing. That is what God has called you to do, and he will bless you for it.

DAILY DEVO
I fight back with gloves of love.
Kids fight. Parents fight. Even nations fight. A good fight is when you're fighting for the truth of God with his strength. A bad fight is when you're fighting for revenge—to get even—in your own strength. Don't try to get back at others for what they've done to you. Leave that to God. Instead, do the unexpected: Love them. Learn to fight with God's boxing gloves from above. Pray for those who have hurt you the most and leave them in the hands of God. Then ask God for the strength to do or say something nice to them . . . today. You see, if you want God's blessing on your life, you've got to get out of the revenge business.

MAKE IT STICK
Name all the different kinds of gloves you can think of. Talk with your dad or mom about each kind of glove: how and when it's used, what it's made of, where you'd keep it, and so on. The next time someone says something mean to you, take a deep breath and silently pray this daily devo to God. Ask him for strength not to say anything mean in return.

PRAYER
Dear God, it's really tough being nice to someone who's mean to me. But I know that's what you want. So please help me put on your gloves of love and fight back with kindness. In Jesus' name, amen.

CLICK-ER: GLOVES
Whenever you see, wear, or think about *gloves*, let this daily devo fit like a glove on your heart as it clicks and sticks. Peter Panda the 1st with his three-is-the-key reminds you that the devo is from 1 Peter, Chapter 3.

1 PETER, CHAPTER 4 (VERSE 8)

Most important of all, continue to show deep love for each other, for love covers a multitude of sins.

DAILY DEVO

God's love is a quilt that covers all my guilt.

Quilts are made from many small pieces of fabric sewn together to form a pattern. God's love is like a beautiful hand-stitched quilt. It's warm, cozy, and big enough to cover anyone. Peter reminds us to love one another deeply, because love—God's kind of love—covers many sins. Think about it. How many of your sins has God forgiven, covered up, and hidden forever? Every single one! If he's covered ALL of yours, is it too much for you to forgive someone else? You can love like God by forgiving again and again. Then God's love will flow through you and come out like a giant quilt that covers others' guilt, as well as your own.

 **MAKE IT STICK**

Use crayons to turn a sheet of paper into a beautiful quilt by completely filling it up with patches of color. Now write a couple of your sins on slips of paper and hide them under your paper quilt. Can't see them anymore, can you? That's a picture of what God has done for you and what he's asking you to do for others. As you think deeply about this teaching, say this daily devo.

PRAYER

Thank you, God, for your love, which covers up all my sins. Please help me to forgive others so that same love can flow through me and cover their sins too. In Jesus' name, amen.

CLICK-ER: QUILT

Whenever you see, use, or think about a *quilt*, let your heart snuggle up with this daily devo as it clicks and sticks. Peter Panda the 1st with his four-on-the-floorboard reminds you that the devo is from 1 Peter, Chapter 4.

WEEKEND ACTIVITY IDEAS

(1) Highlight the verses for Week 49 in your Bible. (2) Find the HoneyWord animal in each picture for this week and identify the chapter-number symbols. (3) Add to your collection of Click-ers. (4) Say the daily devos for Week 49. (5) Check out Thursday of Week 4 for a related devo on the scapegoat who took your "sin coat."

CHEW BAMBOO

Pandas have big appetites and can eat up to 40 pounds of bamboo a day. Giant pandas can eat twice that much.

1 PETER, CHAPTER 5 (VERSES 8-9)

Stay alert! Watch out for your great enemy, the devil. He prowls around like a roaring lion, looking for someone to devour. Stand firm against him, and be strong in your faith. Remember that your Christian brothers and sisters all over the world are going through the same kind of suffering you are.

DAILY DEVO

My knees hit the floor when I hear the devil roar.

Have you ever heard of Nero? He's definitely nobody's hero. He was the fifth Roman emperor and ruled for 14 years, from AD 54 to 68. He became famous for killing Christians. He would let lions attack and kill believers in front of large audiences. Satan is like a lion, ready to pounce on people who believe in Jesus. Interestingly, God never commands us to directly attack the enemy, but our heavenly Father does ask us to hold our ground against Satan's roaring air raids. How? By never giving up our faith. When you hear the devil roar during difficult times, you can stand firm by letting your knees hit the floor in prayer. God will see you through your troubles and keep your faith from dying.

MAKE IT STICK

Before you go to sleep tonight, kneel by your bed and pray that God will help you be strong against the attacks of the devil. Use this daily devo in your prayer. Over the next few days, watch to see how God keeps your faith alive and strong.

PRAYER

Heavenly Father, I really don't understand why you let the devil live. But help me trust you with this and keep my faith strong when Satan tries to get me down. In Jesus' name I pray. Amen.

CLICK-ER: KNEES

Whenever you touch, bend, or think about your *knees*, let this daily devo kneel in your heart as it clicks and sticks. Peter Panda the 1st with his five-on-a-hive-hat reminds you that the devo is from 1 Peter, Chapter 5.

Week 50, Tuesday

BOOK OF 2 PETER

Peter Panda the 2nd

Panda begins with the same letter as *Peter*. The black eyes and boxed ears of the giant panda are a picture of the sufferings Peter challenged believers to endure as they held on to their faith. When you see Peter Panda the 2nd in a picture, you'll know the daily devo is from 2 Peter. Connected to Peter Panda the 2nd are number symbols. (See page 15.) They make the chapter location of the devo click and stick.

It's hard to believe, but even in the church there are some people who will try to lead us away from God. Whether it's beatings from those outside the church (the message of 1 Peter), or wrong teachings from those inside it (the message of 2 Peter), every kind of knockout punch hurts a lot. So for the second time, Peter, like a giant panda, put his arms around God's people and comforted them. Having weathered black eyes and boxed ears himself, Peter encouraged the believers to bear in mind the importance of holding on to their faith. His message is for all of us. Knowing God's Word helps us know what to believe.

 MAKE IT STICK

Make a tab to mark the book of 2 Peter in your Bible. (See Week 1, Monday, for directions.)

Work with your family to make a list of the top 10 daily devos you like most. Write the Click-er for each one on a small slip of paper and place the papers in a bowl or basket. Now take turns pulling out the Click-ers, one by one, and seeing who can remember the daily devo along with the book and chapter location of that passage of Scripture. Keep going until someone gets all the answers right. Then let that person gather with the rest of your family for a group bear hug.

Whenever you see a panda and picture it wearing the number *two*, remember Peter Panda the 2nd and the book of 2 Peter.

JUST FOR FUN

Read 2 Peter, Chapter 3 (verses 3-5) for a quick summary of how God created the heavens and the earth. What did you learn that you never knew before?

PRAYER

Lord, I really do love learning your Word whenever I sit down and read it. But sometimes other things get in the way. Please help me to meet with you at the same time every day so we can become even better friends. In Jesus' name, amen.

2 PETER, CHAPTER 1 (VERSE 3)

By his divine power, God has given us everything we need for living a godly life. We have received all of this by coming to know him, the one who called us to himself by means of his marvelous glory and excellence.

DAILY DEVO

I glitter **God's glory.**

Have you ever made dazzling designs on paper with glitter? It's fun to see something you've made glisten and glimmer, isn't it? Creating a glittery picture helps us understand how God's glory (his greatness) works in our lives. When we believe in Jesus and follow God's ways, he showers his glory on us like glitter. Then God uses his glitter on us to brilliantly attract others to himself. It's a beautiful plan, isn't it? But it's not automatic. We must choose to receive God's glory so we can live godly lives. Peter says that getting to know God better is the only way to tap into his divine power and glory. Talk to God often. Read his Word and learn how to obey it. Then glitter his glory wherever you go.

MAKE IT STICK

Respectfully ask your dad or mom to buy you some glitter from a discount store or craft shop if you promise not to make a mess. When you get your glitter, put down a lot of newspaper. Then have fun creating a glorious design by doodling glue on paper and covering it with glitter. As you make it, say this daily devo.

PRAYER

Dear God, I like the idea of glittering your glory. It sounds like fun. And I'm trusting you to help me learn to be more like you. In Jesus' name I pray. Amen.

CLICK-ER: **GLITTER**

Whenever you see, use, or think about *glitter*, let this daily devo glisten in your mind as it clicks and sticks. Peter Panda the 2nd with his one-on-a-bun reminds you that the devo is from 2 Peter, Chapter 1.

2 PETER, CHAPTER 3 (VERSES 8-9)

You must not forget this one thing, dear friends: A day is like a thousand years to the Lord, and a thousand years is like a day. The Lord isn't really being slow about his promise, as some people think. No, he is being patient for your sake. He does not want anyone to be destroyed, but wants everyone to repent.

DAILY DEVO

God's clock is tick-tock-ticking on time.

Come on! Hurry up! Let's go!" are lines we've all heard—and used—a million times. In a world that lives on instant pudding, Minute rice, and fast-food restaurants, impatience is widespread. But that's not even close to the way God is. He's very, very patient. Like a faithful grandfather clock, he's slowly tick-tock-ticking off the seconds to eternity. He's delaying Jesus' return to the earth so more people can have time to say they're sorry for their sins and turn away from them. You see, God wants everyone to live with him in heaven someday. Have you put your faith in Christ? If not, "Come on! Hurry up! Let's go!" God's clock won't tick-tock-tick forever.

MAKE IT STICK

If you have a grandfather clock at home, sit and watch it for a while. You'll be fascinated. If you don't have one, which most people don't, politely ask a parent to take you to the clock section of a department store at the mall. At least one store will probably have a grandfather clock. When it's time to go, say this daily devo.

PRAYER

Thank you, God, for being so great that you are in control of time. Thanks for never being too early or too late. And thank you for giving me the time to tell you I'm sorry for my sins. In the name of Jesus I pray. Amen.

CLICK-ER: GRANDFATHER CLOCK

Whenever you see, hear, or think about a *grandfather clock*, let this daily devo tick-tock-tick in your ticker as it clicks and sticks. Peter Panda the 2nd with his three-is-the-key reminds you that the devo is from 2 Peter, Chapter 3.

Week 50, Friday

BOOK OF 1 JOHN
Johnny Giraffe the 1st

Giraffe starts with the same sound as *John*. A baby giraffe is the animal that best pictures the long, warmhearted reach of John in this little letter. When you see Johnny Giraffe the 1st in a picture, you'll know the daily devo is from 1 John. Connected to Johnny Giraffe the 1st are number symbols. (See page 15.) They make the chapter location of the devo click and stick.

John wrote this short book when he was an old man. Known as "the apostle of love," John wrote again about the life-changing power of God's love. John was direct and clear. Loving God means loving people. And loving people means loving God. Sounds simple, but it can be very hard. That's why John used simple words and sharp contrasts—light and darkness, truth and error, God and Satan, life and death, love and hate. Like a giraffe, John reached up and grabbed high thoughts about God, then brought them down to our level. So enjoy these spiritual cookies he put on the lower shelf just for you!

MAKE IT STICK

Make a tab to mark the book of 1 John in your Bible. (See Week 1, Monday, for directions.)

Show your love for God and for one or more of your Christian friends. Write a note, make up a song, or draw a picture for each one. When you're finished, take it or mail it to them and see how they respond.

Whenever you see a loving baby giraffe and picture it wearing the number *one*, remember Johnny Giraffe the 1st and the book of 1 John.

JUST FOR FUN

Read what John says about loving God and loving people in 1 John, Chapter 4 (verses 19-21). Have you ever thought about this before?

PRAYER

Thank you, Lord, for loving me first. It makes me want to love you back. Teach me to show my love for you more and more each day by really loving my family and friends. In Jesus' name, amen.

1 JOHN, CHAPTER 1 (VERSE 9)

If we confess our sins to him, he is faithful and just to forgive us our sins and to cleanse us from all wickedness.

DAILY DEVO

His soap gives me hope.

Soap comes in many forms: bars, flakes, grains, liquids, tablets. And we use it for cleaning all kinds of things: hands, hair, clothes, dishes. Daily bathing with soap keeps dirt and body oils from clogging the pores of our skin. In this verse, John reminds us that everybody also needs spiritual cleansing. But if we want God to forgive us and clean away our sins, we first have to confess them. That simply means sincerely praying a one-sentence prayer: "I was wrong, and I'm sorry." Then, because God's Son, Jesus, has already died for our sins, God forgives us. That one requirement doesn't seem like too big of a deal. But you'd be amazed at the number of people who refuse to come clean with God. Don't be like them. Admit your dirt. And then let Jesus' soap scrub you clean and give you hope.

 MAKE IT STICK

Politely ask your dad or mom to help you safely and carefully carve the name *Jesus* in a big bar of soap. Then say this daily devo tonight as you use it to bathe.

PRAYER

Dear God, I'm glad you clean me up inside, just like soap cleans me up outside. I'm sorry for all the things I've done that hurt you. Please forgive me and clean away my sins. In Jesus' name, amen.

CLICK-ER: SOAP

Whenever you see, use, or think about *soap*, let this daily devo wash your heart clean as it clicks and sticks. Johnny Giraffe the 1st with his one-on-a-bun reminds you that the devo is from 1 John, Chapter 1.

WEEKEND ACTIVITY IDEAS
(1) Highlight the verses for Week 50 in your Bible. (2) Find the HoneyWord
animal in each picture for this week and identify the chapter-number symbols.
(3) Add to your collection of Click-ers. (4) Say the daily devos for Week 50.
(5) Check out Wednesday of Week 47 for a related devo on getting clean in a
supernatural washing machine.

FALLING INTO PLACE
Weighing between 120 and 150 pounds, a baby giraffe is
six feet tall and drops five feet to the ground at birth.

1 JOHN, CHAPTER 5 (VERSE 18)

We know that God's children do not make a practice of sinning, for God's Son holds them securely, and the evil one cannot touch them.

DAILY DEVO

Jesus holds me tight like a kite.

After you do something that isn't right, do you wonder if you're still a member of God's family? John wanted all who believe in Jesus to know that Satan can't pull us away from our forever family. Sometimes we *will* do wrong things. But because we love Jesus, we'll feel bad and confess what we did. See 1 John, Chapter 1 (verse 9). Then Jesus will help us stop sinning. Before you placed your faith in Christ, you were like a kite on the ground with no strength to fly. Then it was as if Jesus picked you up, tied a long string around your heart, and set you aloft. He'll never let go of you or let you crash to the ground. He permanently holds you tight. So enjoy the flight. You're on your way up, up, up to heaven, and that's worth shouting about with all your might.

 MAKE IT STICK

Draw a kite and attach a string to it, or have fun flying a real kite. Then thank Jesus for forgiving you, holding you tight, and helping you follow him instead of doing wrong things again and again. Repeat this daily devo as you run with your kite.

PRAYER

Lord Jesus, thank you for holding on to me and keeping me from sinning again and again. And thank you for protecting me from Satan. I love you with all my heart and want to follow you every day. Amen.

CLICK-ER: KITE

Whenever you see, fly, or think about a *kite*, let this daily devo fly high in your heart as it clicks and sticks. Johnny Giraffe the 1st with his five-on-a-hive-hat reminds you that the devo is from 1 John, Chapter 5.

Week 51, Tuesday

BOOK OF 2 JOHN
Johnny Giraffe the 2nd

Giraffe starts with the same sound as *John*. A baby giraffe is the animal that best pictures the long, tenderhearted reach of John in this second little letter. When you see Johnny Giraffe the 2nd in a picture, you'll know the daily devo is from 2 John. Connected to Johnny Giraffe the 2nd are number symbols. (See page 15.) They make the chapter location of the devo click and stick.

John wrote this super-short book when he was an old man. Known as "the apostle of love," John once again pointed to the life-changing power of the love of God. In a letter only 13 verses long, John's simple style kept things short and sweet: Loving one another is the key to Christian living. And real love, said John, cannot be separated from truth and obedience. Anyone teaching anything different is a false teacher. Like a giraffe, John reached up and grabbed high thoughts about God, then brought them down to our level. So enjoy these spiritual cookies he put on the lower shelf just for you!

 MAKE IT STICK

Make a tab to mark the book of 2 John in your Bible. (See Week 1, Monday, for directions.)

Verse 12 of John's letter is the only place in the Bible that mentions paper. The process of making paper was invented around the time Jesus lived on the earth. Someone figured out how to slice the flower stems of the papyrus plant into sections, press them together, and let them dry into a flat sheet. Click on "Images" in a search engine to look up *papyrus* on the Internet.

Whenever you see a baby giraffe and picture it wearing the number *two*, remember Johnny Giraffe the 2nd and the book of 2 John.

JUST FOR FUN

Read 2 John, Chapter 1 (verse 12), and then write your favorite daily devo "with paper and ink."

PRAYER

Dear Lord, thank you for those who worked hard to invent paper and ink. Because of them, I can read your Word and know what you're like. And thanks for those who put together this book. Bless everyone who helps me understand your ways. In Jesus' name, amen.

2 JOHN, CHAPTER 1 (VERSE 6)

Love means doing what God has commanded us, and he has commanded us to love one another, just as you heard from the beginning.

DAILY DEVO

It's fun to funnel God's love.

The Bible is a long book. If you would read about four pages a day, it still would take you more than a year to read it all. But here's a secret shortcut. God had John give us three little words that tell how he expects us to respond to the big message of the entire Bible: Love one another. Simple, isn't it? And it's fun to do when you get the hang of it. You see, as tough as it is to really love someone, it actually fills your heart with joy and peace when you choose to do it. That's because we can't drum up God's love on our own. It's only when our hearts stay open to receiving this love that we can funnel it to others so they can feel it.

 MAKE IT STICK

The next time you take a bath, politely ask your dad or mom for a funnel and two plastic cups. Fill one cup with water and set the empty one in a corner on the edge of the tub. Now hold the funnel over the empty cup and pour the water through it. That shows how the love of God flows through you to others. Each time you let it gush through, say this daily devo.

PRAYER

Heavenly Father, I'm thankful for all of the people who love me. As I learn about love from them, teach me how to pass it on to others. In Jesus' name, amen.

CLICK-ER: FUNNEL

Whenever you see, use, or think about a *funnel*, let this daily devo flood your heart as it clicks and sticks. Johnny Giraffe the 2nd with his one-on-a-bun reminds you that the devo is from 2 John, Chapter 1.

Week 51, Thursday

BOOK OF 3 JOHN
Johnny Giraffe the 3rd

Giraffe starts with the same sound as *John*. A baby giraffe is the animal that best pictures the long, softhearted reach of John in this third little letter. When you see Johnny Giraffe the 3rd in a picture, you'll know the daily devo is from 3 John. Connected to Johnny Giraffe the 3rd are number symbols. (See page 15.) They make the chapter location of the devo click and stick.

This tiny 15-verse book is the third one John, "the apostle of love," wrote as an old man. He praised his friend Gaius for being a great guy and a good example of how to welcome people into our homes. In those days, church leaders traveled from town to town starting new congregations. They depended on other believers for food and shelter. Today, Christian workers, teachers, and missionaries still need this kind of help. Opening our homes to them makes us partners in their ministries. As in his other letters, John, like a giraffe, reached up and grabbed high thoughts about God, then brought them down to our level. Enjoy these spiritual cookies he put on the lower shelf just for you!

 MAKE IT STICK

Make a tab to mark the book of 3 John in your Bible. (See Week 1, Monday, for directions.)

The big theme of this little book is how we're to care for those who do the work of the Lord. Talk with your family about what you can do to bless the staff members at your church or a missionary your church supports. It doesn't have to be something big for them to feel loved. It's the little stuff, like writing a letter or taking them a treat, that makes all the difference. Whatever you decide, do it today.

Whenever you see a softhearted baby giraffe and picture it wearing the number *three*, remember Johnny Giraffe the 3rd and the book of 3 John.

JUST FOR FUN
Read 3 John, Chapter 1 (verse 4) to learn what gave John his greatest joy.

PRAYER
Dear God, thank you for all the people in your family who work hard at teaching and preaching your Word. Show me creative ways to bless them. And then give me courage to follow through on what you tell me to do. In Jesus' name I pray. Amen.

3 JOHN, CHAPTER 1 (VERSE 5)

Dear friend, you are being faithful to God when you care for the traveling teachers who pass through, even though they are strangers to you.

DAILY DEVO

You can hang your hat over my welcome mat.

Bible-time evangelists, prophets, pastors, and teachers usually didn't have much money. So as they started new churches in different places, they depended on other believers to care for them. Gaius (GUY-us) had a special ability from God called the gift of hospitality. He was good at welcoming God's people into his home. John wrote to let him know how important that was. Maybe your family would like to pray about opening your home to Sunday school teachers, pastors, and missionaries who would appreciate a meal or a place to stay. You'll find it's fun to let others "hang their hat" over your welcome mat.

MAKE IT STICK

On a piece of cardboard, use paints, markers, or crayons to make a cool welcome mat. After you place it by your bedroom door, invite a friend or someone in your family to your room. Have fun pretending to hang up your guest's hat and offering something good to drink. Explain that you're practicing hospitality. Then say this daily devo.

PRAYER

Dear God, when guests visit my family, please help me do my part to make them feel welcome—like hanging up their coats or serving them something cold to drink. In Jesus' name, amen.

CLICK-ER: WELCOME MAT

Whenever you see, wipe your feet on, or think about a *welcome mat*, let your heart warmly welcome this daily devo as it clicks and sticks. Johnny Giraffe the 3rd with his one-on-a-bun reminds you that the devo is from 3 John, Chapter 1.

Week 51, Saturday/Sunday

BOOK OF JUDE
Jude the Donkey Dude

Donkey Dude rhymes with *Jude*. Like a donkey, Jude stubbornly kept warning Christians to defend the faith at all costs. When you see Jude the Donkey Dude in a picture, you'll know the daily devo is from Jude. Connected to Jude the Donkey Dude are number symbols. (See page 15.) They make the chapter location of the devo click and stick.

What animal won't move when you want it to? The donkey. Right? And if one of these dudes digs in, you can't dynamite it off its spot. Jude, a half brother of Jesus', was like a don't-move donkey dude in the best possible sense of the term. His don't-budge-no-matter-what letter is a wonderfully stubborn warning for Christians to defend the faith at all costs. If something is true, it doesn't matter how many people say it's not. The Bible will always be true—it's God's unchanging Word. The book of Jude is only 25 verses long, so you can read it quickly. After you've done that, join Jude's Donkey Dude Club and stand your ground.

MAKE IT STICK

Make a tab to mark the book of Jude in your Bible. (See Week 1, Monday, for directions.)

Donkeys are stubborn like Jude. But they are also sturdy and sure-footed like the one that carried Jesus into Jerusalem. Enjoy playing pin the tail on the donkey, and remember to thank God for all the cool animals he's created.

Whenever you see a donkey or a picture of one, think about Jude the Donkey Dude and the book of Jude.

JUST FOR FUN

Jude wrote a really good prayer of praise to God in Chapter 1 (verses 24-25). Pray it out loud as your own prayer of praise to God, who can help you keep on believing the truth.

PRAYER

Dear God, I don't even want to think about the possibility of falling away from you and your truth. Please do whatever it takes to keep me strong in you and believing what is true. In Jesus' name, amen.

WEEKEND ACTIVITY IDEAS

(1) Highlight the verses for Week 51 in your Bible. (2) Find the HoneyWord animal in each picture for this week and identify the chapter-number symbols. (3) Add to your collection of Click-ers. (4) Say the daily devos for Week 51. (5) Check out Saturday/Sunday of Week 3 for a related devo on being in the crowd that follows God's cloud.

LEND ME YOUR EAR

Standing only four feet high at the shoulders, the donkey has huge ears—the largest ears of any member of the horse family.

JUDE, CHAPTER 1 (VERSE 22)
You must show mercy to those whose faith is wavering.

DAILY DEVO
I'm a lifesaver **for those who waver.**

Waver is a big word that means to move back and forth unsteadily because you're unsure of yourself. It's like losing your balance. We all waver a lot in the Christian life. If you waver from time to time, going back and forth about what you believe, just know you're perfectly normal. What's important to God is that you let him help you get back up so you can help others do the same. We can be like lifesavers, helping each other stay afloat and follow God for a lifetime. Hear this loud and clear: It's okay if you waver once in a while, but don't ever give up and stop believing in Jesus.

MAKE IT STICK

Life Savers candies look like those O-shaped life preservers that lifeguards throw to people who are drowning. Politely ask your dad or mom to let you buy a roll of them. Say this daily devo before you pop the first one in your mouth. Then offer one to someone else. As the person reaches out and takes it, silently think about how Life Savers are a picture of showing kindness by helping someone who is wavering.

PRAYER
Heavenly Father, please show me how to be kind to everyone I know. I want the kind things I say and do to help someone keep believing in you. In Jesus' name I pray. Amen.

CLICK-ER: LIFESAVER
Whenever you see, touch, or think about a *lifesaver* (a real one or a Life Savers piece of candy), let this daily devo keep your heart from drowning as it clicks and sticks. Jude the Donkey Dude with his one-on-a-bun handle reminds you that the devo is from Jude, Chapter 1.

Week 52, Tuesday

BOOK OF REVELATION

Rev. the Rooster

Rooster begins with the same letter as *Revelation*. John, who was kind of like a reverend or preacher, writes his revelation from God as a cock-a-doodle-doo wake-up call about what we are to doodle-do during the last days of the world. When you see Rev. the Rooster in a picture, you'll know the daily devo is from Revelation. Connected to Rev. the Rooster are number symbols. (See page 15.) They make the chapter location of the devo click and stick.

Roosters love raising a ruckus and waking everybody up. The beloved old apostle John, who was sent to live on the island of Patmos, wrote to some churches about God's revelation to him. God showed, or revealed, things that will happen at the end of the world. Like a rooster, John crowed about what we are to doodle-do before the end comes. His main point was that God will win and the devil will lose. Someday soon God will reward Christians with eternal life and others with eternal punishment. Until then, God has everything carefully planned and perfectly timed. So don't worry, but do let Rev. the Rooster wake you up. The time to love God is now.

 MAKE IT STICK

Make a tab to mark the book of Revelation in your Bible. (See Week 1, Monday, for directions.)

Play "sleeping musical chairs" with your family. Set up one less chair than the number of people playing. Each time you play, set an alarm to ring on a different number of seconds. Pretend to walk in your sleep as you walk around the chairs. When the alarm goes off, everyone tries to grab a chair. The one left standing has to *cock-a-doodle-doo* like Rev. the Rooster.

Whenever you see a rooster or a picture of one, think about Rev. the Rooster and the book of Revelation.

JUST FOR FUN

Read Revelation, Chapter 3 (verse 20). Why does Jesus knock on the door of your heart? Have you let him in? If you're not sure how to do it, check out the Bike Hike to Jesus on page 17.

PRAYER

Lord Jesus, I'm so glad you keep knocking on the door of everyone's heart. Please come into my life right now and be my friend. I'm ready to follow you to heaven. Amen.

REVELATION, CHAPTER 3 (VERSES 15-16)

I know all the things you do, that you are neither hot nor cold. I wish that you were one or the other! But since you are like lukewarm water, neither hot nor cold, I will spit you out of my mouth!

DAILY DEVO

I'm hot sauce for the one true Boss.

Most of us are acquainted with mouth-sizzling hot sauce, especially those of us who like Mexican food. It really brings out the flavor of the food, doesn't it? Now listen to this: God loves hot sauce, and he wants us to be like it. You see, tasteless, fizzless, cold Christianity makes God sick. He just can't stand it. In fact, he'd rather you be ice cold any day instead of lukewarm every day. Don't be distasteful to God. Tickle his taste buds by being a faithful follower of Jesus each day. Being hot sauce for the one true Boss of the entire universe is the only cool way to live.

MAKE IT STICK

The next time you have some tortilla chips, try dipping one in some lukewarm water. It's pretty tasteless and soggy, isn't it? Now dip a chip in some hot sauce. All you need is a tiny drop. Brings out the salty flavor, doesn't it? When we're excited about following Jesus, it's as thrilling to God as if he were eating tortilla chips totally covered with hot sauce! Say this daily devo as you try another chip.

PRAYER

Lord Jesus, I'm so excited to be following you! Please keep my heart from turning cold toward you or others. Remind me to shout and sing praises to you every day for the rest of my life! In Jesus' name, amen.

CLICK-ER: HOT SAUCE

Whenever you see, taste, or think about *hot sauce*, let this daily devo heat up your heart as it clicks and sticks. Rev. the Rooster with his three-is-the-key reminds you that the devo is from Revelation, Chapter 3.

REVELATION, CHAPTER 7 (VERSE 17)

The Lamb on the throne will be their Shepherd. He will lead them to springs of life-giving water. And God will wipe every tear from their eyes.

DAILY DEVO

One day God will wiper-blade every tear I've ever made.

Can you imagine driving in a rainstorm without wiper blades on the windshield? You wouldn't be able to see a thing and would probably get lost or hit something. Just like cars need wiper blades, we need caring parents to wipe our tears when we get hurt. Their comfort clears our eyes and keeps us from running off the road of life. But loss and pain, sadness and sorrow, get old after a while, don't you think? During those times when you're crying and really hurting, look up toward heaven. And look forward to the time when God will wiper-blade every tear you've ever made. After you've cried your last cry on earth, there will be no more tears once you get to heaven. So hang on, heaven is coming. It's closer than you think!

 MAKE IT STICK

The next time you're riding in the family car, ask your dad or mom to please turn on the windshield wipers. If it's not raining, politely ask your parent to spray a little bit of window washer so the wiper blades have something to wipe. Now say this daily devo as you follow the rhythmic *swish-swash-swishing* of the wipers.

PRAYER

Dear God, I don't like feeling sad or getting hurt. I don't like anything that brings me pain. So thanks for your promise that a day is coming when I never need to cry again. In Jesus' name, amen.

CLICK-ER: **WIPER BLADES**

Whenever you see, watch, or think about *wiper blades*, let this daily devo wipe away the tears of your heart as it clicks and sticks. Rev. the Rooster with his highway-seven-to-heaven sign reminds you that the devo is from Revelation, Chapter 7.

REVELATION, CHAPTER 21 (VERSE 21)

The twelve gates were made of pearls—each gate from a single pearl! And the main street was pure gold, as clear as glass.

DAILY DEVO

Let's meet on Easy Street!

Heaven is so out of this world that God tells us in Revelation, Chapters 21 and 22, as much about what's *not* there as what *is*. There's no death, sorrow, crying, or pain. No hunger or thirst. No sun or moon. No night. And best of all, no evil. On the flip side, everything will be new and perfect. God will live among us, and worship will be nonstop. The gates will be made of giant pearls, and the main street will be made of gold. You might wonder, *Do we get to play games all the time? And after the first million years, then what?* The Bible does the best it can to describe something so wonderful that we'll never really be able to picture it until we get there. For now, let's just agree to meet on that golden Easy Street and take it from there. See you soon!

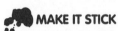 **MAKE IT STICK**

Draw a street sign on a piece of paper and print the words "Easy Street" on it. Around it, draw what you think heaven might look like. From this day forward, each time you read a street sign, say this daily devo as a reminder of your home in heaven.

PRAYER

Dear Lord, it's so much fun just thinking about how beautiful and perfect heaven will be. I'm really looking forward to meeting you there face to face. In your name I pray. Amen.

CLICK-ER: **STREET SIGN**

Whenever you notice, read, or think about a *street sign*, let this daily devo direct your heart toward heaven as it clicks and sticks. Rev. the Rooster with his two-blue-shoes and one-on-a-bun reminds you that the devo is from Revelation, Chapter 21.

REVELATION, CHAPTER 22 (VERSE 13)

I am the Alpha and the Omega, the First and the Last, the Beginning and the End.

DAILY DEVO

Jesus is my friend to The End.

Most of us are pretty lousy friends. We shove our way to the front of the line. We serve ourselves the biggest cookies. And we wait for others to be friends with us first. But as someone has wisely observed, "The only way to have a friend is to be one." And Jesus knows how to be one. He is the best friend anyone will ever have. He came to earth so we could go to heaven. He became poor so we could become rich. He died so we could live. He was our friend even while we were his enemies. And he promises to be our friend all the way to The End. No matter what. Now that's something worth standing up and hollering about.

 MAKE IT STICK

The next time you come to the end of a book, movie, or video, think about this daily devo and say it quietly to yourself. Remember that your life is like a story line. It has a starting point, a middle, and an end. Since Jesus is the Alpha and the Omega *(A and Z* in the Greek alphabet), the First and the Last, he is the only One who stays with you all the way, from beginning to end.

PRAYER

Dear Jesus, you were with me even before I was born. You're with me now. And you've promised to be with me forever. You're the best friend a kid could ever have. Thanks, Jesus! Amen.

CLICK-ER: THE END

Whenever you see, read, or think about the words *The End*, let your thoughts finish with this daily devo as it clicks and sticks. Rev. the Rooster with his two pairs of two-blue-shoes reminds you that the devo is from Revelation, Chapter 22.

WEEKEND ACTIVITY IDEAS

(1) Highlight the verses for Week 52 in your Bible. (2) Find the HoneyWord animal in each picture for this week and identify the chapter-number symbols. (3) Add to your collection of Click-ers. (4) Say the daily devos for Week 52. (5) Check out Monday of Week 51 for a related devo on how Jesus holds you tight like a kite to the end.

TRUE ALARM

A rooster crows at the beginning of each day as the sky begins to get light. He does this to let all other roosters know that this is his space, and the hens here belong to him. Roosters also crow during the day. And sometimes they crow at night if the moon is shining brightly.

THE HONEYWORD CLICK-ERS

Note: This list of Click-ers includes the following cross-references.

(Word in parentheses) = the actual word in a daily devo when it is different from the Click-er.

Word in italics = a word that is an incomplete part of a Click-er or daily devo, such as *airplane*, *dew*, and *oven*.

OLD TESTAMENT

airplane: see "twin engine plane"	1 Samuel 18:3-4	85
alcohol bottle (alcohol)	Proverbs 20:1	164
arrow (arrows)	Nehemiah 2:4-5	115
ball	Genesis 1:1	20
basket	Exodus 2:3	30
baton	Psalm 78:5-6	140
beach ball (beach)	Job 12:7-8	125
bed	Proverbs 26:13-14	169
birthday cake (birthday)	Isaiah 49:1	188
(blocks): see "wood block"	Numbers 22:32	55
(bloom): see "rose bloom"	Jeremiah 1:5	192
boat (lifeboat)	Genesis 7:18	23
boomerang	Ecclesiastes 11:1	174
bowl	2 Kings 23:2	100
bowling pin	Proverbs 24:16	167
brick wall	Exodus 5:13	33
broom	Zephaniah 1:2	230
bush	Exodus 3:4	31

NEW TESTAMENT

ALPHABETICAL LIST OF HONEYWORD ANIMALS

OLD TESTAMENT

Amos the Moose	Amos	212
Captain Kingaroo the 1st	1 Kings	94
Captain Kingaroo the 2nd	2 Kings	97
Dan O. Saur	Daniel	203
Davey Cricket the 1st	1 Chronicles	101
Davey Cricket the 2nd	2 Chronicles	107
Doodlebug-eronomy	Deuteronomy	56
E. Zeek Eel	Ezekiel	201
Eagle-easy-astes	Ecclesiastes	171
Elks-odus	Exodus	29
Esther the Starfish	Esther	119
Ezra-triever	Ezra	112
Genny the Jellyfish	Genesis	19
Habakkuk the Hawk	Habakkuk	226
Haggai the Hedgehog	Haggai	231
Hosea the Horse	Hosea	208
Isaiah the Irish Setter	Isaiah	178
Jaws-chew-ya (shark)	Joshua	65
Jerry the Jackrabbit	Jeremiah	191
Joe B. Buffalo	Job	124
Joel the Mole	Joel	210
Jonah the Moan-ah Fish	Jonah	218
Judge the Jaguar	Judges	71
Levi the Lamb	Leviticus	40
Mala-gator	Malachi	237
Mama Llama	Lamentations	198
Micah the Cat	Micah	222
Na-hum-ing-bird	Nahum	224
Nehemiah the Butterfly-ah	Nehemiah	114
Num-Bee	Numbers	48

NEW TESTAMENT

TIPTOP HONEYWORD TOPICS